Genesis of Symbolic Thought

Symbolic thought is what makes us human. Claude Lévi-Strauss stated that we can never know the genesis of symbolic thought, but in this powerful new study Alan Barnard argues that we can. Continuing the line of analysis initiated in *Social anthropology and human origins* (Cambridge University Press, 2011), *Genesis of symbolic thought* applies ideas from social anthropology, old and new, to understand some of the areas also being explored in fields as diverse as archaeology, linguistics, genetics and neuroscience. Barnard aims to answer questions including: when and why did language come into being? What was the earliest religion? And what form did social organization take before humanity dispersed from the African continent? Rejecting the notion of hunter-gatherers as 'primitive', Barnard hails the great sophistication of their complex means of linguistic and symbolic expression and places the possible origin of symbolic thought at as early as 130,000 years ago.

ALAN BARNARD is Professor of the Anthropology of Southern Africa at the University of Edinburgh, where he has taught since 1978. He has undertaken a wide range of ethnographic fieldwork and archaeological research in Botswana, Namibia and South Africa, participated in the British Academy Centenary Research Project 'From Lucy to Language: The Archaeology of the Social Brain' and serves as Honorary Consul of the Republic of Namibia in Scotland. His numerous publications include *History and theory in anthropology* (2000) and *Social anthropology and human origins* (2011). In 2010 Professor Barnard was elected a Fellow of the British Academy.

Genesis of Symbolic Thought

Alan Barnard

Professor of the Anthropology of Southern Africa
University of Edinburgh

CAMBRIDGE UNIVERSITY PRESS

CAMBRIDGE UNIVERSITY PRESS
Cambridge, New York, Melbourne, Madrid, Cape Town,
Singapore, São Paulo, Delhi, Mexico City

Cambridge University Press
The Edinburgh Building, Cambridge CB2 8RU, UK

Published in the United States of America by
Cambridge University Press, New York

www.cambridge.org
Information on this title: www.cambridge.org/9781107025691

© Cambridge University Press 2012

This publication is in copyright. Subject to statutory exception
and to the provisions of relevant collective licensing agreements,
no reproduction of any part may take place without
the written permission of Cambridge University Press.

First published 2012

Printed in the United Kingdom at the University Press, Cambridge

A catalogue record for this publication is available from the British Library

Library of Congress Cataloging-in-Publication Data
Barnard, Alan (Alan J.)
    Genesis of symbolic thought / Alan Barnard.
    p. cm.
    Includes bibliographical references and index.
    ISBN 978-1-107-02569-1 (Hardback) – ISBN 978-1-107-65109-8 (Paperback)
 1. Symbolic anthropology. 2. Language and languages–Origin.
 3. Human evolution. 4. Thought and thinking. I. Title.
    GN452.5.B37 2012
    306.4–dc23
                                                            2011052551

ISBN 978-1-107-02569-1 Hardback
ISBN 978-1-107-65109-8 Paperback

Cambridge University Press has no responsibility for the persistence or
accuracy of URLs for external or third-party internet websites referred to
in this publication, and does not guarantee that any content on such
websites is, or will remain, accurate or appropriate.

Sociology cannot explain the genesis of symbolic thought, but has just to take it for granted in man.
C. Lévi-Strauss

>

Contents

List of figures	*page* viii
List of tables	ix
Preface	xi
1 Introduction	1
2 Stones, bones, ochre and beads	15
3 Kinship, sociality and the symbolic order	40
4 Ritual and religion	59
5 The flowering of language	83
6 Conquering the globe	104
7 After symbolic thought: the Neolithic	122
8 Conclusion	142
Glossary	151
References	173
Index	190

Figures

2.1 Southern African archaeological sites with early symbolic culture	page 16
2.2 Mary Douglas' grid/group boxes (with examples)	30
2.3 Wissler's age-area hypothesis: dating change within a culture area	37
3.1 'Iroquois' and 'Eskimo' terminologies	43
3.2 The four Kariera sections and their symbolic associations	45
3.3 A moiety structure	53
4.1 Radcliffe-Brown's two theories of totemism	68
5.1 Time line for the genus *Homo*	101
6.1 Major prehistoric human migrations, with approximate dates BP	108
6.2 The consensus view: African genetic diversity and global migration	116
6.3 Dziebel's view: American cultural diversity and global migration	117
7.1 Hunter-gatherer versus Neolithic ideologies	124
7.2 Biological and cultural evolution	135
8.1 Genesis of symbolic thought	147

Tables

2.1 Hominin fossil species	*page* 18
2.2 Grahame Clark's modes of lithic technology	24
2.3 'Stone Age' archaeological periods	26
4.1 Radcliffe-Brown's (1951) examples of moiety or related opposition (in the order he mentions them)	69
7.1 Humankind: the most recent 500,000 years	139

Preface

When I finished writing *Social anthropology and human origins*, I wanted to explore one area of human origins in greater depth. The earlier book looked to a great extent at primates, fossil hominins and the archaeology of humans living long before language, art, symbolism or religion. It touched too on these later developments, but the present subject, the genesis of symbolic thought, cries out more than any other for engagement with social anthropology. It is as much part of our discipline as it is of any other, and exploring it is not only to the benefit of, say, archaeology, but also to the benefit of social anthropology itself. Indeed, the genesis of symbolic thought is not even always in the past: symbolic thought is generated every time a person thinks symbolically. In this book, though, I am concerned primarily with new developments in the study of human origins. Much of what I say also reflects both on humanity's present and on anthropology's glorious past.

Proto-humans certainly had, in some sense, sophisticated communications skills with which to deal with practical matters. They had collective behaviour: they had society. They also had 'culture', but they did not think symbolically. The origin of symbolic thought is one of the great questions of social anthropology, as indeed it is of archaeology. However, for the last hundred years or so, mainstream social anthropology has not confronted it. When last we did, both social and biological anthropology and archaeology too were very, very different from what they are now. Intelligence was being measured with callipers, and we were being told that the missing link was a strapping young Englishman called *Eoanthropus dawsoni*, with a big head and an ape-like jaw, who long ago lived on the Sussex Downs and played cricket. This book is a twenty-first-century history of the last 200,000 years, and more significantly (at my guess) the last 130,000 years or so, when humans began to think symbolically.

Let me comment briefly on terminology. In general, given the choice I tend to prefer the more English-sounding terms and to use traditional labels where appropriate, but modern place names. In English, I prefer the traditional Neanderthal to the modern German spelling Neandertal. There is only one correct Linnaean Latin term, which is *Homo neanderthalensis*. 'Rhodesian Man' is now archaic and goes in inverted commas, but *Homo rhodesiensis* is the correct Linnaean Latin. One cannot change either to incorporate the word Zambia, the modern name for the colony of Northern Rhodesia in which the fossil was found. However, I use the modern name Kabwe for the specific place where it was found, rather than its colonial name Broken Hill. The most complex problem is what to call the hunter-gatherers of southern Africa. Both Bushman (which in my usage is gender-neutral) and San (which, correctly used, should be common gender plural) are in common English usage, and I use them interchangeably or according to context. There is no 'correct' term though. In Khoekhoegowab, the language from which it comes, San (actually, Saan) can be as derogatory as Bushman, and many Bushmen object to being called San. Alternatives like Khoe, Ju/'hoan, Kua and so on never work in English, since they can all have more specific ethnic meanings as well as generic ones. In the past, I have sometimes used N/oakhoe or Ncoakhoe (Naro for 'Red Person') or Basarwa (which is the usual term in Setswana, etymologically: plural prefix (noun class for humans) – San – diminutive suffix), but the use of these terms creates similar problems, at least whenever they are used in any languages other than Naro or Setswana.

I will not name *all* the many individuals who have helped, in various ways, to allow me (often unknowingly) to stand on their shoulders, but I am grateful to them all the same. A social anthropology of human origins, even with respect to the genesis of symbolic thought, is utterly dependent on research in other disciplines: from genetics to linguistics, from archaeology to art history, from neuroscience to comparative anatomy, from folklore to religious studies. But, of course, it is dependent too on ethnography and anthropological theory, not just in the present, but through the history of social anthropology. Therefore, let me acknowledge collectively my sometime collaborators and close colleagues, my teachers, my intellectual ancestors and the many passing acquaintances whose impact on the development of my ideas is greater than they know. If I may pick out just a few, I am grateful to Fred Coolidge, Robin Dunbar, Tecumseh Fitch, Chris Henshilwood, Jean-Marie Hombert, Jim Hurford, Tim Ingold, Wendy James, Chris Knight, Adam Kuper, David Lewis-Williams, Dan Sperber and Tom Wynn for their inspiration and, in some cases, simply for being at exactly the right place at the right time. However, none of them has had a direct input to what I have written here, and some may disagree profoundly with my arguments – but, I hope, not too much.

Thanks also go to colleagues in conferences and seminars where I have talked on the issues touched on here, specifically in Bern, Edinburgh, Halle, London, Montreal, Oxford, Stellenbosch and Utrecht, both for offering me the chance to present ideas on early symbolic thought and for providing the necessary feedback on my more idiosyncratic ideas. And thanks too to my wife Joy (whose training is in archaeology and in law) for aiming to temper my more extreme theoretical speculations with common sense and the demand, at each stage, for evidence – however hard it is to come by.

1 Introduction

In his novel *Before Adam*, Jack London presents recollections in the 'racial memory' of his narrator:

> We had no conjugation. One judged the tense by the context. We talked only concrete things, because we thought only concrete things. Also we depended on pantomime. The simplest abstraction was practically beyond our thinking; and when one did happen to think one, he was hard put to communicate it to his fellows. There were no sounds for it. (London 1908: 34–5)

Whether gesture or speech came first is open to debate, though the prevailing view seems to favour gesture, that is, gestural language rather than literally pantomime, even if the former stems in part from pantomime (see Corballis 2002, Arbib 2005). But what did early *Homo sapiens* do with gesture or speech? Assuming speech had evolved by the time of early *H. sapiens*, what did people say to each other? And above all, when did they start communicating in more intricate ways, with difficult sentences, concrete details and abstract thoughts? Is this the origin of art, of religion, of thinking beyond the self, of thinking beyond immediate needs? We all know that living hunter-gatherers spend less time in work-related activities than we food-producing peoples do (see Sahlins 1974: 1–39). Was the same not true of their, and our, *H. sapiens* ancestors?

This first chapter concerns some philosophical, linguistic and anthropological questions that may serve as background to our bigger problem: the genesis of symbolic thought. Later chapters will refine these and touch on data from social anthropology and from many other disciplines, and especially on some recent findings from archaeology and genetics. The time span of my earlier book *Social anthropology and human origins* (Barnard 2011) was roughly from the purported common ancestor of humans and chimpanzees, *Sahelanthropus tchadensis* (from about 7,400,000 BP) to the early days of symbolic culture. When these 'early days' might be is in dispute, but it is according to most who hazard a guess within the last 200,000 years. This book picks up where that book left off. It tells the tale of these more recent times in greater detail and brings to the fore what it means to be fully human. And it presents, I hope, a picture of the many facets of human life, particularly the sway of the ethereal over the material, that has occurred since the dawn of *human modernity* in its broadest sense.

Symbol, mind and human thought

I am very interested in the origins of linguistic complexity and in the origins of cultural complexity. These, it seems to me, are related. But what is cultural complexity? For some anthropologists, thoughts of cultural complexity might conjure images of social complexity or even political complexity. That is *not* of particular concern to me, at least not in this book. Every linguist knows that a hunter-gatherer living a 'primitive communistic' existence may well speak a language as rich and complex as that of an astronaut or a nuclear physicist. Every anthropologist should know that a hunter-gatherer may have just the same facility for cultural expression as an astronaut or nuclear physicist. What it means to be human is something embedded at least as much in hunter-gatherer social life as it is in the age of iron, steam or electronics. Perhaps even more so. Hunter-gatherers may today number only a very small percentage of the earth's population, but hunting and gathering are the 'natural' means of subsistence of our species, and were at the time of the genesis of symbolic thought too. I do not regard *Homo sapiens sapiens* hunter-gatherer existence as in any way less sophisticated than my own, but rather as an expression of the human condition that is more real to me than today among many of my fellow non-hunter-gatherers. Richard Lee and Irven DeVore (1968a: ix) recognized this in their famous statement: 'We cannot avoid the suspicion that many of us were led to live and work among hunters because of a feeling that the human condition was likely to be more clearly drawn here than among other kinds of society.'

Neither Lévi-Straussian 'untamed thinking' nor even Lucien Lévy-Bruhl's notion of 'mystical thought' impose any restriction on the quality or richness of cultural expression, and neither is confined to 'primitive peoples' in any sense. On the contrary, these anthropological abstractions are broadly characteristic of humanity in general. In the words of the much maligned French philosophical anthropologist, 'mystical thought ... is present in every human mind' (Lévy-Bruhl 1975 [1949]: 101). This book is an attempt to look back to the origins of that form of thought, and to the beginnings of communication (with nature, with the spirit world and among humans) through symbols. Many species communicate, but only humans have language, and only humans communicate through symbols. To use symbolism is to be human. It follows that to think in symbols is to be human too. However chimps might 'think', however australopithecines and early *Homo* might have 'thought', even however creative they might have been, they do not or did not possess the capacity for the making of metaphor, symbolism or art that can communicate. Nor can they conjure mystical ideas that can be pondered or shared. These things differentiate not only chimpanzees from humans, but also early humans, like *Homo erectus*, from ourselves. I would even go one tiny step further: in some ways, we humans who grow grain and keep livestock, who live in towns and write things down, in other words, who are Neolithic or post-Neolithic, have lost some of our 'humanity'. Hunter-gatherers, in general, can and often do retain more symbolic aspects of humanity: these are the things which make us truly human.

I will not belabour that point, but in this book I shall argue that the search for the beginnings of symbolism, and all that goes with it, is possible. It is also fruitful for social anthropology and for a widely conceived four-field anthropology too: social anthropology (cultural anthropology), biological anthropology, prehistoric archaeology and anthropological linguistics. These are the four divisions of the broad-based anthropology practised in most North American departments, if not in most other places, including my own British one. I write from a social anthropological point of view, but it is together with our sister sub-disciplines that social anthropology's contribution comes into its own. I prefer the phrase 'social anthropology' rather than 'cultural anthropology', but the two are essentially synonymous. Symbolism is our subject matter, that is, the subject matter of social anthropology. So too is the anthropology of art, the anthropology of religion and so on. We must, of course, rely on archaeology, on genetics, on neuroscience, on linguistics, or whatever, to provide data and many understandings: but it is up to social anthropology to complete the picture.

If thinking through symbols is human, consider some of the implications. In *Social anthropology and human origins*, I held back in discussing theory of mind, and beyond that, levels of intentionality. But let me touch briefly on these here. These concepts though are masterfully dealt with by Robin Dunbar (2004: 41–76), and they help us to understand in general why humans are different from other intelligent animals. They also help us to understand child development, for human children acquire a theory of mind only at the age of about four and a half. Symbolic thought is a few stages beyond that, and religion, defined as including collective action based on common belief, possibly even more so (2004: 184–6). A theory of mind is the understanding that someone else thinks differently from oneself. Chimpanzees can have it, and humans at five years old normally have it. But at four years old things are different. Psychologists have several tests for it. For example, the 'Sally-Ann test' involves two dolls, named Sally and Ann, and a ball. The psychologist acts out a scene for the child: the doll called Sally puts the ball under a cushion and then leaves the room. In her absence, the doll called Ann retrieves the ball and places it in a toy box on the other side of the room. Then Sally returns. The four-year-old child is asked: 'Where does Sally think the ball is?' Invariably, the four-year-old will say that Sally thinks the ball is in the toy box. But, of course, Sally could not know this, because she was out of the room when Ann placed the ball there. A five-year-old child, however, will get it right: the five-year-old will know that Sally lacks the knowledge that the psychologist, the child and the doll called Ann all share.

Theory of mind is the second level of intentionality. First-level intentionality is that of believing something, and second-level is believing that someone else believes something. Experiments with chimps show that they have it (e.g., Towner 2010), and Dunbar (2004: 190–2) has used cranial capacity to plot the highest probable levels of intentionality of fossil hominins. Very simply, australopithecines, like chimps, acquired second-level intentionality; *Homo erectus*, third-level; and what Dunbar prefers to classify as 'archaic' *Homo sapiens* (*Homo heidelbergensis*), about 500,000 years ago, fourth-level. Fifth-level intentionality is confined to 'anatomically modern' humans, and Dunbar suggests it first occurred no more than 200,000 years ago. Third-level intentionality is thinking that someone else thinks something about what a third party thinks or wants. Say, Fred thinks that Jane believes that Jim fancies her. Gradually, at fourth and fifth levels, things get more complicated. For example, Fred thinking that Jane believes Jim fancies her, but that she nevertheless intends to play coy in the hope of Jim fancying her even more.

Symbolic thought entails a consciousness of the aesthetic. It also entails the wish to communicate this, one would imagine, to someone else, with the view to influencing that person's perceptions. Religion entails all that plus the presumption, at least in some religions, of consciousness beyond mortal consciousness. It presumes also, as I have suggested above, a commonality among believers, and a recognition of common belief in a spiritual entity that, itself, recognizes what humans are thinking. Dunbar (2007: 44–5) tells us that in order to have religion a fifth level of intentionality is required, and that anything less than that implies that we have less than a religion. When these layers cease to seem tautologous, then indeed we may have the development of some kind of 'theology'. Whether fifth-level might in fact *require* some kind of religion in order to come into being is an open question. Certainly, we have language at fifth-level, and to my mind this is in fact what *full language* was originally for: the expression of complex thought through myth, or at the very least in narrative that leads ultimately to mythological expression. I will explore this in depth in Chapter 5.

Genesis and language

Claude Lévi-Strauss (1945: 518) commented that sociology, and by implication social anthropology too, cannot explain the genesis of symbolic thought. His remark appeared in a critique of one of Émile Durkheim's more evolutionist ideas.

In *Incest: the nature and origin of the taboo* (1963 [1898]) and in *The elementary forms of the religious life* (1915 [1912]), Durkheim had argued (especially with reference to Aboriginal Australia) that religion reflects society. His opponent in the original debate was Sir James Frazer, who in *Totemism and exogamy* (1910) held the reverse: the social order is built on religious belief. My argument is that all three are wrong, Durkheim, Frazer and Lévi-Strauss alike. Neither religion nor society came first, nor do we just have 'to take for granted' the genesis of symbolic thought. Symbolic thought emerges along with changes in the brain, in society and in communication. It reflects language, including both its communicative and its non-communicative aspects. By non-communicative aspects, I simply mean those that exist as art forms in their own right, such as mythology and other examples of narrative, and also poetry and song. Of course, these communicate, but they do so in a quite different way than communication of stone tool techniques and where to find game animals or to dig tubers.

Complex or full language is far richer in every aspect of meaning than it has to be for ordinary communication. Complex morphology and syntax came into being long before writing, and long before humans learned to domesticate livestock or till the soil. We know this, not least, because the languages spoken by hunter-gatherers are every bit as complex as those of any others. My own primary language of ethnographic fieldwork, Naro (spoken by hunter-gatherers in Botswana), has at least eighty-six person-gender-number markers, making it among the most complex in the world in this respect, while other languages spoken by San or Bushmen vie for being the most phonologically complex. Probably !Xóõ wins out on that score, with 126 consonant phonemes (Traill 1994: 13), and Ju/'hoan is not far behind. The richness of Inuit grammars and those many Amerindian languages is well known too: the mean number of affixes in an Inuit dialect seems to be around 450 (Dorais 1990: 219).

But why should languages be so complicated? The short answer is that it is in our genes, certainly not merely in 'culture'. On the other hand, there is no reason except the prejudice of the literate, the agricultural and the technologically 'advanced' that might suggest that a Bushman or an Inuit hunter-gatherer might be any less cultured than a European, Euro-American or Japanese farmer or a computer wizard. Lévi-Strauss (1968: 351) once commented that by 200,000 years ago (more precisely, 'over two or three hundred thousand years ago'), there were people of the intellect of as a Plato or an Einstein, only their specialized knowledge was not in philosophy or physics, but probably in kinship. I would suggest it was also in grammar, and in those forms of human knowledge that require grammar: especially mythology. On the other hand, there are extremes at the other end. Mandarin Chinese is not complicated. And, notoriously, a Native South American language, Pirahã, seems to be the simplest in the world. According to Daniel Everett (2005), who has spent some years studying that language, it has no numbers at all, nor any concept of quantification. It has no colour terms, it has the simplest pronominal system ever recorded and it has no recursion: the embedding of one grammatical form into another. Culturally, Pirahã is said to possess the simplest kinship system ever recorded and one of the simplest living material cultures, and there is an individual memory of only two generations and a complete lack of drawing and no other art. Again, according to Everett (formerly a missionary), it also completely lacks creation myths and has no fiction, and in spite of 200 years of contact with surrounding Amerindian groups who speak much more complicated languages, the Pirahã do not learn them. Yet, by his own admission, in all these things Pirahã is an exception, and the case is utterly extreme – if indeed Everett is correct. In Chapter 5 we will explore the other extreme, the southern San language /Xam, which has one of the richest mythologies ever recorded and some of the most extreme cases of recursion, which in turn implies, both in factual narrative and in fiction, a highly complex mental mechanism of levels of intentionality.

A very great deal has been written about early phases of language. These phases most certainly are related to primate communication. They are also related to grooming (picking nits out of hair) among primates, which is a primary means of communication among them. Grooming of a similar kind occurs among humans too, but in most societies it is confined to close relatives or intimate partners (see

Dunbar 2004: 126–8). There is an overlapping trajectory of evolution here that we might summarize as: from *grooming* (e.g., Dunbar 1996) to *gestural communication* (e.g., Corballis 2002 and 2003) to *music* (e.g., Mithen 2005) to *spoken language*. Of course, grooming has not died out, modern sign language is not directly related to gestural communication and music still communicates. Yet to look for the origins of language only in these things is to miss those relatively recent origins that are found in the relation of language to symbolic thought. I am speaking here not of proto-language or rudimentary language, but of full or true language with its potential for complicated grammars and enormous vocabularies (Barnard 2009). *Homo erectus* certainly communicated, but members of this species did not possess language as we know it.

On the basis of the development of the brain and fourth-level intentionality, Dunbar suggests an origin of some kind of 'language' at roughly 500,000 years ago. In this scenario, *Homo antecessor* or *H. heidelbergensis* may have had a primitive sort of language, but I would look further. The full development of complex grammar, in the sense of an ability to learn such grammars, if not to possess one in your own language, is a *H. sapiens sapiens* characteristic. Its relation to the use of complex language in myth and possibly in narrative generally is so strong that I would look for clues on the origins of full language among the earliest users of symbols and of expressive and symbolic communication, and in the development of mythological systems. Obviously, myth requires complex language. Whether complex language requires myth is more difficult to ascertain, but Lévi-Strauss' guess that by 200,000 years ago we find 'Platos' and 'Einsteins' does not seem that far off the mark. If my guess is that it could be slightly more recently, at least we are in the same ballpark.

Symbol and metaphor

Once humans acquired language, we acquired the ability to communicate over long distances. Of course, this is or was important, not only for humans today, but for our ancestors – both those who stayed in Africa and tamed the continent, and those who migrated out to Asia,

Europe and beyond. But, as I have suggested above, real language is rather more than mere communication. Through complex grammar we can explore meanings within our symbolic systems, including, for example, in mythology. More to the point, complex grammar helps us to construct mythologies and to 'enact' them in the mind. Myth, religious thought and ritual are all related.

But take one step beyond this. Symbols are, in a sense, metaphorical. Like metaphorical words, they enable us to play with meaning, to use analogy, to be creative. This kind of creativity is yet one step beyond that enabled by music or visual art. Music, in particular, may be deeply embedded in our biological makeup. Musical creativity implies social and cultural processes, but it is also a blend of the cognitive with the physiological (Blacking 1976: 7). Creativity through symbolism and through language is a conscious step beyond that. It requires more thinking, as well as requiring perhaps the emotion that may exist in the appreciation of any visual art, and which most certainly exists in music.

Metaphor through words is yet another step beyond symbolism. In their seminal *Metaphors we live by*, George Lakoff and Mark Johnson (1980) tell us that metaphor is part of everyday language. It is not just for poets. For example, consider that 'ideas are plants'. We have in English, to name but a few expressions of this metaphor: 'He views chemistry as a mere *offshoot* of physics. Mathematics has many *branches*. The *seeds* of his great ideas were *planted* in his youth. She has a *fertile* imagination' (1980: 47). Possibly language itself is always metaphorical? Much the same has been suggested about symbolism, in very different ways by rather different anthropological thinkers, for example the French cognitive anthropologist Dan Sperber (1975) and the American symbolic anthropologist Roy Wagner (1986).

Symbols communicate with reference to other symbols, and not necessarily with direct reference to non-symbolic objects (either physical ones or otherwise). In Saussurian terms, the sign is truly arbitrary. Its meaning exists only within a context of other symbols (see Saussure 1974 [1916]: 65–78; Barnard 2000: 121–4). That radical Saussurian position is not necessarily one that I hold, but it can be a useful way to think of the relations between words and symbols and between symbols and other symbols.

Theories of society, culture and nature

Tim Ingold (1999) has argued that hunter-gatherers have sociality, but, at least in some sense, *not* society. It is worth remembering, though, the imprecision of these very words, as well as their changing meanings. This is part of Ingold's point, although he emphasizes instead the difference between hunter-gatherers and others in terms of the immediacy of social relations of hunter-gatherers (that is, their lack of long-term commitments), their personal autonomy and their ideology and practice of sharing. For me, even a notion like 'hunter-gatherer sociality', or 'hunter-gatherer society', is not to be taken for granted. Those are fundamentally economic concepts, and therefore could have had little meaning before society was defined economically, as it came to be specifically in eighteenth-century Scottish writings (Barnard 2004). In seventeenth-century England, society was defined not economically but politically. Thus for Thomas Hobbes (e.g., 1991 [1651]), there could be no such thing as hunter-gatherer society or even hunter-gatherer sociality, because: (1) Hobbes had no notion that hunter-gatherers could be anything other than brutes, and (2) society required a social contract, and this he equated with the state. And hunter-gatherers, of course, do not create states.

In the seventeenth century, the word 'sociality' existed, but not in English. It occurred notably in the Latin writings of Samuel Pufendorf (1927 [1682]), in the form *socialitas*. This is almost invariably rendered in English as 'sociability', the ability to be sociable. In contrast, Hobbes does use the English word 'society', but he uses it not as a count noun but as an abstraction – with no indefinite article. In Hobbesian usage, people may live 'in society', but they do not live 'in societies'. In other words, Hobbes' notion of 'society' is at least approximately equivalent to Ingold's or Pufendorf's 'sociality' or *socialitas*. What we call 'societies', Hobbes called 'commonwealths', or, more accurately, 'the commonwealth'. Biologists reinvented the term 'sociality' in the twentieth century, and Ingold's vision of it is derived from that.

For me, hunter-gatherers not only live not only in society, but in societies. To accept that some but not all human groups are 'societies' seems to me a difficult position to maintain. No democratic society could ever be as societal as Hobbes conceived a true 'commonwealth' to be, and hunter-gatherer societies *do* represent a form of democracy. Decision-making is by consensus, and allegiance is to land-owning units. These may be bands or what in some ethnographic literature (especially with reference to Aboriginal Australia) are characterized as 'hordes', but more usually, the land-owning unit is a cluster of bands related through ties of kinship, language and, most importantly, association with the land itself. Society and the land-owning unit may be the same thing (Barnard 2002: 13–18).

Culture is more difficult to define. For me, this is also the concept which is difficult to conceive of as a count noun. In much of my earlier work I did so, but Adam Kuper's (1999) arguments against this view have persuaded me that there are no 'cultures', even if sometimes we have to act as if there are. The concept is too static. Radcliffe-Brown's (1952: 3–5) concept of 'cultural traditions' gets around this problem to some extent, but the fact of counting them at all still leaves us with a rather messy situation. There can be no pure 'cultures' or 'cultural traditions'; all cultures or cultural traditions are mixed. This, however, does not prevent us from using the word 'culture' with reference to stone tool traditions, in other words, 'culture' in a much narrower sense than is typical particularly in American 'cultural anthropology'. Nor should it prevent us from using it in an adjectival form, even with reference to cultural difference, for example the phrase 'cultural difference' itself, or the phrase 'cultural anthropology'. The best use of the word, though, is with reference to human 'culture', which is to say those aspects of the human makeup which are ubiquitous but not innate, and universal but not biological. Bruno Latour (1993: 103–9) has a more complicated answer to the question of whether or not 'cultures' exist, though his assertion that it is always possible to see peoples as possessing 'nature-cultures', rather than 'cultures' as distinct from nature, merely obscures the question of diversity among supposed 'cultures'. That said, he is right that all 'nature-cultures' define the human, the non-human and the divine (1993: 106), each 'nature-culture' through its own symbolic system.

Latour is an original thinker. Nevertheless, like all of us he draws on ethnography to aid his analytical sense in matters such as the divide, or lack of it, between nature and culture. In particular, he seems to draw on South American ethnography, or at least his theory evokes images of Amazonian and other non-Western explanations of the intertwined relations among nature, culture and society (cf. Descola 1994 and 2005). When once in the early 1980s I organized a seminar series on the nature/culture divide, I wrote to a number of social anthropologists to speak. The eminent Oxford anthropologist Rodney Needham wrote back that he did not wish to, because he found that nature–and–culture 'is an ill-founded and perhaps even a rhetorical opposition' (Needham, pers. comm.). He did not come to speak, nor give any deeper explanation, but his comment has proven correct. Latour found it so, as have many others. I shall return later to the ideas of society, culture and nature, and, of course, to symbol, metaphor, thought and language as well.

The human revolution

In 1964, Charles Hockett (a structural linguist with an interest in animal communication) and Robert Ascher (an archaeologist) put the case for an early 'human revolution' (Hockett and Ascher 1964). I remember their paper well: it was probably the first scientific article I read as an undergraduate, and it generated huge interest and debate. This was true not only at the time, but much later too among those who since the 1990s have looked again at possible origins for language – one of Hockett and Ascher's main concerns. Some have examined aspects of the original thesis, including human divergence from 'the apes', and similarities and differences between animal communication and human. However, the prevailing view today seems to favour or take an interest in a later 'revolution'. Some call it the 'symbolic revolution', and date it to within the last 100,000 years, or not long before. For these writers, 'language' means language as we know it today, and it is associated with the flowering of art, religion and so on. I count myself among the latter group, and this book argues the case from a social anthropological point of view.

In fact, my own view is slightly more complicated: there have been several revolutionary advances in human cultural and linguistic evolution. Hockett and Ascher were looking to one (now dated to 7,000,000 or 5,000,000 BP). I, along with others, am more interested in another, for the sake of argument, perhaps 130,000 BP, maybe 120,000 BP, maybe, as most claim, rather later. Many say around 50,000 BP, and some even later still. Adam Brumm and Mark Moore (2005: 157) refer to a 'commonplace' assumption of a symbolic revolution at between 50,000 and 40,000 BP, and this seems at first glance to trouble them in view of their wish to explain cultural evolution in Australia. That took place over the 50,000 or 40,000 years since first colonization of the continent, without much new input from the outside world since. Symbolic behaviour, including widespread use of personal ornaments (32,000 BP), pictorial art (17,000 BP) and so on, seems to have developed since then, and material culture evolved from Lower to Upper Palaeolithic in parallel with that of Africa and Europe through these past tens of thousands of years.

This book deals with that latter revolution, the symbolic revolution (as opposed to the 'human revolution' of Hockett and Ascher), when symbolism blossomed and when language became (or gradually began to become) something more than a simple system of communication. I do tend to call it the 'symbolic revolution' in order to differentiate it from Hockett and Ascher's. This terminology is not necessarily an agreed one though, and how fast or slow it might have been is an ever present issue. To me, the revolutionary nature of the change is more important than the speed of it, and for that reason, I favour an earlier date for symbolic thought if possibly a later one for *full language* and all that that entails. I have seen too many changes of such dates over the last couple of decades to stick by these as truly significant for exact origins. Usually, with new discoveries and further constraints (for example, genetic findings, the date of the Toba volcano in present-day Indonesia, the populating of Australia or the Americas or archaeological discoveries) they seem to change from a later one to an earlier one. For that reason, my suggestion of 130,000 or 120,000 years for a symbolic revolution should at best be taken as educated guesswork. They must have occurred before the Toba explosion (about 74,000 years ago, or within five years of that) or Blombos Cave in South Africa (around the same time) – both of which almost certainly post-date symbolic thought, if not language. In fact, a good argument could be made at least for *looking for* symbolic culture from 130,000 or 120,000 years ago, dates which mark the approximate beginnings of the Eemian interglacial period and the Late Pleistocene geological epoch. The dates may simply be coincidental and the boundaries quite arbitrary, but the image is clear: the Late Pleistocene is the epoch of 'modern' humanity and symbolic thought. As we shall see in Chapter 7, the Holocene (from 10,000 BP to the present) is, in a sense, the epoch of a kind of 'postmodernity': the Neolithic and all that followed.

One authoritative conference volume edited by archaeologist Paul Mellars and palaeo-anatomist Chris Stringer (1989) is called *The human revolution*. Most of its 800 pages fall broadly within the sphere of my concerns, and with the time frame of the 'symbolic revolution' more than with Hockett and Ascher's 'human revolution'. That volume deals with, among other topics, the emergence of *Homo sapiens sapiens*, regional versus Out of Africa theories of its evolution and geographical origin, the extinction of the Neanderthals, changes in behaviour implied in the Upper Palaeolithic archaeological record and the original colonization of the Australian continent. A subsequent, even more wonderful, conference volume, *Rethinking the human revolution* (Mellars *et al.* 2007), examines a wealth of issues in genetics and demography, in the cognitive sciences, including neuroscience and linguistics, and especially in archaeology. It also deals with the later revolution. Sadly, there do not seem to have been any social anthropologists among the seventy-four participants and contributors, although many of our number feature among those cited in the papers. Most of these social anthropologists are ethnographers of living hunter-gatherer populations, and I hope that this book serves in part to redress that balance by bringing a social anthropological perspective to archaeological data, as well as data and ideas from within social anthropology and linguistics to larger audiences.

There is no doubt though that this later revolution, whatever we call it, was truly the great one. It was the one which generated symbolic thought, and, more to the point, symbolic culture – which is the ultimate mark of humanity.

2 Stones, bones, ochre and beads

The discipline that has had the most to say about early symbolic thought is archaeology. Yet, archaeology has no internal means of interpreting its material findings. It relies on speculation, on ethnographic comparison and on theories drawn, at least implicitly, from social anthropology. If social anthropology (or 'sociology', as Lévi-Strauss saw it) cannot explain the genesis of symbolic thought, then what can?

This chapter outlines recent archaeological discoveries and provides my own explanations, as well as those presented by archaeologists themselves. Important findings include etched red ochre from Blombos Cave, about 100 metres from South Africa's Indian Ocean coast, and beadwork made from shells, also found at Blombos. Both are dated to around 77,000 or 75,000 BP (see, e.g., Henshilwood 2009). There are also engraved ostrich egg shell fragments from Apollo 11 Cave in southern Namibia, dated at 83,000 BP (Miller *et al.* 1999). Even finds interpreted as non-*Homo sapiens* are possibly relevant too: for example, the Mousterian perforated cave bear femur found in Slovenia and described, controversially, as a 'Neanderthal flute' (see, e.g., d'Errico *et al.* 2003: 36–9). There are suggestions of ochre use much earlier than at Blombos, between 270,000 and 170,000 BP at Twin Rivers in Zambia (Barham 2002), possible ritual burial among *Homo heidelbergensis* around 320,000 BP in Spain (Bermúdez de Castro *et al.* 2004), and various changes in stone technology early in the African Middle Stone Age that might indicate creativity reminiscent of symbolic thought. There are even claims of 'rock art' that could be 290,000 or even 700,000 years old, specifically cupules at Auditorium Cave, Bhimbetka, in Madhya Pradesh, India (see, e.g., Bednarik 1996). These were

16   *Stones, bones, ochre and beads*

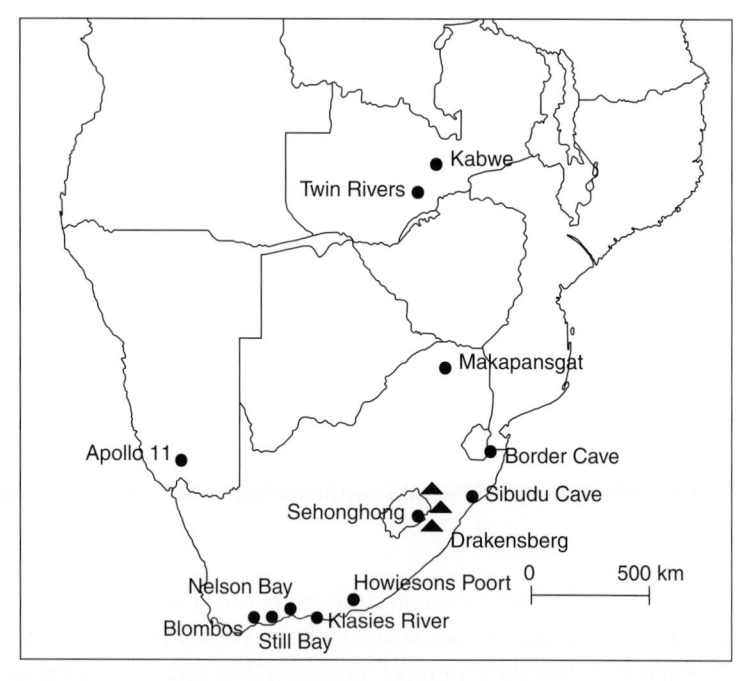

Figure 2.1. Southern African archaeological sites with early symbolic culture

discovered in the early 1990s, but beyond that not much can be said about their origins. The beautiful rock paintings found in the same area are much more recent. Robert Bednarik has published very extensively on evidence of early 'art' in many forms, on all inhabited continents, and broadly his conclusion (e.g., Bednarik 2003) is that Asia has the earliest of all the world's rock art and art objects. Some will differ, and for various reasons southern Africa remains the subcontinent where rock art has gained most prominence.

Figure 2.1 shows the locations of southern African sites where early symbolic culture is found or reported. The question is: how far should we go? Some archaeologists have gone much, much further. For example, there is the jasperite cobble which appears to have the face of a man. This, the earliest proclaimed 'art object', was collected by a hominin, possibly an *Australopithecus africanus*, at Makapansgat, in South Africa. This was some 2,300,000 or possibly even 3,000,000 years ago (Bednarik 1998), and the pebble lies well away from any natural source. Yet, in my view, this is going too far. After all, any material culture can have some kind of meaning, look like something else or have aesthetic value, at least to modern eyes. We might wish to distinguish such things from truly symbolic culture, although I would nevertheless be reluctant to define the 'symbolic' too specifically. It may be better to think in terms of three cultural levels: *material culture* (fashioned artefacts), *aesthetic culture* (which may include culturally understood objects, whether fashioned or not) and *symbolic culture* (whose meaning is both cultural and deeper). Material culture is obvious. Aesthetic culture is often hard to decipher, let alone to interpret. Symbolic culture, although it may be deeper in its meanings, is nevertheless both more obvious and more profoundly interesting. It is the main subject of this book.

The hominin fossil record

In order to appreciate early symbolic thought, we need first to understand the hominin fossil record and the technological advances which accompanied human evolution. Some technological advances enabled humans to spend more time planning, playing and in the pursuit of the arts. Among these were the bow and arrow, in Australia the boomerang, and in South America the atlatl. Hafting of stone points onto spears has been dated at 285,000 BP in eastern Africa and in continuous use in southern Africa for the past 100,000 years. Bow and arrow technology has been dated, if but arguably, at 64,000 BP at Sibudu Cave in South Africa (Lombard and Phillipson 2010). No doubt, also, earlier advances in stone, bone, antler, leather and wood tool-making abilities facilitated greater efficiency in hunting and other 'work'-related activities. Many of such material advances may also have had aesthetic implications too. However, ultimately I am not concerned with any of these here except as forerunners of symbolic culture. Therefore, let me simply offer a brief summary of human prehistory, by way of background. Further background information is, of course, available in many other sources, including my own *Social anthropology and human origins*, Chapter 3 (Barnard 2011: 33–52).

The hominin fossil record consists of twenty or more species, depending on how we count them (see, e.g., Sarmiento 2007). Some of the key ones

Table 2.1. *Hominin fossil species*

Species	Time	Location	Cranial capacity	Discovered (described)
Early species				
Sahelanthropus tchadensis	7 mya	Chad	360–70 cc	2001 (2002)
Orrorin tugenensis	6.1–5.7 mya	Kenya	unknown	1974 (1975)
Ardipithecus kadabba	5.7–5.2 mya	Ethiopia	unknown	1997 (2001)
Ardipithecus ramidus	4.4–3.9 mya	Ethiopia	unknown	1992 (1994)
Australopithecines				
Australopithecus anamensis	4.2–3.9 mya	Kenya, Ethiopia	unknown	1965 (1967)
Australopithecus afarensis	3.9–2.9 mya	Ethiopia, Kenya	380–550 cc	1935/1973 (1974)
Australopithecus bahrelghazali	3.6 mya	Chad	unknown	1993 (1995)
Kenyapithecus platyops	3.5–3.2 mya	Kenya	<400 cc	1999 (2001)
Australopithecus africanus	2.8–2 mya	South Africa	400–500 cc	1924 (1925)
Paranthropus aethiopicus	2.7–2.5 mya	Ethiopia	410 cc	1985 (1985)
Paranthropus boisei	2.6–1.2 mya	Tanzania, Kenya	500–50 cc	1959 (1959)
Australopithecus garhi	2.5 mya	Ethiopia	450 cc	1996 (1999)
Paranthropus robustus	2–1.2 mya	South Africa	410–530 cc	1938 (1938)
Australopithecus sediba	2–1.8 mya	South Africa	420–50 cc	2008 (2010)
Early Homo forms				
Homo habilis	2.3–1.4 mya	Tanzania, Kenya, Ethiopia	590–687 cc	1959 (1962)
Homo gautengensis	2 mya–600 kya	South Africa	unknown	1977 (2010)
Homo erectus	2 mya–300 kya (or until 50 kya)	Indonesia, China, Africa, etc.	850–1,100 cc	1891 (1892)
Homo rudolfensis	1.9 mya	Kenya	c. 700 cc	1972 (1986)
Homo ergaster	1.9–1.4 mya	Kenya, South Africa	502–909 cc	1971 (1972)
Homo georgicus	1.8 mya	Georgia	610–775 cc.	1991/1999 (2002)
Homo floresiensis	74–13 kya	Indonesia	380–417 cc	1965/2003 (2004)
More modern species				
Homo antecessor	1.2 mya–800 kya	Spain, England, Algeria	1,000–150 cc	1995 (1997)
Homo heidelbergensis	880–250 kya	Europe, Africa	1,100–400 cc	1907 (1908)
Homo neanderthalensis	600–30 kya	Europe, Africa	1,200–740 cc	1829/1856 (1856)
Homo rhodesiensis	300–125 kya	Zambia	1,100 cc	1921 (1921)
Homo sapiens sapiens	200 kya	worldwide	average 1,450 cc	– (1758)
Homo sapiens idaltu	160 kya	Ethiopia	1,450 cc	1997 (2003)

are outlined in Table 2.1. While, technically, hominins (the Linnaean tribe Hominini) include chimps and bonobos as well as members of the subtribe Hominina, only the latter are included here. *Sahelanthropus*, found in Chad, is said to be the last common ancestor of chimps and humans. *Orrorin*, found in Kenya, was certainly not an ancestor of the chimpanzees, but closer to the line from which we humans are descended. The Ethiopian fossil *Ardipithecus* was another possible human ancestor, but was arboreal if probably largely bipedal. Through the years, a number of classifications have changed, and this goes on all the time. The rules on naming are detailed and technical (see Ride *et al.* 2000). Just two rules are worth noting here: (1) when species are reclassified, the older name takes precedence over the newer, and (2) one may abbreviate genus names but not species names unless they are also identified by a subspecies name. For example, if we classify Neanderthals together with (other) humans they are *Homo sapiens*, or more specifically *H. sapiens neanderthalensis* or *H. s. neanderthalensis* (and ourselves, *H. sapiens sapiens* or *H. s. sapiens*). In this text, *Homo* is abbreviated where appropriate, but never *sapiens*. Likewise, for example, although humans may be 'apes', if ever humans and chimps were to join the same genus, chimps (*Pan troglodytes*) become *Homo troglodytes*. Humans do not become *Pan sapiens*. This is simply because the classification *Homo* is older and therefore, according to the rules, takes precedence.

The australopithecines exhibited considerable sexual dimorphism. Therefore, their social organization was probably more ape-like than human-like: families living polygynously, a dominant male with more than one female partner. This is perhaps more likely with *Australopithecus africanus* than with *A. afarensis*, about whom there is some debate on this issue. The human sexual dimorphism of pelvis size, also found among australopithecines, may have to do with changes required in lumbar support for pregnant females who walk on two legs. There is an assumption today of possible tool use with some australopithecine species, notably *A. garhi*, although *Homo habilis* (by definition, 'handy man') is credited with using and being the first to fashion stone tools. In Table 2.1, the split date on *Australopithecus afarensis* reflects the discovery of a Kenyan specimen by Louis Leaky in 1935 (identified as *A. afarensis* only in 1979) as well as the famous discovery of 'Lucy' by Donald Johanson at Hadar, Ethiopia, in 1973.

Australopithecines are classified either as *Australopithecus* (southern ape) or more commonly, as members of separate genera though still loosely referred to as australopithecines or australopiths. *Paranthropus boisei* was originally classified as *Zinjanthropus* (nut-cracker man), then reclassified as *Australopithecus*, and now more commonly given the genus name *Paranthropus* (beside human). Those classified as *Paranthropus* are often called robust australopithecines, and those classified as *Australopithecus* are often referred to as gracile australopithecines. Robust australopithecines had a diet consisting largely of grasses, while gracile species ate more fruits and tubers. Recent work has suggested that southern Africa gave rise to *Homo*, through descent from a newly discovered *Homo*-like australopithecine called *A. sediba*, from Malapa, a cave site near Johannesburg in South Africa (Berger *et al.* 2010; Pickering *et al.* 2011).

Since the 1960s, the earliest member of the genus *Homo* has been assumed to be *H. habilis*, or possibly *H. rudolfensis* (represented by the controversial 'Skull 1470', discovered in 1972). However, the recent reclassification of skull fragments discovered in 1977 in the Sterkfontein caves, near Johannesburg, has given us an earlier *Homo* species: *H. gautengensis* (Curnoe 2010). This, of course, fits in with the suggestion that southern, rather than eastern, Africa is where *Homo* might have originated, although it seems likely that some of the earliest branches of *Homo* did migrate northwards to eastern Africa while others evolved in the south. Less than a metre tall, *H. gautengensis* apparently spent much time in the trees, and charred animal remains were found in association with the fossils (indicating the possible use of fire). It is today assumed that we are all descended from *H. ergaster*, a close cousin of *H. erectus*. *H. erectus* is, of course, quite unique in its long duration, and therefore variety, with some eight recognized subspecies: *H. erectus erectus*, *H. erectus yuanmouensis*, *H. erectus lantianensis*, *H. erectus wushanensis*, *H. erectus nankinensis*, *H. erectus pekinensis*, *H. erectus palaeojavanicus* and *H. erectus soloensis*.

Homo erectus was the first hominin to venture out of Africa, and specimens have been found in Indonesia ('Java Man', in 1891), China ('Peking Man', in 1923) and, depending on classification of various remains, in Israel, Georgia and Spain, as well as in southern, eastern and northern regions of the African continent. *H. erectus* made tools, made fire and cooked. Some subspecies, such as *H. erectus pekinensis*, relied more on vegetable foods, while other subspecies lived extensively by hunting, it is presumed, in task-specific hunting groups. The relevance of all this to later humanity is that humans had *culture* long before we had *symbolic culture*. The divergence of the human line from chimpanzees is now reckoned by many geneticists to have been somewhere between 6,300,000 and 5,400,000 years ago. This is about twice as recent as once thought. Humans were making tools by 2,500,000 BP, and there is recent evidence of tool use by *Australopithecus afarensis* by 3,390,000 BP (McPherron *et al.* 2010). Chimps make tools today, although we have no idea how long ago they started doing this. The evolution of *Homo* was slow, apparently without appreciable biological adaptations of any kind that affected cognitive abilities, and without much progress in toolmaking techniques until *Homo heidelbergensis*, *H. neanderthalensis* and, really, until *H. sapiens* (see also Gamble 2007; Coolidge and Wynn 2009).

Multiregional Continuity Model versus Recent African Origin

There are two main theories of modern human population origins. The Multiregional Continuity Model (MCM) is now argued by very few palaeontologists, and in my view can no longer be sustained. This theory is in fact reliant on palaeontological evidence, and proponents see the evolution of humans through fossil finds in continuity within regions of the Old World. In this view, *Homo sapiens* evolved from *H. erectus* not once nor in a single location, but independently on several continents. Thus, crudely, the 'races' of humankind reflect very ancient evolutionary developments: Asians and Native Americans from 'Peking Man', Australian Aborigines from 'Java Man', Europeans from Neanderthals and Africans from *H. ergaster*. The theory, in one form or another, was propagated originally by Franz Weidenreich (1947), later in a more purist and racialist form by Carlton Coon (1962) and later still by a number of palaeo-anthropologists active especially in the early 1980s. While there may be evidence of slight genetic continuity, for example, from Neanderthals to some modern populations of Eurasia, palaeontological evidence for widespread continuities is today unsustainable in light of massive genetic breakthroughs since the 1980s (see, e.g., Cann *et al.* 1987). Those today who adhere to some version of the multiregional hypothesis do so only in part, and generally as explaining only some genetic material believed to be carried from earlier population groups down to modern ones.

The Recent African Origin (RAO) or Out of Africa theory is the accepted model – or what Chris Stringer (2011: 261) has labelled the 'mostly out of Africa' model, in deference to the fact that only 10 per cent of the human genome is represented by those who left the continent. We may all be Africans, but some of us are more African than others. African populations account for some 90 per cent of the genome. In a somewhat controversial rendition of the model, the Israeli geneticist Doron Behar and his team argue that all humanity is descended in a common matriline from a small group of Africans who lived something between 210,000 and 140,000 years ago (Behar *et al.* 2008: 6). Of more than forty mtDNA lineages in African populations, only two were part of the Out of Africa migration (or migrations). The team argue further that kinship was probably matrilineal, but this seems unlikely to me. Much more probable would have been uxorilocality, leading at best to *de facto* matriliny among some groups. Their date for an Out of Africa migration and dispersal of the rest around Africa is between 70,000 and 60,000 BP, with a split among Khoisan populations of between 150,000 and 90,000 BP. All these dates refer to matrilines only, since they are entirely based on mtDNA evidence.

With a theory of the common origin of humankind more or less in place, the next question is: what happened before Out of Africa? One may quibble over the minutiae, but my money is broadly on the explanation provided by Sir Paul Mellars (2006). His summary of events goes like this. Between 200,000 and 150,000 years ago, genetically and anatomically modern human populations emerged in Africa. Then around 110,000 or 90,000 BP, there was a dispersal of these modern populations, with both Middle Palaeolithic technology and elements of symbolic culture, into southwest Asia. Those populations died out but left traces in the archaeological record. Between 80,000 and 70,000 BP, there were rapid climatic and environmental changes in Africa, and these were associated with technological advances and with economic and social transformations in the eastern and southern parts of the continent. From 70,000 to

60,000 years ago, an expansion of population from a small source area gave rise to what we now know as modern humanity. From 60,000 years ago, part of this population left Africa and spread, mainly along coastlines, into Asia and Europe. In another paper, Mellars (2002: 31) refers to 'seemingly explicit evidence for fully symbolic expression' in Africa by 80,000 or 70,000 BP at the latest. In his comparison there between Europe and Africa, he notes that the appearance of symbolic elements in the archaeological record in Africa is more gradual, and in Europe, more sudden. To me this makes the significance of symbolic elements no more or less revolutionary, although the use of the term 'revolution' for something that might be slower than expected admittedly causes problems for some archaeologists. Crucial African finds cited by Mellars (2002: 37–40) include multiple-barbed bone spear points from three sites in Katande in the Democratic Republic of Congo, controversially dated at 90,000 BP, bifacial projectile points possibly from 80,000 or by 70,000 BP at Blombos, the famous intentionally designed abstract engravings on ochre in the same period, and perforated ostrich egg shell beads dating possibly from 50,000 BP at Mumba in Tanzania and definitively from 40,000 BP at Enkapune ya Muto in Kenya. He also notes two sites 'immediately to the north of Africa' (2002: 40), in Israel, of grave goods including a deer antler clasped in the arms of a deceased person and perforated sea shells, possibly decorative or 'symbolic' (Mellars' inverted commas), securely dated at between 110,000 and 90,000 BP.

Mellars' (2006) theory is, perhaps, driven to some extent by his background as an archaeologist, but it is utterly consistent with the findings of population genetics, known environmental factors and so on, all of which are incorporated into the model. Humans developed symbolic culture in Africa, at least some aspects gradually, long before the dates of 50,000 BP or so that many writers assume, and small numbers of these early *Homo sapiens* migrants left Africa carrying their African traditions to the other continents.

'Stone Age' prehistory

In global terms 'stone ages' are divided into three or five: Lower Palaeolithic, Middle Palaeolithic, Upper Palaeolithic, Epipalaeolithic

Table 2.2. *Grahame Clark's modes of lithic technology*

Mode	Technology	Archaeological periods (African/world/other label)
Mode 1	Choppers and flakes struck from pebble cores	Early Stone Age/Lower Palaeolithic/ Oldowan industry
Mode 2	Bifacial flaked cleavers and hand axes from large cores	Early Stone Age/Lower Palaeolithic/ Acheulean industry
Mode 3	Flaked tools made from prepared cores	Middle Stone Age/Middle Palaeolithic/ Mousterian industry
Mode 4	Retouched punch-struck blades	Later Stone Age/Upper Palaeolithic/ Aurignacian industry
Mode 5	Composite artefacts with microliths	Later Stone Age/European Mesolithic/ Microlithic industry

(North African and southern European) or Mesolithic (essentially northwestern European) and Neolithic. The southern African equivalents (also relevant to much of central and eastern Africa) do not map onto these very closely. For this reason, a number of recent overviews of African and especially southern African prehistory have favoured instead Sir Grahame Clark's (1969: 24–47) set of five modes of lithic technology. Among recent works using Clark's classification scheme are the overviews of African archaeology by David Phillipson (2005), Pamela Willoughby (2007) and Lawrence Barham and Peter Mitchell (2008). However, my concern in this book is not with lithic technology, but rather with symbolic thought, and less with Africa as a whole or African technology compared to European, and much more with the material evidence for symbolic thought, which is particularly evident in southern Africa. Therefore, like Mitchell (2002) in his earlier overview of southern African archaeology, and like the authors in Colin Renfrew and Iain Morley's (2009) edited volume on prehistoric spiritual culture, I prefer the traditional African (or southern African) classification. This dates from the 1920s and is still widely in use. Clark's 'five modes' are more useful for those whose primary concern is with lithics *per se*. For the sake of comparison, though, Clark's classification is shown in Table 2.2. (The Neolithic is not included among his five modes.)

The southern African designations are the Early Stone Age or Earlier Stone Age (roughly the Palaeolithic, especially the Lower Palaeolithic), the Middle Stone Age (roughly the Middle and Upper Palaeolithic), and the Later Stone Age. The last is sometimes said to correspond loosely with the European Mesolithic, but is ongoing, in the sense that modern, living African hunter-gatherers are often said to be 'Later Stone Age'. Such a designation is, of course, misleading, but it tends to refer to their social organization through its long duration, which in turn is related to their hunter-gatherer lifestyle, and *not* to their present-day tool kit. Their implements now are invariably made of iron. In the traditional classification, southern Africa and some other parts of Africa have no Neolithic, just as they have no Bronze Age (the European age between Stone and Iron). However, this traditional understanding is changing, since some archaeologists writing today (e.g., Sadr 2003) prefer to employ the term 'Neolithic' for the development of economies of livestock domestication. Such economies are characteristic of Khoekhoe cattle and sheep herders over the last 2,000 years or so, and this classification distinguishes them both from pure hunter-gatherer ones and from those of the Iron Age agro-pastoralists who form the majority populations of southern Africa today.

For those who do *not* employ the word 'Neolithic' in this way, the rough equivalent of the European Neolithic would represent part of the (late) Later Stone Age of Khoekhoe-speaking herders living in migratory hierarchical communities, and also, more usually, part of the (early) Iron Age of Bantu-speaking agro-pastoralists living in homesteads and well-organized villages. Therefore, while it is meaningful to speak of the earlier stages in global terms, it is useful to remember that although humankind began in Africa, when some moved out of Africa things began to change. Population groups around the world exhibit considerable diversity in economic activities associated with subsistence. The rough equivalents of each of these archaeological periods are shown in Table 2.3.

Fortunately, since our concern is not with *all* the ages described in Table 2.3, but pretty much only with the middle ones, the differences here should not cause much difficulty. The most important thing to remember is that 'Middle Stone Age' or 'MSA' does not mean 'Mesolithic'. Indeed, the meaning of 'Mesolithic' has changed through time, especially in its earliest usage, whereas 'Middle Stone Age' has had a

Table 2.3. *'Stone Age' archaeological periods*

Worldwide archaeological periods (and cultural developments)	Southern African archaeological periods (and cultural developments)
Lower Palaeolithic 2,600,000–100,000 BP Oldowan and Acheulean industries Early *Homo*, at first only in Africa *H. erectus* Out of Africa migration	**Early Stone Age 2,600,000–300,000 BP** Oldowan and Acheulean industries Early *Homo* and further human evolution
Middle Palaeolithic 300,000–30,000 BP Mousterian and subsequent industries Stone-tipped spears Neanderthals, *H. sapiens* *H. sapiens* Out of Africa migration	**Middle Stone Age 300,000–50,000 BP** Still Bay and Howiesons Poort industries Flaked tools, from prepared cores Early symbolic culture: beads, ochre (Development of language)
Upper Palaeolithic 45,000–10,000 BP Diversity of artefacts, bow and arrow Figurines, rock art Domestication of animals	**Later Stone Age 50,000 – recent** Robberg, Oakhurst, Albany, Wilton, Smithfield, etc. Industries. Acquisition of modern hunter-gatherer Lifestyles. Extensive rock art: painting and engraving Development of 'Neolithic' (herding) lifestyles
Mesolithic 22,000–5,900 BP Microliths, development of ceramics	Contact with Iron Age agro-pastoralists
Neolithic 12,700–5,300 BP Farming, urbanization	

relatively consistent meaning since its first use in the 1920s (Deacon 1990). 'Middle Stone Age' is taken today to constitute not only the technological tradition of the period of roughly 300,000 to 50,000 years ago, but the very early stages of symbolic expression, as it is found in the archaeological record. In the broadest terms, the African Middle Stone Age can be equated in time depth and material culture to the Middle Palaeolithic, and in symbolic culture (including early rock art) both to the Middle Palaeolithic and also to the Upper Palaeolithic.

As there remain both differences in the usage of such terms and differences in the timing and geographical distribution of archaeological cultures, it is always best to be cautious about inferring precise meaning to them. There have been several attempts to replace the southern African system of Early, Middle and Later Stone Age (Underhill 2011). These include various archaeological congresses, including notably the Pan-African Congress of Prehistory held in Tenerife in 1963, the Burg-Wartenstein Symposium held in an Austrian castle in 1965 and the Pan-African Congress at Dakar in 1967. They also include books and articles by prominent South African archaeologists like Revel Mason and Garth Sampson in the 1970s, arguing against the traditional classifications, and perhaps implicitly, too, against the changes in theoretical approach which marginalized such classification schemes.

Then too came a shift towards later periods within the South African archaeological establishment, as leading archaeologists and their students sought, especially in the 1970s and 1980s, to identify with the anti-apartheid struggle. David Underhill (2011: 8–9) identifies thirteen different classification schemes in South Africa from 1911 to 1999, and many of these reflected regional differences (in the choice of period names from the names of sites, alongside Early, Middle and Later) or reflected simply 'bad' chronology. Therefore, caution should be exercised in the use of any such labels, although when we talk of the 'Middle Stone Age' today it is a fair bet to say that we are at least looking, legitimately, for symbolic thought.

Evidence of symbolic thought

From before humanity to behavioural modernity

As is well known, perhaps the most important hominin ever to be discovered in Africa was *Australopithecus africanus* or 'Dart's child', found at Taung, in South Africa, in 1924. This species lived more than 2,000,000 years ago, and was very different biologically and culturally, and, of course, cognitively, from the many *Homo* species which followed. (I use 'followed' here, both in terms of human ancestry and in terms of fossil discovery.) *A. africanus* was important because it proved Darwin right: humanity's origins were in Africa, not in Asia.

However, *A. africanus* was not the first African discovery. That honour goes to 'Rhodesian Man' or 'Broken Hill Man', discovered in 1921 at the Broken Hill lead and zinc mine in what was then Northern Rhodesia, now Zambia. Ironically, Broken Hill was named after a mine in the interior of New South Wales, Australia. It is now called Kabwe, and the find is known as *Homo rhodesiensis* or, much more commonly, as *H. heidelbergensis*. This is the same species as that found at Heidelberg, Germany in 1907, but it lived more recently in Africa, between 300,000 and 125,000 years ago. The significance of the find may lie in its cognitive abilities. This species is also known as 'archaic' *H. sapiens*, or in any case, one of the 'archaics' (Neanderthals also being 'archaic' *H. sapiens*). The term 'archaic', though, is not as common as it once was. Like 'modern', and even more so like 'behavioural modernity', it is perhaps best either avoided or used very carefully (see also Shea 2011).

All this begs the question not only of when 'behavioural modernity' might have begun, but when it became possible. The evidence of ritual burial at 320,000 BP (Bermúdez de Castro *et al.* 2004) certainly suggests it was indeed at least possible. That was among *H. heidelbergensis*. There is plenty of evidence of ritual disposal of the body, often with de-fleshing, and of burial proper among Neanderthals, and similarly among *H. sapiens idaltu* at Herto in Ethiopia (at 160,000 or 150,000 BP), among *H. sapiens* at Skhūl in Israel (between 130,000 and 100,000 BP) and with *H. sapiens* at Klasies River Mouth in South Africa (around 110,000 BP and later). There is similar evidence in the Djebel Qafzeh in Israel (100,000 to 90,000 BP), at Border Cave in South Africa (definitely by around 82,000 and possibly as early as 170,000 BP), at Taramsa in Egypt (60,000 to 50,000 BP), on Lake Mungo in Australia (both a burial and a cremation, variously dated at 60,000 or 40,000 BP, originally dated at between 32,000 and 25,000 BP) and so on. These and many other cases of ritual mortuary activity are argued in depth in recent work by British archaeologist Paul Pettitt (2011). The fact that numerous Neanderthal sites (Pettitt 2011: 78–138), as well as *H. sapiens sapiens* ones, are attested or argued, and from as long ago as 75,000 BP, looks pretty convincing as evidence for some kind of ritual. Thinking in terms of a 'single species model', even for the *origin* of behavioural modernity, may be incorrect (d'Errico *et al.* 2003: 19). Whether they had 'Neanderthal flutes' or not, Neanderthals both buried the dead and produced and presumably used pigment crayons: in short, they seem to have possessed some kind of ritual and some kind of decoration, as well as, possibly, some kind of music.

I will not dwell further here on burials or cremations, but turn now to other evidence of symbolic thought: specifically that of some key sites in southern and eastern Africa. These regions hold the key to understanding early symbolic thought both because they are indeed older than sites elsewhere in the world and because they lie in the part of the world from which modern humans emerged. In light of such material, it is also interesting to see how archaeologists have interpreted their sites: with ever-more increasing reliance on anthropological theory and today often with bold assumptions about symbolic thought.

Twin Rivers and Mumbwa Caves, Zambia

Near Lusaka are sites known as Twin Rivers and Mumbwa Caves. As I noted earlier, they are significant because of the presence of ochre and its presumed use in some kind of symbolic activity (Barham 2002 and 2004). This could be as early as 270,000 years ago, with Middle Stone Age (MSA) flaked tool technology even earlier. Yet, for me, the most interesting thing about the material from these sites is not so much how early it is, but how creatively it is interpreted by its principal investigator, Lawrence Barham (see, e.g., 2000 and 2007).

Other sites in Zambia are similar in their indication of gradual changes in behaviour which seem to point to a relation between environmental exploitation, material remains and social life. Barham sees these in comparative perspective and argues a long development from the dawn of the MSA to recent times. Both Barham and Robert Foley (2004) develop comparative models of innovation, and they base these on Dame Mary Douglas' grid/group analysis (Figure 2.2). This is a structuralist theory and method for differentiating either whole societies or social groups within a society according to two axes: 'grid' (those representing constraints of social hierarchy) and 'group' (those representing constraints of group solidarity). The cross-cutting axes generate four 'boxes': low grid and group (individualism and competition), low grid with high group (strong group solidarity), high grid with low group (isolation or constraint by the system itself), and high grid and group (strong group solidarity with social hierarchy). In small-scale societies, the method works particularly well for explaining

30   *Stones, bones, ochre and beads*

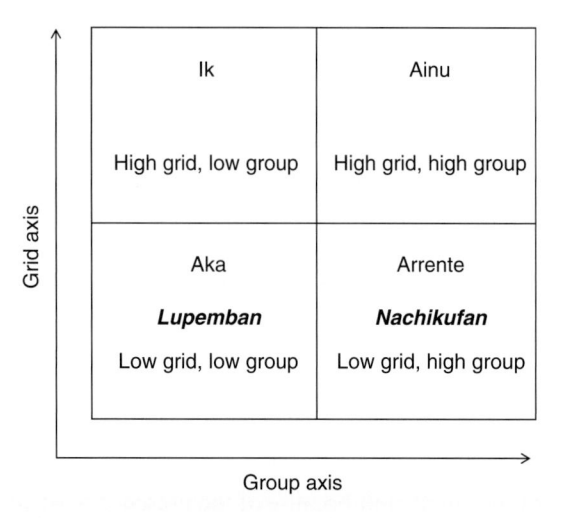

	Ik	Ainu
	High grid, low group	High grid, high group
	Aka	Arrente
	Lupemban	**Nachikufan**
	Low grid, low group	Low grid, high group

(Grid axis / Group axis)

Figure 2.2. Mary Douglas' grid/group boxes (with examples)

things like the use of symbols and the constraints implied in ritual activity (see Douglas 1969 and 1982). It also works well in specific situations, like, for example, the comparison of differently organized science laboratories (Barnard 2000: 152–6), although I am sceptical of its use in many of the situations that Douglas herself suggested. I illustrate it here with Barham's (2007: 171–3) contrast between Nachikufan and Lupemban industries and with some examples of hunter-gatherers today, gleaned from the pages of *The Cambridge encyclopedia of hunters and gatherers* (Lee and Daly 1999).

Lupemban industries were spread throughout central and western regions of Africa from about 32,000 to 17,000 BP. They were characterized, among other tools and weapons, by long, thin bifacial and two-pointed blades. Through most of this period, population density was low and symbolic behaviour does not seem to have been significant. Barham argues the case for the Lupemban as low grid and group. But during this time also, the bow and arrow came into use within this industry. Barham suggests that this might have led to great population density and ultimately to the Nachikufan. Nachikufan industries were centred in Zambia and characterized by the development of small blades, followed by scrapers and bored stones: from about 20,000 to 10,000 BP. These industries coincide with a period of environmental stress, and they also mark the appearance of geometric rock art. Barham speculates that the group solidarity implied by the appearance of the art may suggest high group solidarity.

The Aka (Bayaka or Mbenjele) seemingly have no strong environmental or social constraints: they associate with whom they please, including non-hunter-gather 'patrons' of their choice. The Ik (Teuso) of Uganda, a former farming group, reverted to hunting and gathering in the 1960s, and with this to individual isolation and mistrust, because of drought and the loss of their lands. The Arrente (Arunta or Aranda) of the Australian interior are a highly structured but (apart from age and gender considerations) otherwise egalitarian society. The Ainu are hierarchical, traditionally with inherited chieftaincy and headmanship and with, in the recent past, their holders maintaining political, judicial and spiritual roles.

Foley (2004) employs the grid/group method in order to differentiate societies according to the probability of geographical isolation and the diversity of resources within an environment. These factors operate according to rates of cultural boundary formation, and they can give different results from Barham's or mine (Foley's has the Arrente as low in habitat diversity, analogous to 'group', as well as low in geographical isolation, analogous to 'grid'). The application of such tools of social anthropological method as this, and the implications here of Douglas' insistence on a close relation between society and cosmology, is indeed intriguing. It offers a useful means with which to conceptualize change in archaeological 'cultures', without the encumbering specificity of more precise anthropological and sociological models.

Apollo 11 Cave, Namibia

Apollo 11 Cave was first excavated at the time of the Apollo 11 space mission, in 1969, hence its name. Among the most significant finds there are pieces of mobile rock paintings of animals (Wendt 1976; see also Masson 2006). They have been dated between 27,500 and 25,500 BP. The well-known Upper Palaeolithic animal paintings at Lascaux in France and Altamira in Spain date only from around 17,000 BP, although recent discoveries have yielded similar paintings at Chauvet Cave in France which are earlier, between 32,000 and 30,000 BP.

At Apollo 11 there are numerous cupules, circular engravings and paintings, mostly more recent than 25,500 BP. As an art form, portable pieces are rare in the world and those of Apollo 11 are the oldest ever discovered. Both the paintings and the engravings have been interpreted quite definitively as fitting the pattern typical of shamanic rock art of southern Africa (Masson 2006: 84–5). There are engraved 'lines of power', 'power spots' and so on related to animal depictions in the art, and these are believed to be indications of a trance performance and associated rain-making and curing rites. These, of course, are well documented among Kalahari San groups (e.g., Marshall 1999), and there is almost certainly a cultural continuity between the rock art of southern Africa and the present-day hunter-gatherer inhabitants of the Kalahari. Some of the material culture of Apollo 11 is related to the Howiesons Poort archaeological tradition, and there are traces of pigments dating possibly from as early as 49,000 BP (Masson 2006: 87).

Blombos, South Africa

The supreme significance of Blombos is without doubt. This is perhaps all the more true, given recent and compelling evidence (Henn *et al.* 2011) that southern Africa, rather that eastern Africa, is where *Homo sapiens sapiens* evolved. That evidence is based on genetic studies of both southern and eastern African living hunter-gatherer populations. The researchers were able to cut through the influence of 5,000 years of admixture with pastoralist and agro-pastoralist populations from elsewhere in Africa to examine geographic patterns of population diversity. While the detailed analysis is probably accessible only to experts, their conclusions are clear and the implications for symbolic culture are obvious. Assuming Brenna Henn and her colleagues are right, then symbolic thought and culture must have evolved with the populations of southern Africa. These authors offer climatological and archaeological evidence, including evidence from Blombos (Henshilwood *et al.* 2001), for additional support.

Eastern Africa experienced massive droughts between 135,000 and 75,000 BP (Scholz *et al.* 2007). The southern African climate was much more hospitable to humans during this period, and it remained more hospitable probably until about 60,000 years ago. This is exactly the period that Blombos material and symbolic culture was evolving. Of course, it is not possible to correlate Blombos specifically with the ancestors of the living hunter-gatherers of southern Africa. A much more reasonable proposition is to read the conclusions of Henn and her colleagues as implying something quite different: Blombos is indicative of an early form of symbolic culture, which began in southern Africa during the period of the eastern African droughts and rapidly spread northwards and across the globe. The droughts do not necessarily mean that people could not have passed through eastern Africa in those millennia, but, rather, simply that they probably did not evolve there. There will have been population bottlenecks, and continual habitation in the drought areas may have been difficult even for scattered hunter-gatherers. Migrating groups will have gone through to the north and onwards to Asia and Europe, first through eastern Africa and then across the available land bridges. At least some of these population groups must have carried the common cultural heritage of humanity that we all share with our Blombos ancestors.

Blombos has yielded as many publications as it has finds, and it has yielded plenty of finds! The most important discoveries there are the pieces of etched red ochre which have become iconic of cultural modernity (e.g., Henshilwood *et al.* 2009). The first two pieces of red ochre, discovered in 2002 and dated at 77,000 BP, are now joined by others, with fifteen pieces altogether, from levels from 100,000 to 75,000 BP. Christopher Henshilwood and his colleagues claim for them this title of *cultural modernity* precisely because they indicate also what we might describe as *symbolic modernity*. To a social anthropologist, what is at least as interesting as the ochre pieces themselves is the debate that seems now to be increasing in both complexity and sophistication. Much of it involves what is or is not 'modernity', and the degree to which it is important to have symbolism as well as advanced lithic technology in the mix. A key player at the level of general theory has been Lyn Wadley, notably through her key paper (Wadley 2001) asking the simple question 'What is cultural modernity?' She and others have argued that it is not invention, or technology itself, that creates modernity, but the definition of individual or group identity, and the negotiations that must have taken place with reference to artefacts or ochre, brought from a distance and stored. Christopher Henshilwood, who discovered the site (on his family farm) at Blombos takes this line too. And in spite of arguments against the assumption of language at Blombos, Henshilwood and his colleague Curtis Marean (2003: 636) hold that: 'Language and symbolic systems would also have facilitated trade or exchange and aided movement and contact between subdividing populations.'

For me, the evidence is gradually coming to be more convincing, not just because of the finds but because of the arguments for social complexity and the development of language earlier than once thought: some say that there was even language among Neanderthals (e.g., Krause *et al.* 2007). Indeed, even archaeologists who have excavated at Blombos and co-author papers on the site differ in their interpretations of it, with some looking to language and full symbolic expression, others less so, and others perhaps inclined towards a rather more open view on the plausibility of Neanderthal symbolic thought. The evidence for symbolic thought among Neanderthals is all the more evocative in view of Neanderthals in the modern European imagination, but it is also a genuine issue in view of suggestions on flute playing, hunting magic, the treatment of cave bear skulls, the use of pigments and perforations on bone and teeth, as well as burials (see Renfrew 2009).

Other sites: beyond Blombos

Christopher Henshilwood and Benoît Dubreuil (2011) comment on the relation between the two complex Middle Stone Age traditions in southern Africa. More significantly, they relate these two traditions, sites of the Still Bay or Stillbay tradition and the slightly later, more widespread and more numerous Howiesons Poort or Howieson's Poort (or simply HP) sites. Still Bay is usually dated from around 77,000 to 72,000 BP, and Howiesons Poort, or at least the eponymous site, from 66,000 to 59,000 BP. Both traditions include the use of non-local raw materials, hafted lithics, bone tools, hafted bone tools, engraved bone and the extensive processing of ochre. The Still Bay tradition exhibits bifacial points, abstract engravings on ochre and pierced shell beads, while the Howiesons Poort one contains crescent-shaped stone tools and abstract engravings on ostrich egg shell (Henshilwood and Dubreuil 2011: 377). Nelson Bay was inhabited by both Middle and Later Stone Age populations.

The richness of the finds over the last decade or so has even led Henshilwood and Dubreuil to speculate, at least tentatively, on possible migrations within southern Africa, on the transfer of ideas between peoples and on the increase in population in the times of the Howiesons Poort sites (2011: 379). Steven Mithen (2005: 250) has suggested that Howiesons Poort culture marks the beginning of 'modern thought and behaviour and by implication, language'. It may well do, although the argument depends on an enormous degree of nuance in how we define modern thought, modern behaviour and also (modern) language – that is, language as we know it. As we shall see later, I believe that modern language emerged with the coincidence of its use in symbolic thought, especially symbolic expression embedded in narrative. It did not emerge in utilitarian speech (see also Barnard 2010a). The latter, utilitarian speech, simply does not have the necessity to build grammars of the kind living languages possess. In short, one sense of the concept 'modernity' is in essence the Middle Stone Age, and more precisely either Howiesons Poort or Still Bay. The etched red ochre pieces at Blombos were found in Still Bay layers.

Debates, as well as edited collections, on cognition among hominins, early humans and MSA southern Africans have been emerging in recent years (d'Errico and Backwell 2005), with the focus now to a great extent on the very real possibility of the emergence of symbolic thought along with the advanced cognitive capabilities of the earliest *Homo sapiens sapiens* (Beaune *et al.* 2009; Renfrew and Morley 2009). While some urge caution in the assumption of symbolic thought and practice (e.g., Wynn and Coolidge 2009), particularly among Neanderthals, the search for archaeological evidence for both symbolism and language is on the increase. This profound shift in archaeological thinking is due more than anything else to the recent finds in southern Africa, but due too to similar work elsewhere in Africa and in the Near East, Europe, India and Australia as well. I would predict that in the near future the commonly cited date of around 50,000 BP for the emergence of language, together with similar if slightly earlier dates for symbolic thought, will be pushed back to nearer the dates for the earliest *Homo sapiens sapiens*.

Recent dating methods and the age-area hypothesis

Today, archaeologists can date sites by means such as the decay of radioactive isotopes (see Renfrew and Bahn 2008: 121–74). The best known is radiocarbon dating (also known as carbon dating, carbon-14 dating), which measures the amount of this isotope in a sample of organic material from an archaeological site. This enables the archaeologists to calculate a date before the present for that organic material (such as bone, plant remains or charcoal). Carbon-14 decays into nitrogen at a constant rate, and it works back to about 60,000 BP. For earlier dates, potassium-argon (K-Ar) dating has been used. This measures the decay of a potassium isotope into argon in rock, and the most recent material that can be so dated is around 100,000 years old. Newer methods, such as argon-argon (40Ar-39Ar) dating, are both more accurate than K-Ar and possible for much younger rock specimens. Other methods include thermoluminescence and optical dating, which can in effect measure the time since geological material was last exposed to heat or sunlight.

However, radiocarbon dating was only invented in 1949, and all the many other methods are much more recent in invention. So what did archaeologists do before 1949? In fact, there was a method, or more accurately a hypothesis, which enabled not absolute dating (in terms of number of years) but relative dating (in terms of which of two things happened first). This was Clark Wissler's (e.g., 1923: 58–61) age-area hypothesis, which is closely related to the culture-area concept of the heyday of classic American cultural anthropology (e.g., Wissler 1927; Kroeber 1931). I believe it is still useful, although, of course, it is no longer necessary for use by archaeologists wishing to date bones, pottery or samples of rock that lie above their strata. That is because its use need not be confined to material remains, and can in theory be employed to work out the relative dates or direction of the spread of things such as myths, totemic beliefs, kinship systems or languages.

Recent dating methods and the age-area hypothesis

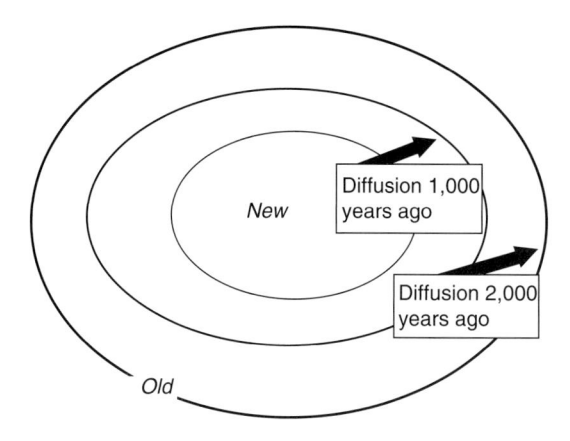

Figure 2.3. Wissler's age-area hypothesis: dating change within a culture area

Archaeologists no longer need Wissler's method, but perhaps social anthropologists do. Wissler did intend it mainly for material culture, but in the absence of a social anthropological equivalent of carbon-14 it is worth at least considering it as an alternative precisely when it is non-material remains we want to date. Such 'remains' could include any non-material, cultural artefact.

Often when teaching courses in the history of anthropology, I ask students which is more likely:

(a) Older aspects of culture are more likely in the centre of a culture area;
(b) Older aspects of culture are more likely on the periphery of a culture area; or
(c) Older aspects of culture are equally likely in the centre or the periphery.

Each year, the majority of students get it wrong. The 'correct' answer, according to Wissler, is (b), older things are found on the periphery. That is because things supposedly change in the centre, and diffuse outwards towards the periphery (see Figure 2.3). While the periphery may have contact with an adjacent culture area and take in foreign elements, nevertheless the elements indigenous to the culture area itself will be expected to be older than those at the ever-changing centre. Wissler was thinking mainly of changes within a culture area. Yet, the hypothesis makes sense too, for example, of aspects of language, even between culture areas. One will find, say, archaic features of the English language in the linguistic periphery of Scotland, Ireland or even North America, but not in London. The language of London or the southeast of England has lost some vocabulary still in existence elsewhere, and it has lost pre-consonantal and post-vocalic /r/ (in words like 'car' or 'cart'). These changes affecting southeastern England reached the English dialects of the periphery only later. A similar case can be made for the English of North America. In general, it is archaic, and Boston and New York have changed in ways the backwoods of Maine or West Virginia have not (see, e.g., Wells 1982: 218–22).

Clark Wissler (1923) explained the distribution of prehistoric artefacts of North America in terms of the development and expansion of culture areas. But what of the wider applicability of the hypothesis? As I have suggested, to a degree it works for non-material aspects of culture too, like language. But does it work between culture areas? Can we use it to speculate on, for example, the oldest kinship system, or the oldest religion? Will these also be found on a global periphery: the last land area occupied or the continent to which people migrated, rather than the one they came from? Is South American culture, or Australian, older than African? These very questions were characteristic of German-Austrian anthropology in the late nineteenth and early twentieth centuries, and present-day American cultural anthropology is descended from this tradition (see Barnard 2000: 47–60). For the moment, I merely raise this as a grand question and clearly one that lies beyond stones, bones, ochre and beads.

Broadly, my own answer to that grand question is both 'yes' and 'no'. The age-area hypothesis works sometimes, but not always. It is a tool to think with, but will not always produce the 'correct' answer. And other factors, such as known evolutionary sequences, will have to override it. Still, its existence and its continued relevance as such a tool should remind us never to underestimate the value of the history of the anthropological sciences. In this case, even a tool rendered useless to archaeologists by the invention of absolute dating methods remains good to think with within those branches of anthropology that have no such method. If sociology cannot explain the genesis of symbolic thought, then perhaps Wissler's hypothesis can give us something to conjure with.

3 Kinship, sociality and the symbolic order

In their seminal paper, Hockett and Ascher (1964) explained human society through its emergence from what we now call *hominin society*. I prefer to begin much later, with the evolution of *Homo sapiens* from *H. heidelbergensis* or *H. rhodesiensis*. Not much can be said about the social organization of any human ancestors directly from the archaeological record, but we can infer some things through comparative primatological studies, and through a number of theoretical works in both archaeology and social anthropology since the 1970s (see Barnard 2011: 18–32). We can also see it through comparisons among present-day human societies, and this will be my main focus.

At the very least, we should be able to assume that the attributes common to all human societies must lie at the base of *H. sapiens* sociality. Furthermore, I believe that those attributes common to all hunter-gatherers, but not to non-hunter-gatherers, can tell us something inherent in that lifestyle that the rest of us (the non-hunter-gatherers) have lost. I have recently written on this (e.g., Barnard 2010b), and my argument is that during the Neolithic transition we non-hunter-gatherers literally lost something of our humanity. This chapter explores the possibilities, and it tells what we know about things like decision-making, family and band structures and inter-group relations among fully human, fully 'modern', hunter-gatherers. There is, of course, no possibility of meeting any other kind, although we know that humans who were not quite like humans today did exist within the last few hundred thousand years. It is worth remembering that all humans alive today not only speak fully modern languages, but have done so since long before computers, literacy or the domestication of animals and plants. Language, in all its beauty, richness of vocabulary and grammatical complexity, was completely a hunter-gatherer invention. Knowing this will lead us to the possibilities we might envisage for fully modern hunter-gatherer societies in early stages of development, and towards an understanding of sociality among early symbolic humans.

Marriage: the root of *Homo sapiens* sociality

According to two primatologists, Duane Quiatt and Vernon Reynolds (1993: 261), 'Marriage evolved as a powerful structural linking mechanism, and undoubtedly had advantages in the bringing about of extensions of the communicative network between palaeolithic groups.' At first glance, it may seem odd to begin a chapter on kinship, sociality and the symbolic order with the evolution of marriage, but this quote puts that institution in perspective.

Marriage is communication. Lévi-Strauss repeatedly said something similar, notably in his great treatise, *The elementary structures of kinship* (Lévi-Strauss 1969c [1949]). Women are 'communicated' as wives, or (he added later) men are 'communicated' as husbands. All human social life is communication, and we must never suppose that marriage is something that exists merely between a husband and a wife. Of course, it can be that, especially in Western societies, but ethnography across the globe teaches us that more often than not, marriage unites kin groups as well as uniting individuals as spouses. For a Lévi-Straussian, marriage literally defines kin groups: they take on their meaning through the marriages that connect them to each other. One could say that marriage is that form of communication which defines human sociality, and, in essence, human society. It is not so much the collection of couples that is significant, but the sets of families that are related through couples. Families may also be related though some form of polygamous marriage or even 'group marriage', a communal form that at least nineteenth-century thinkers imagined as existing at the beginning of the institution.

As Robin Fox (1967: 54) once said, while every teenager knows the difference between sex and marriage, some anthropologists seem to muddle them up. The incest taboo is universal among modern humans, and therefore can be presumed to have an origin either in human biology or at the dawn of symbolic culture. Marriage presumably began later, and it is possible to allow sex between relatives that are forbidden as spouses. It follows that group marriage in its true form is not the same as promiscuity. The precise definition of incest (which relatives are forbidden does differ from society to society), and the regulation of incest along with the requirement to marry someone of some particular category, while not identical, are the twin pillars of what we might think of as symbolic sociality.

We should not confuse *communication* with *language*. Although the metaphor of society being 'a language' or being 'like a language' is common in structuralist writings, language is not communication except in some similar metaphorical sense. Language evolved in part from primate communication (Tomasello 2008: 13–55, 319–45). Yet, primate communication is just that; it is not really an incipient form of language at all, because language is much, much more than that. I will have much more to say about this in Chapter 5. Also, there are in fact many other forms of communication in human societies. Marriage communicates, and through this communication it creates bonds which may be enduring, or not, and which have the propensity to establish sets of relations which are both systematic and culturally understood. We call these sets of relations *kinship systems*, and kinship systems do share something with language. They have grammar. They share something else too. They have words, and words that can be attached to other words. These form metaphorical 'sentences', as well as sets of words that can also form parts of real sentences: 'mother's brother's daughter' (MBD) or 'father's sister's daughter' (FZD), for example.

We see the systematic nature of kinship ties in rules of marriage, such as MBD to FZS, or FZD to MBS. Marriage between people in these particular genealogical positions (that we call cross-cousins) is very common around the world. These so-called 'Iroquois' kin terminology structures are, in fact, rather more common than that of English, which has the so-called 'Eskimo' structure (see Figure 3.1). A kinship system is made up of such sets of words within a terminology structure; customs of postmarital residence (e.g., husband moves to the wife's place); rules for the transmission of group membership (e.g., a child belongs to the

Kinship embedded in cosmology?

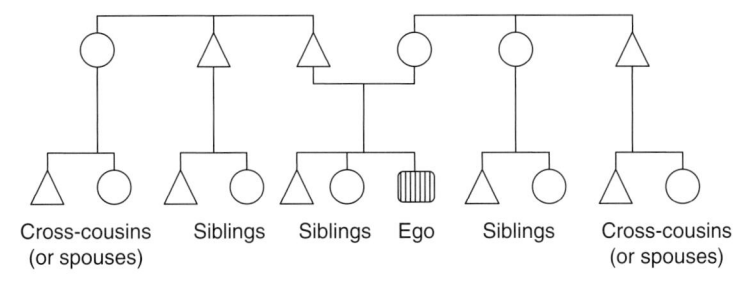

Cross-cousins (or spouses) — **Siblings** — **Siblings** — **Ego** — **Siblings** — **Cross-cousins (or spouses)**

'IROQUOIS' STRUCTURE

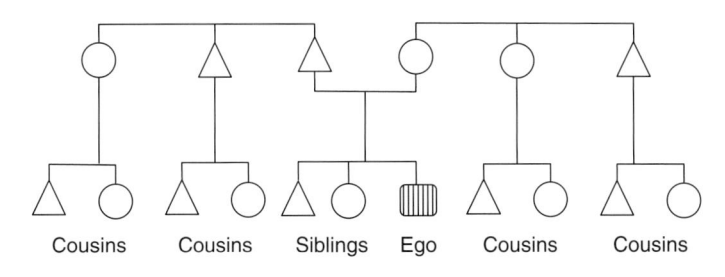

Cousins — **Cousins** — **Siblings** — **Ego** — **Cousins** — **Cousins**

'ESKIMO' STRUCTURE

Figure 3.1. 'Iroquois' and 'Eskimo' terminologies

group of its mother) and for the inheritance of property; rules constraining or permitting marriage to relatives; a host of behavioural norms; and the symbolic relations that govern the whole system.

Kinship embedded in cosmology?

I have argued elsewhere (Barnard 2008) that in the earliest symbolic times kinship became structured. However, ethnographic evidence from living hunter-gatherers is not quite conclusive. At one extreme, we have Australian Aborigines (e.g., Maddock 1972: 72–108), whose kinship systems remain the most structured in the world, in both the egocentric domain and the socio-centric: egocentric meaning in terms of relatedness to a given person (kin terms), socio-centric meaning in terms of categories the same for all (such as clans, moieties or sections). At the other extreme, we have groups like Andaman Islanders (Radcliffe-Brown 1964 [1922]: 22–87) and Mbuti Pygmies (Turnbull 1968, 110, 268–72), who extend kin classification only to close relatives, and are not concerned with categories like marriageable/non-marriageable. Like Westerners, they count people as 'close kin', 'distant kin' or 'unrelated', rather than all as members of all-embracing categories, extended throughout society. In the Mbuti case, even relationship terms for close kin are said to have no particular significance.

An in-between form is that of most Kalahari Bushman or San groups. This form is in between in the sense that these people recognize only egocentric categories, but there is a twist. That is, their systems share with the systems of Australia, South America and many other places the practice of universal kin categorization (Barnard 1978). There exist no 'non-kin'. Everyone in society belongs, in relation to any other individual, to some category or other. Even strangers *must* be fitted into the system: strangers, including ethnographers, have local or Bushman 'kin' as well. Such a system is, in fact, found in nearly all hunter-gatherer societies, in Africa, South Asia, Southeast Asia, Australia, North America and South America. It is also found in very small-scale cultivating communities from South Asia and Southeast Asia to the Americas. I cannot prove it, but I believe that this type of system is reminiscent of the primal, post-symbolic revolution kinship system.

Kinship can be unstructured, or it can be structured. But structured kinship can also exist within larger structures which comprise virtually everything. In other words, kinship is not always a separate realm, but can exist in systematic relation to totemic, mythological, cosmological and natural thought. This is the norm in traditional Australian Aboriginal religion. It is illustrated, for example, in the writings of C. G. von Brandenstein (1970 and 1982), a linguist who deciphered the presumed 'meanings' of the names and symbolic associations of the four sections of Kariera society (see Figure 3.2). The Kariera are a people much written about, but whose population was decimated by disease in the early twentieth century, and whose descendants no longer recall the traditional knowledge that made up symbolic aspects of their section system. Part of von Brandenstein's reconstruction of symbolic meanings is based on etymology. In the social sphere, Banaka men marry Burung women, who give birth to

Kinship embedded in cosmology? 45

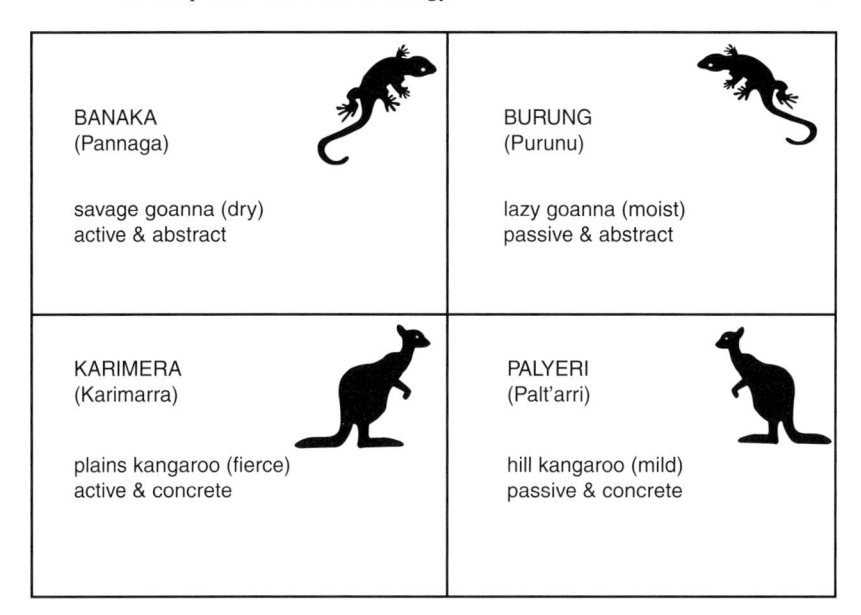

BANAKA (Pannaga) savage goanna (dry) active & abstract	**BURUNG** (Purunu) lazy goanna (moist) passive & abstract
KARIMERA (Karimarra) plains kangaroo (fierce) active & concrete	**PALYERI** (Palt'arri) hill kangaroo (mild) passive & concrete

Figure 3.2. The four Kariera sections and their symbolic associations

Palyeri children. Burung men marry Banaka women, who give birth to Karimera children. Palyeri men marry Karimera women, who give birth to Banaka children. And Karimera men marry Palyeri women, who give birth to Burung children. Banaka and Palyeri are connected through patrlineal descent, in a moiety (half of society) which in part reflects group structure. Likewise, Burung and Karimera are in the other patrilineal moiety. Banaka and Karimera are connected through an imaginary matrilineal moiety, deduced by anthropologists but not recognized by the Kariera themselves. Burung and Palyeri are in the other, imaginary matrilineal moiety. Thus, a man belongs to the same section as his father's father (and son's son), and a woman to that of her mother's mother (and daughter's daughter). What all this means is that if I am, for example, a male Banaka, so too are my siblings and my parallel cousins (and my paternal grandfather, my sons' sons, my sisters' daughters' daughters, etc.), and we marry Burung (who include our cross-cousins, etc.). We Banaka, that is, my sister and I, are represented by the savage goanna and have the characteristics of activity and abstractness, and our Burung spouses are represented by the lazy goanna, a different species, and are passive but also abstract, and so on.

A related question concerns the degree to which kinship is embedded in cosmology, or vice versa. Australian systems represent a world order of which kinship is a part. However, it is possible to have 'kinship systems' and even flexible cosmologies, neither of which has moiety, section or subsection structures, nor any kind of rigid rules of marriage or obligation. When kinship is embedded, it can be very much the *opposite* of the configuration we might find in Aboriginal Australia. Order and embeddedness do not necessarily go together, as the idea of 'kinship' with nature or with animals tells us. In Aboriginal Australia, one defines oneself as 'related' to others through a totem animal. In another sense, one may be related to an individual animal such as a dog. An entire species of animal, such as goanna or kangaroo, may belong to a 'section' or what in early Australianist literature was called a 'marriage class', and so too may an individual dog. Many hunter-gatherer peoples express 'kinship' with animals, or with nature. Nurit Bird-David (1990) makes this point in her paper, 'The giving environment'. Within ethnography and indeed in writings about ethnography, we have beautiful examples such as this one from Colin Turnbull (1985: 25): 'In explaining why they address the forest in this way, the Mbuti say: "Like our father and mother the forest gives us food, shelter, clothing, warmth, and affection."' The word the Mbuti use for 'affection' here is *kondi*, which means both 'love' and 'need', concepts which, Turnbull tells us, the Mbuti seldom differentiate.

Not only hunter-gatherers, but many other peoples too shy away from the separation of kinship from other realms. The case of East African pastoralists is so well known as to be trite in anthropology, so let me use *another* example. In the Arab world, it is said, there is sometimes a reluctance to accept universal values such as the rule of law. In Arab society, even what is understood as 'right and wrong' is dependent on kinship, in the form of group solidarity, and, more importantly, group opposition (Salzman 2008). One has not only loyalty to one's own group, but its very definition in terms of its structural opposition to groups of the same order of segmentation. This, of course, does not make Arabs any more culturally dependent than anyone else, nor incapable of understanding or indeed also holding the universalistic values claimed by liberal Westerners. But it does perhaps make some Arabs, in certain circumstances, cautious – because *other* principles, namely such oppositions between kin groups, are in play. According to Philip Carl Salzman (2008: 197–212), this creates a dilemma for those who see right thinking in both spheres: loyalty to kin group versus acceptance of common humanity.

Of course, this is not an 'Arab problem'. It is a universal problem, and a classic dilemma in social anthropology too. Human beings are at once the same the world over, but nevertheless profoundly but subtly different culturally, in thought and social behaviour (Barnard 2000: 99–119).

Symbolism and emotion

Kinship theory has gone through several phases in its history, from evolutionism to functionalism and structuralism, from descent to alliance, from an interest in groups to the slow growth of an interest in categories. In 1968, however, there was a revolution – from which kinship studies, some say, have not quite recovered. This was the publication of David M. Schneider's *American kinship* (1980 [1968]).

What Schneider did was simple. He jettisoned both the functionalist preoccupation with intra-familial roles and the structuralist concern with kinship structures as the outcome of marriages. He substituted instead a focus on symbolic dimensions, which he saw as more part of 'culture' than of 'society'. Much of Schneider's argument that kinship, in the words on the dust jacket, concerns 'systems of symbols and meanings' rests on the words and euphemistic phrases that white middle-class Americans use to describe kinship. Phrases like 'by blood', 'by birth', 'by marriage', 'the facts of life', 'man of the house', 'Smith blood in their veins', 'natural child', 'real mother', 'in-laws', 'meet my family', 'I have no family', all cited by Schneider at different points in his book, are examples. American (Euro-American) kinship is decidedly cultural and symbolic, but it is predicated on a notion of some imprecisely defined aspects of biology and of nature.

The primary unit of American kinship is 'the family' (Schneider 1980: 30–54). This is predicated on two kinds of 'love', one a euphemism for sexual intercourse, and the other its antithesis, the kind that stems from childbirth and close 'blood' bonds. American kinship is ultimately about genealogical 'proximity' versus 'distance', a fact mentioned though not emphasized by Schneider (1980: 25). In this, it is fundamentally different from most kinship systems in the world, which rather are based on categories such as parallel relative and cross-relative (Barnard 2011: 123–6). As shown in Figure 3.1, parallel relatives in the 'Iroquois' system are those related through a same-sex sibling link (for example, father's brother or father's brother's child), and cross-relatives are those related through an opposite-sex sibling link (for example, father's sister or father's sister's child). American kinship does not make this distinction but a lineal versus collateral one, and is also characterized by a distinction between genealogical relationships, foster ones (e.g., step-mother) and metaphorical ones (e.g., priest as 'father') (Schneider 1980: 99–102).

Whether or not one agrees with Schneider that all this is useful for the analysis of American kinship, or that similar emphases are useful for the analysis of other kinship systems, nevertheless, his approach is revealing. It is revealing not least as a means of conceptualizing alternatives, such as emphasis on category over distance, or the necessity to classify all as some kind of kin, rather than to distinguish metaphorical from 'real' kin usages. With that in mind, consider the implications of Schneider's *American kinship* for prehistory. Prehistoric peoples had two choices. They could either classify cross-cousins differently from parallel cousins, or they could emphasize genealogical proximity over marriageability and distinguish, for example, cousins from siblings (see Barnard 2011: 137–41). Classification creates, at the very least, the potential for taboos. Why else classify, unless one is to treat a cross-cousin differently from a parallel cousin? The only way to treat them differently is to allow some latitude towards one category that is forbidden towards the other.

The recognition of cross-cousins is not a matter of pure genealogical distance, unless the culturally recognized proximity of same-sex over opposite-sex siblings of one's parents is somehow symbolically important. It is much more reasonable to suppose that the purpose of the distinction in prehistory is the same as in virtually every society today that makes a parallel/cross distinction. Parallel cousins the world over are commonly classified as if siblings and treated as such: they are prohibited as mates. Cross-cousins the world over are commonly classified differently, as 'joking partners', equivalent to grandparents (not to parents), as possible mates, or even as already classificatory 'spouses'. That is, the word for 'cross-cousin', or one word for this kind of relative, may be the same as that for 'husband' or 'wife'.

Apart from these symbolic dimensions, there are also affective or emotional ones. Bronislaw Malinowski (1930: 19) once wrote that for the 'average anthropologist', kinship is 'a matter of flesh and blood, the result of sexual passion and maternal affection, of long intimate daily life, and of a host of personal intimate interests'. He was questioning the growing tendency of kinship specialists in the 1920s, himself included, to explain kinship instead in terms of 'mock algebra', kin term extension, social relations, clan structures and so on. Much later, Janet Carsten's (e.g., 2000) work on 'relatedness' has suggested ways to cut through the nature/culture problem by placing the emphasis on indigenous thought. She rejects the supposedly Western orientation of traditional kinship studies. Her work, in many ways, is a follow-up of criticisms made by Schneider (1984) of the directions that kinship travelled from before Malinowski until Schneider's own time. Really fundamental cultural assumptions are involved in all this, as evidenced, for example, by Schneider's (1984: 19) remark that Americans pray to God directly, whereas the Yapese (the inhabitants of the Micronesian island of Wa'ap or Yap, with whom he had done fieldwork in the later 1940s) pray to God through their deceased kinsfolk. Obviously, the notion of kinship itself, and perhaps both the social relations to kin after their death and the emotional attachment to them, are affected by the religious meaning of ancestry.

Meanings of the 'father'

It is a fundamental property of relatedness that it is defined culturally, that is, defined differently within different 'cultures'. Let me give two examples. My first concerns biological (genetic) fatherhood, and my second, social fatherhood.

In his book *Arguments about Aborigines*, L. R. Hiatt traces the history of social anthropology through the controversies of the meaning and interpretation of Australian Aboriginal society and belief. One such controversy was the one he discusses in the chapter cleverly entitled 'Conception and misconception' (Hiatt 1996: 120–41). The saga begins in 1905, when Sir James Frazer announced he had discovered the origin of totemism (reprinted in Frazer 1910: I, 139–72). He traced this to a custom of the Arrente of central Australia, a group of peoples who have lived in that area for some 20,000 years. They recognize a form of totemism Frazer called 'conceptional'. Frazer regarded it as ancient, and once general among humankind. According to the early ethnographers of the Arrente, Baldwin Spencer and Frank Gillen (1899: 123–5), Arrente had explained that although sexual intercourse 'prepares' a woman for birth, conception occurs through the entry of a spirit from the land she walks upon. The spirits represent species, each associated with a site where they had settled with their sacred stones in the Dreamtime. In other words, the earliest totemism was like that of the Arrente, who then knew nothing of the 'facts' of conception. The entity responsible for conception was not the woman's husband, but the totem of the site of conception. The father, or woman's husband, was another entity entirely.

Meanwhile, according to Hiatt, Andrew Lang was correcting the proofs of *The secret of the totem* (Lang 1905) when Frazer's account appeared. He left his text unchanged, but added a chapter to his book (Lang 1905: 188–201) to refute Frazer's theory. Lang's theory of the origin of totemism was that it began when humans gave names to groups, in order to differentiate them from one another. From this, followed religious association of the (species) name and the group, as well as mythology to explain it, plus a notion of shared kinship among holders of the same totem, and a consequent exogamous principle. Through the decades that followed, numerous anthropologists entered the fray and extended the notion to other ethnography and even to ethnography of other parts of the world. Some, including, famously, Malinowski (1916), took essentially Frazer's line, that 'primitive peoples' were ignorant: Malinowski's Trobriand ethnography supposedly also showed this people to be entirely ignorant of physiological paternity. Others supported Lang's view, that indigenous statements on such issues must be merely symbolic. The battle lasted at least until the late 1960s, when Melford Spiro (1968) supported an updated Frazerian view, and Edmund Leach (1967), with comparisons to Christian notions of 'virgin birth', supported Lang's view. Lang's captured well the paradigm of the later times: Leach was Lang with a structuralist twist, rather than with an evolutionist hypothesis at the root of anthropological explanation.

My second example is social fatherhood among the Aka, a Pygmy group of the Republic of Congo and the Central African Republic. Barry Hewlett has devoted his career to the study of fatherhood among this people and to cross-cultural comparison of the institution of fatherhood. His findings indicate that Western notions are not always what is found ethnographically. It may be relevant, too, that the Aka are particularly egalitarian and highly individualistic – low grid, low group in Mary Douglas' grid/group terms (see Figure 2.2). Conformity to cultural expectations may be prevalent, but individual variation even in religious belief is considerable. The Aka fall at an extreme in their high paternal involvement in the upbringing of their children, and are indulgent: children are free from infancy to do as they like. Hewlett (e.g., 1991) reports that although this is not really a child-centred society, Aka infants spend a great deal of time with their parents. Most of this time, naturally, is with the mother. However, an Aka father spends 47 per cent of his waking hours within an arm's reach of his infant child, and when holding his children the father is more likely to hug and kiss them than is the mother. Hewlett's comparisons show that an Aka father will spend 22 per cent of his time holding an infant and 14 per cent holding an older child. Other hunter-gatherers spend significantly less time, and farmers less still. While exact comparison is difficult because the ages of children vary in different studies, comparable figures show ranges from 2.6 to 4 per cent of their time for other hunter-gatherers, and 0 to 2 per cent for farmers. Interestingly, too, Aka fathers spend 88 per cent of their time in view of their children, and Ju/'hoansi (a hunter-gatherer population of Botswana and Namibia) spend 30 per cent. The figures for farming and fishing populations of Kenya, Mexico, the Philippines, Japan, India, Nepal, Samoa, Belize and Micronesia range from 3 per cent to 14 per cent (Hewlett 1991: 134–5).

Of course, one extreme example is not enough to make statistical correlations, but it would seem to be the case that hunter-gatherers are quite different from farmers. Hewlett's comparative data also show differences between societies with few accumulated resources and those with many, those that are monogamous and those that are polygamous, those that are more egalitarian and those that are less so, and among hunter-gatherers between those in which subsistence is co-operative between the sexes (like the Aka) and those in which it is not (Hewlett 1991: 133–41). In short, exactly what it means to be a 'father', socially, is dependent on cultural criteria, and particularly on the subsistence basis and economic structure of society.

What it means to be a 'father' biologically depends on a theory of conception. What 'we' take for granted depends on our own theory, and we ordinary people must never forget that we are dependent on what scientists tell us. Whatever alien or early kinship systems might have entailed, the belief systems that underlie them will be different from ours today in any number of ways. As John Barnes (1973) once reminded us, 'sophisticated' Western-educated people believe that conception occurs when a spermatozoon penetrates an ovum. Spermatozoons were discovered in 1677 and ova in 1828. The entry of a spermatozoon into an ovum was first observed, it was claimed, in 1853. How they combine was first described in 1875. Thus, for most of Western history, never mind Aboriginal or Pygmy history, 'the uniqueness of physical paternity was a cultural construct for which there was very little conclusive evidence' (Barnes 1973: 66). And all of this is still a very long way from public 'knowledge' of chromosomes and DNA.

The Aka example shows us that we should be careful about assuming the naturalness of social practices: it is not that Aka are in any way primeval, but perhaps the opposite. In the late Pleistocene, 120,000 years ago, males in fact contributed more to subsistence and therefore probably less to childrearing than in later times, among hunter-gatherers, among horticulturalists or among intensive farmers (Hewlett 1991: 151–3). If Aka practice is 'natural', it perhaps represents not a primitive form but an advanced form of human nature.

The earliest kinship systems

The problem

At the dawn of symbolic culture, we had the potential for two types of kinship system. I will call these Type I and Type II. I had earlier labelled them 'African' and 'Australian' (Barnard 1999), but now, for various reasons, I think it best to avoid geographical labels. My own view is that Type I (African) is rather more likely to be the earlier, although this should not preclude the identification of some Type I characteristics in Australia or anywhere else. The difference is that Type I is based on flexibility in social organization, and an equivalent flexibility in other spheres, too, including kinship and the symbolic domain.

However, other scholars have proposed one variation or another on the Type II (Australian) possibility. Among these are Claude Lévi-Strauss (1969c [1949]) and more explicitly Nicholas Allen (e.g., 2008) and Ruth Manimekalai Vaz (2010; 2011). Lévi-Strauss (1969c: 214–20) saw the evolution of at least some kinship structures as stemming from moieties, with a member of group A allowed to marry only a member of the other group, group B (see Figure 3.3). From moieties, cross-cutting descent lines evolved and these generated either sections (group A marries group B, and they have children C and D) or, where descent and residence coincide, generalized exchange (male A marries female B, male B marries female C, and so on). Sometimes, a combination of the two appeared, giving yet more evolved structures. However, Lévi-Strauss (1969c: 142–5) also cautioned against too much reconstruction and argued that evolution cannot necessarily be deduced from logical

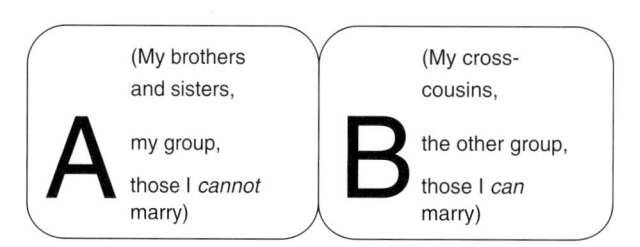

A (My brothers and sisters, my group, those I *cannot* marry)

B (My cross-cousins, the other group, those I *can* marry)

Figure 3.3. A moiety structure

simplicity. Allen sees the four-section system as the logically simplest and *therefore* the original form of social structure across much of the globe. In his view, it is simplest because it does not require one to keep track of line of descent or generation (more technically, *genealogical level*) since descent lines and generations are implicit in the section structure. In other words, it regulates incest avoidance *sui generis*, without requirement of a special rule prohibiting sex between parent and child – as would be required in a moiety system. Vaz, who works with the Hill Madia of central India, agrees with Allen that a tetradic (four-category) structure is characteristic of Dravidian-speakers, but argues that it is not the simplest but rather the one with clearest symmetry, and that it is generated by patrilateral cross-cousin marriage. This very unusual feature, marriage to the category defined as that of father's sister's daughter, is found among the Hill Madia and virtually nowhere else on earth. In her view, moieties came first, and four-category structures evolved from these.

Among those rejecting this hypothesis is Robert Layton (2008), whose vision is very similar to mine. Layton suggests that in thinking about early kinship, we have to envisage social units such as modern hunter-gatherer bands, within which sharing is not only commonplace but in fact advantageous for the individuals who make up the bands. There is plenty of ethnographic evidence to support the view that this is the norm for the physical condition of hunter-gatherer humankind. Sharing enables access to material wellbeing more effectively than hoarding, since pooling resources evens out unpredictable successes and since it ensures that surpluses do not go to waste. Layton slips easily into general conclusions on pre-*Homo sapiens* as well as *H. sapiens* society, but his focus is clearly on the latter. He echoes Lévi-Strauss' (1969c: 70, 144) position that binary thought is common, if not (as Lévi-Strauss saw it) universal, and that this led to the repeated rediscovery, time and time again, of cross-cousin marriage. Cross-cousin marriage enables exchanges, and it also defines groupings. Layton points out that cross-cousin marriage is *not* found among all hunter-gatherers, and I would add that its incidence is not necessarily an indicator of rigid structures of the kinds required in Lévi-Strauss' moiety-based model, Allen's section-based one or Vaz's evolving one.

Intriguingly, whereas Allen (2008: 112) sticks his neck out for a 60,000-year-old origin of tetradic structures, in Africa before human dispersal, Layton (2008: 122) much more cautiously proposes that such structures spread through Australia only in the last 5,000 years and reached central Australia just 1,500 years ago. With them, spread new associations between people and land and new forms of rock art. Similarly, totemism in the Northwest Coast of North America, Layton argues, also first appears in rock art about 1,500 years ago, after transformations in social organization as a result of environmental change. As for which came first, patrilineal or matrilineal descent, Layton (2008: 123–6) opts for neither: humans first entered the Americas with flexible group structures based on bilateral descent. I am in agreement. There exists today the possibility of reconstructing prehistoric residence patterns, and possibly descent structures, through the 'virtual archaeology' of genetic studies. This has already proven successful in 'digging up' an uxorilocal norm throughout the Austronesian ethno-linguistic area, north of Australia from Indonesia to Melanesia, Micronesia and Polynesia (Jordan *et al.* 2009). Unfortunately, though, the methodology would seem to be limited in time depth. The suggestion of uxorilocality for the Austronesian area allows inference only back to the earliest days of the language family, about 4,500, perhaps 5,000, years ago.

Type I kinship structures

In my paper, 'Modern hunter-gatherers and early symbolic culture' (Barnard 1999: 65–6), I noted six characteristics of San or Bushman society. Let me use this as an example of what I am calling here 'Type I'. (1) The first characteristic is that San are essentially monotheistic. San peoples may have a pantheon of deities, but these deities merge into one another and are sometimes represented as the moon or the sky. (2) San have a flexible but definable group structure and relation to the land. Band membership may change, but people recognize their belonging to other people and to land which they 'own'. (3) They may have collective symbolic relations to animals, such as through the spiritual forces or the recognition of symbolic power in some animal species, but they rarely recognize totemic spirits. Where totemism exists, it is usually borrowed from neighbouring agro-pastoralists. (4) San lack clans, moieties or any other socio-centric means of categorization. (5) They possess universal kinship. That is, individuals recognize kin relationships to everyone in their society. There may be 15,000 Naro, for example, but every Naro can trace a relationship to every other Naro through namesake links. My own Naro name happens to be !A/e (also spelled Qace). I call every other person named !A/e 'grandrelative', and call his sister 'my sister', and so on. Thus, even ethnographers are brought into the system, because Naro society does not exist except within its 'kinship' framework. If I were really Naro, applying such rules, I would classify a younger person in this way, but an older person would classify me, and I would reciprocate appropriately. Such rules regulate the incest taboo, marriage and even how close two people may sit. (6) Finally, the San world is flexible. Unlike the Australian Aboriginal one, it has no singular coherence.

San-type systems, or let us call them Type I systems, are characteristic of hunter-gatherers and small-scale cultivators in Africa, much of Asia and North America. In some ways, they are also reminiscent of large-scale post-Neolithic societies in their flexibility, although these latter kinds invariably do not classify all members of society as 'relatives'. Universal kinship is found mainly among hunter-gatherers, where it is the norm. With regard to kinship terminology, basically there are two different possibilities. Either people make parallel/cross distinctions (and treat cross-cousins as marriageable), or they do not. Both forms are found among San, and both are found too among Type I structures elsewhere in the world. The key characteristic of a Type I system is its flexibility. The systems with the greatest flexibility are those based on genealogical distance, with marriageability determined by distance rather than by category. However, the constraints are not terribly great in a system like Naro either, because categorization is purely egocentric. That is, unlike in an Amazonian or Aboriginal structure, there are no moieties or other socio-centric categories to divide a society into 'our half' (whom we cannot marry) and 'the other half' (whom we can marry).

Type II kinship structures

In the same paper (Barnard 1999: 60–2), I similarly noted six characteristics of Australian Aboriginal society, and this is my example here of a 'Type II' structure. (1) Aborigines believe in the Rainbow Serpent (a spirit associated mythologically with land, waterholes, fertility and power) and in the Dreaming (a time which is both the beginning and now, associated with creation, land and peoples, and their relations with one another). (2) While in terms of their spatial occupation and use of the land, they may be similar to San, in terms of their symbolic relation to the land they are quite different. Aborigines' sacred sites are associated with the Dreaming, with ceremonies and sometimes with the spirits of 'conception clans' which complement patrilineal and matrilineal ones. Some groups have all three. (3) There is a belief in totemism, and through totems Aboriginal groups are associated with and symbolically represented by animal species. (4) In Australia, there are clan and lineage structures, with lineages possessing rights and obligations in relation to other lineages, for example, in marriage bestowal arrangements and in funeral and reburial rituals. (5) Aborigines recognize elaborate rules of marriage. Aboriginal groups are divided into moieties, into four sections or eight subsections, and such divisions regulate the incest taboo and define marriageable and non-marriageable kin categories. As with the San, classification is universal: everyone in society is some kind of 'kin' in relation to any other, but the system is socio-centric and in theory much stricter. (6) Aborigines classify their world along the same principles. The social units are only a part of this system: categorical oppositions like moon/sun, night/day, fresh water/sea water, activity/passivity, abstractness/concreteness, and so on, map onto one another to create a world order of which kinship and social organization is only part.

Beyond Australia and southern Africa

By now calling these Type I and Type II, I have emphasized what are in fact general principles. The San and Aboriginal examples are general for these regions, although there are, of course, differences within the regions. They are indicative of the types. The detail will differ significantly in the case of some San or Aboriginal groups, but broadly Pygmy ethnography (e.g., Turnbull 1968; Hewlett 1991), Arctic and Subarctic ethnography (e.g., Damas 1972; Helm 1972; Rogers 1972), and the ethnography of many other hunter-gatherer peoples around the world imply attributes of Type I, particularly in their flexibility of kinship and group structure and the lack of fit between kinship and symbolic realms. As I implied earlier in my discussion of flexibility among the Mbuti, Pygmy kinship may indeed represent a more extreme example of Type I than San. Allen's (2008) model and a great deal of classic South American ethnography, both among hunter-gatherer and small-scale cultivator peoples (e.g., Maybury-Lewis 1967; Rivière 1969; Kaplan 1975; Arcand 1977; Rivière 1984), indicate Type II organization. While some ethnography may suggest something in between, nevertheless, it is useful to think in terms of an opposition between two ideal types, one highly structured and the other very flexible.

The question then is: which is primal? A great deal more comparative and theoretical work on this is yet to be done, but if Layton (2008) is right, then the evolution of even the most strongly Type II systems would seem to be recent. If that is true, then the next question is: how recent? And did they evolve independently in South America and Australia? Or are South American and Australian systems historically related? If South American and Australian systems are related, they would have to be related at quite some time depth: at least 40,000 years. To me, that seems unlikely, but Allen's model implies it. The implications of an answer to this question go far beyond kinship, because they suggest that advanced, but primeval human thought (and I assume a hunter-gatherer lifestyle in advanced human thought) is *either* fundamentally flexible, *or* fundamentally structured. One cannot have it both ways.

4 Ritual and religion

Ritual and religion are central to human society. We find evidence of both ritual and religious belief in burials and, more interestingly and more fully, in rock art. As we saw in Chapter 2, other forms of physical remains may also betoken symbolic thought: etched ochre, worked ochre in general, shell beads and even aesthetically worked stone, all well over 70,000 years old and representative of *Homo sapiens sapiens* cultures developing by then in southern Africa. There are also beautiful figurines that may have been crafted by very early European *H. sapiens sapiens* more than 30,000 years ago. Examples in the Aurignacian (European Upper Palaeolithic) include, famously, various 'Venus' figurines, the 'Lion Man of the Hohlenstein Stadel' and other lion therianthropes (human and animal together) in stone and ivory. More recently, we have therianthropic representation in rock art, in both Africa and Europe as well as elsewhere, and a host of interpretations of it. Palaeolithic art can be and has been seen as hunting magic, as mythological or as theistic. It has been interpreted functionally, structurally, psychoanalytically, as reflecting economical conditions, as revealing of the evolution of the mind and so on (see Conkey 1999). Of course, some art may be one thing, and other art may differ in meaning – just as different religions may exist among different populations, or yet in the same population. Even 'a religion' may be a fluid entity, with its meanings malleable and in fact playful (Guenther 1979; Barnard 1988).

Since the nineteenth century, anthropological theory has always had something to say about the interpretation, the mythical or totemic foundation, the structure, the social function or the evolution and diffusion of religious ideas. Social anthropology has also provided a wealth of ethnographic data on all aspects of religion, including ritual and belief. This accumulated body of knowledge, along with the theoretical means to understand it, is one obvious place to start in seeking evidence for the origins of beliefs and rites. Another must be the comparative study of early and later forms of rock art and other material remains. In this chapter, I seek explanations for early religious belief and other associations. Chris Knight (1991; Knight *et al.* 1995) has done this with regard to menstrual and moon symbolism, and their evolutionary social implications. But there are many other possibilities: comparative world mythology, comparative studies of various belief systems (notably animism, totemism and shamanism), beliefs about the heavenly bodies, taboos regarding food and hunting and so on. These are worth consideration too.

As we shall see later in this chapter, rock art for many interpreters came to evoke spirits of an anthropomorphic or therianthropic nature. Totemism came to be a major focus of debate among those looking for 'early' or if not the original religion. So too did theism, and specifically monotheism as 'primal religion'. In the late nineteenth century, many focused on animism. Yet, here we find perhaps too simple an explanation, as indeed we did in totemism (Lévi-Strauss 1969b [1962]), not merely because totemism or animism might be difficult to define cross-culturally, but because especially in the late nineteenth and early twentieth centuries they were interpreted through modern Western eyes.

The original religion?

Among the German-Austrian diffusionists of the late nineteenth and early twentieth centuries, there were two competing theories. One faction hailed Australia as the point of the origin of culture, and the other looked to Africa – Darwin's choice for the origin of the human species. Among the latter was Father Wilhelm Schmidt, who added the intriguing twist that the original culture contained a belief in one god – an idea that he got from Andrew Lang. Schmidt's major work was a twelve-volume treatise entitled *Der Ursprung der Gottesidee*, published between 1912 and 1955. Although it never appeared in English, summaries of relevant theoretical ideas presented there were published in English in *The origin and growth of religion* (Schmidt 1931) and

Primitive revelation (Schmidt 1939). The Scottish folklorist Andrew Lang was an exceptionally prolific writer, but his key book here is *The making of religion* (Lang 1898), which was eventually published in many revised editions.

Schmidt, and Lang before him, criticized arguments of the time, that religion began with animism, fetishism or totemism. They had noticed that hunter-gatherers and others reputed to be especially 'primitive' are not only non-totemic, nor even polytheistic, but often monotheistic. For Lang, this notion of primitive monotheism was probably part of his romanticist, perhaps his 'noble savage', vision. Schmidt (1931: 172–84) pays extensive tribute to him for standing against his contemporaries, especially those who favoured either an animistic origin (such as Sir Edward Tylor, who also looked to dreams as a point of origin) or a naturalistic-mythological origin of religions (such as F. Max Müller). Yet, for Schmidt primitive monotheism was also, in a sense, a mix of his culture-circle methodology and his Roman Catholic belief. He held that God had revealed himself to humanity early in time, and that non-hunter-gatherers had devolved from their earlier monotheistic beliefs (and the true religion) to false polytheistic or totemic notions. 'Primitive monotheism' was part of a 'primal culture' that lay at the foundation of later circles of ever-more complex culture that expanded across the globe. Schmidt's comparative studies of hunter-gatherers, including field studies by a number of missionary colleagues from the Vienna-based Societas Verbi Divini, showed specifically that hunter-gatherers frequently referred to their one God as being the creator and font of goodness. The hunter-gatherer God, like the Christian one, was believed to be eternal and omniscient, acted as a father to humanity, dwelt in the sky and so on. As such notions were part of the 'primal culture', Schmidt and his followers believed that later 'culture circles' produced ideas that may have supplanted these among pastoralists and horticulturalists. Nevertheless, these did not entirely obliterate such beliefs, which sometimes persisted in weaker forms among such non-hunter-gatherers. In Schmidt's view, they have persisted quite strongly among hunter-gatherers to this day.

In fact, part of Schmidt's vision of 'culture circles', or *Kulturkreise*, is not entirely unlike recent notions of Out of Africa migrations and global expansion. Like thinkers today, he looked to Africa (Pygmies and Bushmen) for examples of conservative cultures, and for evidence of the earliest symbolic thought. We might interpret Africa as Schmidtian, and Australia as Durkheimian (e.g., Durkheim and Mauss (1963 [1903]: 10–41), in symbolic thought. And although I do not subscribe to Schmidt's view of the cosmos, nevertheless I agree with him that the beliefs of hunter-gatherers of recent years may well reflect those of the early days of symbolic culture at least as well as, and probably very much better than, those of non-hunter-gatherers today. This is not merely because today's hunter-gatherers are more similar in means of subsistence and have social organization more like that of early symbolic humanity. It is also because, in spite of their diversity, African hunter-gatherers have similar religious notions across the continent. These can be found underlying hunter-gatherer belief systems elsewhere too, including in mythology, in rock art, in shamanic performance and spirituality and in the very fluidity of belief itself (Guenther 1999). Some of these attributes may stem from the ethos of hunter-gatherer life in general, including the social values of egalitarianism and flexibility.

In the late 1990s, Nurit Bird-David (1999) returned to the old problem of animism. She argued that nineteenth-century concerns emphasized the supposed simplicity of animism as a belief system. Supposedly, she said, what Westerners regard as non-animate beings like rocks, trees, thunder or celestial bodies are believed to have 'souls'. This is because in the West, there is an absolute distinction between mind and body, non-material and material, and other such pairings. Tylor (1871) had built his magnificent two-volume treatise on 'primitive culture' on a foundation of animism as the first religion. He had argued that appeasement offerings, elaborate rituals of sacrifice, whether to rock spirits, totem animals or deities, are all derived ultimately from a belief in animism. The same is true of fetishism (where human control of the supernatural comes through a material object) or totemism (where animal and plant species are, or have, souls). Through her own ethnography of Nyaka hunter-gatherers in South India, Bird-David disputes this. She says that Tylor and other protagonists have all misunderstood the nature of the problem. If the Nyaka are to be our model, we should be thinking in the way that *they* do: their beliefs are different not because they have a 'simple' religion, but because they perceive relations among people and between people and their environment differently from Tylor, from Bird-David or from you or from me. Different peoples have different concepts of the 'person'. 'Nature' and 'culture' are not in all 'cultures' epistemological opposites but to be seen as part of a larger, and different, ecological system. I read George Silberbauer's (1981) ethnography of the /Gui San (G/wi or /Guikhoe) in a similar way. In spite of his use of words like 'the habitat', 'social organization' and 'socioecology' in his chapter headings, what he actually describes (especially 1981: 51–137) is a /Gui way of thinking about ecology, society and the spirit world. Society and the spirit world are not separate entities but part of the same indigenously defined ecosystem. Generally speaking, other ecologically oriented anthropologists in the Kalahari do not seem to express their ideas as radically as does Silberbauer, nor Indianists as radically as Bird-David, but such views remind us that hunter-gatherer ways of thinking about science or religion are often at variance with our own. There is no reason to suppose that the same will not have been true in prehistoric belief systems too.

Science within religion

In *Social anthropology and human origins* (Barnard 2011: 102–3), I mentioned the Iatmul myth of origin. Because this topic is so central, in a way, to the theme of the present book, I will give a little more detail here.

The Iatmul live in the swampy area neighbouring the Sepik River of Papua New Guinea. There, land and water are not properly divided, but their creation myth tells that in nature, land and water should be separate: order is created when the agent of randomization ceases his randomizing. The crocodile deity, Kavwokmali, creates disorder, while the folk hero, Kevembuangga, through the killing of the deity allows the order inherent in nature to take its course.

They say that in the beginning the crocodile Kavwokmali paddled with his front legs and with his hind legs; and his paddling kept the mud suspended in the water. The great culture hero, Kevembuangga, came with his spear and killed Kavwokmali. After that the mud settled and dry land was formed. Kevembuangga then stamped his foot on the dry land, *i.e.*, he proudly demonstrated 'that it was good'. (Bateson 1973: 30)

The Western creation myth, that is, the first verses of Genesis, is the opposite: the Agent of Order creates order out of nothing. Without God, nature would be chaos and order unknown. This Western myth is present not only in Judaism, Christianity and Islam, but also as a guiding principle in Western thought more generally (see Bateson 1973: 28–31). It gives us the understanding of the relation between randomization and order that is found, then, not just in religion, but also in that form of Western thought (in its widest sense) that is known as 'science'.

> In the beginning God created the heaven and the earth. And the earth *was* without form, and void: and darkness was upon the face of the deep. And the Spirit of God moved upon the face of the waters ...
>
> And God said, Let the waters under the heaven be gathered together unto one place, and let the dry *land* appear; and it was so. And God called the dry *land* Earth: and the gathering together of the waters called he Seas: and God saw that *it was good*. (Genesis 1:1–2, 1:9–10)

Gregory Bateson's interpretation suggests that Western science, even that practised by scientists who are atheists, has within it Judeo-Christian (or Arabic and Islamic) notions of order and disorder. That tradition has governed Western science at least since the Middle Ages, and it continues to do so: even scientists cannot escape their cultural heritage. But more important to me is Bateson's demonstration that thought is patterned and hierarchical (bigger ideas order the interpretation of smaller ones), that thought stems from earlier and deeply traditional belief and that thought processes differ in profound ways, from one cultural system to another. Bateson emphasizes the difference between the Western and Iatmul creation myths, but for me there is similarity as well: both God and Kevembuangga are the source of order in the universe, and order is 'good'. Different societies explain 'order' in different ways, and the requirement for order in a cosmological system varies from one place to another. In the last chapter, we looked at the Kariera of Western Australia. Their notion of order differs too from the ancient Israelites and the Iatmul. Arguably, the Kariera worldview is the most ordered of the three.

Take another example. Arctic and Subarctic peoples commonly hold that animals wish to be killed, or that a hunted beast is drawn to a hunter by some mystical force. In other words, agency exists not only on the part of the hunter, but equally, or even primarily, on the part of the animal. Tim Ingold (2000: 13–15) comments on the role of social anthropology in unravelling such beliefs. Social anthropology has nothing to say about the truth or otherwise of the beliefs, but situates them within a framework understood through the cultural traditions of the hunter. The true 'understanding' of the situation by the polar bear, caribou or whatever is, of course, irrelevant. Ingold invokes the phrases of others, like 'phenomenology of perception', 'steps to an ecology of mind' (Ingold prefers 'steps to an ecology of life'), 'sentient ecology' or his own phrase 'poetics of dwelling'. He is right, of course: anthropology takes a relativist line always in issues such as this one. The discipline understands worldviews 'from above', through a meta-worldview: the situational logic behind each set of culturally dependent perceptions through which nature is understood.

My point, through these examples, is to suggest ways in which anthropology may reveal either deep or situational understandings. I do not want to imply that primal peoples are likely to have held either Iatmul or Cree (Ingold's key example) beliefs, or even that their worldviews are necessarily the opposite of modern Western ones. Rather, what I am arguing is that the discipline of social anthropology enables us to reflect on numerous possibilities for configuring the relations between culture and nature. We do this through us/them dichotomies, not because there are just two possibilities of anything, but simply because setting what we take for granted against what *someone else* takes for granted highlights the idea of *difference*.

Totemism today: why all these birds?

'Totem' comes from the Anishinaabe or Ojibwa word *odoodem* (root – *ode*; with possessive prefix, *odoodem* or *doodem*; plural, *odoodeman*), which means '[patrilineal] clan' or the animal that symbolizes it. Although described in very early ethnographic texts, the totemic system was wonderfully elucidated by William Whipple Warren (1885), the part-Ojibwa historian who in the middle of the nineteenth century recorded the traditions of his people. He recorded these details in a text, which he completed in 1851. He died in 1853, and the text, 'History of the Ojibway people', was finally published in 1885. According to Warren,

> The first grand division is that of blood and kindred, which has been perpetuated amongst the different tribes by what they call the Totemic System, and dates back to the time 'when the Earth was new'.
>   Each grand family is known by a badge or symbol, taken from nature; being generally a quadruped, bird, fish, or reptile. The badge or Dodaim (Totem, as it has been most commonly written), descends invariably in the male line; marriage is strictly forbidden between individuals of the same symbol. This is one of the greatest sins that can be committed in the code of Ojibway moral laws, and the tradition says that in former times it was punishable by death. (Warren 1885: 41–2)

Through the late nineteenth and early twentieth centuries, many anthropologists took up the question of totemism, and asked if it were the original religion or perhaps a later development – explaining beliefs and customs from North and South America to Australia and Africa. Much later, Lévi-Strauss (1969b [1962]) came to reject the notion that there is a single entity here or a single concept that embraces all these religious ideas, except for the concept of the transition from nature to culture. That, Lévi-Strauss (1969b: 172–7) tells us, is the fundamental problem in anthropology and one anticipated by Jean-Jacques Rousseau. Totemism, in other words, is not the 'anthropological problem' but a Western reading of diverse associations across the globe, though nevertheless ones that have in common a deep concern with the relation between natural and social phenomena. Anthropology had become far too preoccupied with Ojibwa belief as a specific model for the origin of belief in general.

Radcliffe-Brown had two theories of totemism. Radcliffe-Brown's 'first theory' of totemism was, predictably, a functionalist explanation: that totemism evolves from the ritual association of certain species with certain groups. It is a development of the (symbolic) understanding of nature. His paper was called 'The sociological theory of totemism', and it concentrates on his disagreements with Durkheim over the specifics of which came first, social groups' associations with totemic species (Durkheim's view) or rituals involving those species (Radcliffe-Brown's view). The ethnographic basis of the argument is to be found in

Aboriginal Australian society and totemism, and both writers agree that the representation of species as totems follows from the original formation of Aboriginal societies and clans. Radcliffe-Brown first published his paper in 1929, in the rather obscure *Proceedings of the Fourth Pacific Science Congress*, but it became known as one of the addresses reprinted in his classic 1952 collection *Structure and function in primitive society* (Radcliffe-Brown 1952: 117–32).

'Why all these birds?', Radcliffe-Brown (1951: 17) once asked. This is the crucial question which leads to his 'second theory' of totemism. Radcliffe-Brown's 'second theory' comes from his Huxley Memorial Lecture, 'The comparative method in social anthropology' (Radcliffe-Brown 1951). It was too late for inclusion in *Structure and function*, but the lecture and its subsequent publication was to have great impact, not least because the latter so profoundly influenced Lévi-Strauss (1969b: 155–64). Radcliffe-Brown corresponded with Lévi-Strauss on the matter, and as Lévi-Strauss points out, Radcliffe-Brown remained an empiricist in his overall stance. Nevertheless, Radcliffe-Brown's 'second theory' comes very close indeed to Lévi-Straussian structuralism in its vision of totemic thought. Totemic thought signifies sets of relations not just between or among groups, and between a group and its totemic species representation, but also between one totemic species and another. Figure 4.1 illustrates this. By closing the 'circle' (itself a metaphor, represented here by my square, on the right, with its connecting arrows between the eaglehawk and the crow), Radcliffe-Brown demonstrates his move well away from Durkheim, on more than merely points of detail.

So, why all these birds? The question was in fact raised not in relation to Aborigines alone, but in relation to Northwest Coast First Peoples as well. In fact, Radcliffe-Brown (1951) also draws on his own Andaman ethnography and on ethnography from New Ireland (the northeastern islands of Papua New Guinea), and that of Native Americans of California and Nebraska. He draws too on historical texts from ancient Greece and the Middle Kingdom of ancient China, as well as the principle which, in the West, opposes any two competing sports teams, and also (his favourite example) the universities of Oxford and Cambridge. The Chinese example includes not only *yin* and *yang*, but

68   *Ritual and religion*

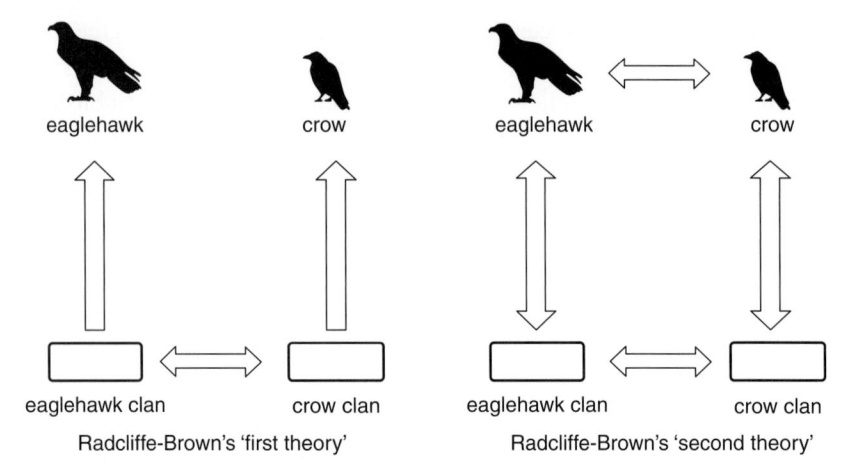

Figure 4.1. Radcliffe-Brown's two theories of totemism

presumed ancient intermarrying moieties. Oxford and Cambridge here must be taken with a pinch of salt, but the notion Radcliffe-Brown introduces is one of a seemingly universal principle reflected especially in the cases of exogamous moieties from various parts of the world. His various examples are listed in Table 4.1.

The crucial thing is that Radcliffe-Brown's consideration of similarities in cases from different parts of the world implies universals. Also, he implicitly denies a 'historical connection' (diffusion) between Australia and the Northwest Coast: the notion of deep cultural connections at a time depth of tens of thousands of years was probably beyond his comprehension. Rather, he sees the connections through what he regards as a first step in 'the systematic use of the comparative method', and in terms of 'the laws of social development'.

Among his examples, it is worth having a closer look at the parallels in mythology or legend. Radcliffe-Brown (1951: 16) notes that among the Haida of British Columbia and Alaska, legend says that Eagle had fresh water and kept it in a basket. Raven had no fresh water, but discovered Eagle's basket and stole it. As Raven flew over the Queen Charlotte Islands (Haida Gwaii), he spilled water from the basket, and now all birds can drink it. Salmon swam upstream into the rivers and lakes so created. The salmon then became the food of the Haida.

Table 4.1. *Radcliffe-Brown's (1951) examples of moiety or related opposition (in the order he mentions them)*

Location or people	Moiety 1	Moiety 2
New South Wales	eaglehawk	crow
Haida (Northwest Coast)	eagle	raven
some parts of eastern Australia	eaglehawk	crow
Victoria (Australia)	black cockatoo	white cockatoo
Western Australia	white cockatoo	crow
New Ireland	sea eagle	fish-hawk
New South Wales	bat	night owl
New South Wales	bat	owlet nightjar
New South Wales (Macleay River)	bat	tree creeper
Western Australia	kingfisher	bee-eater
Western Australia	little red bird	little black bird
Australia	kangaroo	bee
Western Australia	eaglehawk	crow
South Australia	wombat	kangaroo
New South Wales	bat	various animals
Andaman Islands (non-totemic)	fishes	birds
Australia	dingo	wild cat
America	heaven	earth
America	war	peace
America	up-stream	down-stream
Copeño (California)	coyote	wild cat
England	Oxford	Cambridge
Aboriginal Australia and North America	team 1	team 2
Omaha (Nebraska)	moiety 1	moiety 2
Marquesas (Polynesia)	kin of bridegroom	kin of bride
Gusii (Kenya)	kin	enemies/in-laws
Yaralde (non-moiety, South Australia)	own clan	other clans
Victoria	own moiety	other moieties
Tlingit (Northwest Coast)	own moiety	other moiety (in potlatch)
ancient Greece	mortise	tenon
ancient China	*yin*	*yang*
ancient China (Middle Kingdom)	paired clan 1	paired clan 2
New South Wales	'brother' of men	'sister' of women

In an Australian legend, only Eaglehawk had fresh water, and he kept it under a stone (Radcliffe-Brown 1951: 16–19). Crow saw him lift the stone to drink and saw him replace it. But when Crow lifted the stone to drink, he failed to replace it and at the same time he scratched lice from his head. The water therefore overflowed, and the lice became the Murray cod, a freshwater fish, and an important food for the Aborigines in the parts of Australia where this legend is known.

Radcliffe-Brown touches on kinship within totemic notions and within myth several times, as does Lévi-Strauss (1969b: 155–64). The important example that both writers relate is one from Western Australia – where a man marries his classificatory mother's brother's daughter (MBD). In the myth, Eaglehawk is Crow's MBD. Among these peoples, a man has an obligation to provide food for a potential father-in-law. Therefore, Eaglehawk asks Crow to hunt wallaby. Crow does so, but, disrespectfully, he eats the wallaby himself. When later Eaglehawk asks Crow what he has killed, Crow lies and says he got nothing. Eaglehawk catches him out by noting that Crow's tummy is enlarged. Crow lies again, that to ward off hunger he has filled his belly with acacia gum. Eaglehawk does not believe Crow and tickles Crow's tummy until he vomits. And, of course, he vomits out the wallaby. So Eaglehawk rolls Crow into the fire, which makes his feathers black and his eyes red and leads him to call out 'Wa! Wa! Wa!' Thus, he gains his appearance, and Eaglehawk proclaims as law that Crow would forever not be a hunter, but a thief.

Consider again the debate between Frazer (1910) and Durkheim (1915 [1912]), mentioned in Chapter 1, and my suggestion there that symbols are metaphors. Frazer argued that the social order is built on a religious foundation, namely that of totemism. Durkheim argued the opposite: that religion, and totemism in particular, is an ideological expression of the social order. What if we throw myth into the mix? If myth enables metaphor, it also requires it, and so too does totemism. Totemic species are metaphors for social groups. Rather as with the archetypal Chomskyan notion of the emergence of language, fully formed, we have here the potential for a structuralist notion of language, metaphor, mythology, symbolism, totemism and full human sociality (whatever that might entail) all coming into existence more or less simultaneously. Alternatively, we have some sequence of these things, one coming first and the others following.

All this may sound like nineteenth-century speculation, but there are two crucial differences. The two differences reflect the two tools which we have at our disposal, and nineteenth-century anthropologists did not. First, there is a more definitive basis for supposing demographic conditions (population bottlenecks), location (through comparative genetic studies), temporality (through genetics, anatomical and neurological studies and archaeological dating methods) and material conditions (through archaeological discoveries), with far greater material evidence of symbolic thought (e.g., in ochre use). And, secondly, we have not merely the paradigm of evolutionism, plain and simple, but also others to play with – according to our theoretical predilections. The competing paradigms of all social anthropology in the last several decades can be summarized as follows: culture and society are 'language'. *How* they are language, or are like language, depends on how one understands language itself. Is the 'correct' analogy with grammar (as in structuralism) or with translation (as in interpretivism)? In essence, the structuralist sees anthropology as the working out of the grammar of alien thought, while the interpretivist sees anthropology's duty as translating alien thought into meanings intelligible to her readers (Barnard 2000: 175–6). It follows that the establishment of a position on that matter should enable an anthropologist of either disposition to form a view, even sequentially, on the question: 'Why all these birds?'

Back to Frazer, and forwards to Wikipedia

At the same time Frazer was puzzling over Australian totemism, he was also immersed in Roman mythology and especially in pondering customs related to succession to the kinship of ancient Latium. Through the late nineteenth and early twentieth centuries, Frazer compiled a series on this called *The Golden Bough*, whose third edition numbered twelve volumes published between 1906 and 1915. I tend to use the later, abridged, edition (Frazer 1922), which adds no new material but compresses the original into a mere 756 pages. Its scope is seemingly simple: periodically, a (pre-Roman) priest-king is ritually murdered in the sacred grove of Nemi, near Rome. His murderer is his successor, who in his own time will also suffer the same fate. The priest-king (priest of the cult of Diana) is himself sacred, and in Frazer's interpretation he marries Diana – who is the goddess of the moon as well as of the hunt, and who is associated with woodlands and animals. The sacrifice of the king, and Diana's own death at harvest time and her rebirth in the spring each year, are, according to Frazer, at the root of religion in general. He finds parallels in various parts of Europe, in parts of Africa, in India and the East Indies, in Australia and the Pacific, and in North and South America.

The question in my mind, though, is which part of Frazer's findings is the significant one? The moon, the harvest, association with animals, fertility, divinity, sacred place and sacred action, sacrifice and rebirth: they are all there, but to my mind they cannot all be equally significant. Ritual, taboo and tree worship also feature prominently in *The Golden Bough*, and the global connections form part of Frazer's thesis. While commonly categorized as an evolutionist, Frazer can be read with diffusionist spectacles too, and I am not certain at all that this was not part of his intention. There is plenty of historical speculation in *The Golden Bough*, and this certainly reflects the diffusionist premise of common origin, while the assumption that peoples everywhere are coming up with the same ideas independently reflects the evolutionist belief in a psychic unity of humankind. In other words, people everywhere think alike.

The modern version of Frazer is perhaps Wikipedia, which lists some ninety-two lunar deities (Wikipedia contributors 2011). While not necessarily a complete or definitive source, that Wikipedia listing is nevertheless indicative of the importance of lunar deities around the world. Most of them are female or at least in the feminine gender, and whatever the gender of the moon, that of the sun is usually the opposite. In their different ways, many others, including Claude Lévi-Strauss (1978: 211–21) and Chris Knight (1997), have written on this theme too.

Freud vs. Knight

Chris Knight is a controversial character. Today he is probably as well known for his politics and his street theatre as for his anthropology, but I will only touch on the latter here. Sigmund Freud was controversial too. One of the offshoots of his psychoanalytic approach in psychiatry was a theory that was designed to explain the origin of taboos (specifically the incest taboo) and of totemism as an early form of religion. Although they are separated by nearly eighty years, they seemingly are concerned with different sets of supposed events, and they depict quite different points in time in prehistory, I like to see their two theories in opposition to each other. Knight's theory, like Freud's, is an attempt to explain both the origins of society as we know it and the origins of symbolic thought. The difference between the two is that while Freud's theory engages male action, Knight's is dependent on female agency.

Freud's theory lies within an essay on 'The return of totemism in childhood' (1960 [1913]: 100–61). In Freud's mind, the thoughts of European children resemble those of 'primitive' contemporaries such as Australian Aborigines, and also of humans in general at the dawn of symbolic culture. Therefore, he assumes that studies of the former two, especially studies of Australian Aborigines, can lead us to insights into the thoughts and the consequent actions of early humans. Freud is not specific about his time depth, nor even about the degree to which indeed is real time. His text can be read as a metaphor, almost as a kind of 'psychoanalytic Dreamtime' understanding of the genesis of symbolic thought. Nevertheless, I believe he probably did mean it to be taken literally or at least as literally as the works of opposing and supporting theorists he cites – such as J. F McLennan, Sir James Frazer and Andrew Lang.

The crux comes towards the end of the essay (Freud 1960: 140–6), when Freud turns his attention to Darwin's speculations on the 'primal horde' and attempts to explain this through William Robertson Smith's theory of *sacrifice*. The details of these nineteenth-century notions are less relevant to our purposes than how Freud puts them together. Essentially, Freud's argument goes like this: there is a horde made up of a 'primal father' (what would later be called an alpha male), his sons and women. Only the primal father has sexual access to the women, whom he violently protects against the attentions of his (and their) sons. In Freudian thought, men desire their mothers, and this childish desire is in adulthood suppressed and relegated to the subconscious. The actions in the primal horde represent the enactment of this desire coupled with its consequence: murder and (now suppressed) guilt. The band of brothers who were the sons of the primal father killed him in order to have sex with their mother. Then they felt guilty and invented a religion which revered the father, and symbols to support this, along with a taboo on this kind of sexual relationship. Their religion was a totemic one, and the existence of totemism among 'primitive' peoples confirms for Freud his hypothesis. Totemism involves among other things reverence for the species that represents the clan. In other words, it represents the primal father and founder of that clan.

Knight (1991) and his followers believe that symbolic culture (including art and religion) was invented through a Hobbesian 'social contract' perhaps 130,000 years ago, or in his original formulation (1991: 313) perhaps between 60,000 and 40,000 BP. He usually puts the date now at something in between. But unlike Hobbes in his vision of a social contract or Freud in his, Knight and his followers believe it was women, not men, who established this contract. More specifically, Knight (1991: 281–326) argues that women got together collectively in a sex strike, to deprive men of sex, and then to exchange it for meat. Knight claims that after an initial 'revolution' this was done monthly, with the two weeks after new moon for chastity and hunting, and the two weeks after full moon for sex and feasting. He notes that much in the symbolism of hunter-gatherers today (veneration of the moon, menstrual taboos, hunting magic, the use of ochre in body decoration and rock art) all point to this. Aspects of kinship relations in Aboriginal Australia, and taboos on eating food one kills oneself, do as well. For me, the 'own kill rule' (e.g., Knight 1991: 88–121), that one exchanges meat one kills, rather than eating it, is especially significant. It is often related to totemism (not eating one's own totem animal) and to sacrifice, as well as to exchange relations and customs pertaining to in-law avoidance and correct kinship behaviour. This rule is widespread in Australia and South America, and found in various forms in Africa, North America, Oceania and elsewhere. It is a comparative ethnographic generalization of great importance: like the incest taboo, totemism or shamanistic practice. Like exogamy, it enjoins people to exchange and regulates relations between groups. Like any taboo, the own kill rule gives powerful expression to a cultural ethos or a collective consciousness. However, its use as a comparative ethnographic tool is not at all dependent on the rest of Knight's theory. For me at least, its explanatory value is greater.

Knight's project is brilliant in conception, and presents us with a great deal to think about. However, I do not accept it as a model of how things happened. It places far too much emphasis on a single event and, in Knight's view, one we are required to accept in order to make use of his insights. I reject it for a similar reason that I reject Nicholas Allen's (2008) hypothesis that there is a single original kinship system that came into being fully formed. It is too neat and clean. Like Genesis, these models seem to give us order from chaos; but like the Iatmul myth of origin, they present us with a theory of evolution that is in effect chaos from order. For both Allen and Knight, human society as we know it came into being 'in the beginning', but from this state of order, kinship structures and symbolic culture gradually dissipated. To a degree I do accept the gradual withering away of elementary structures of kinship and symbolic association in the Neolithic, but that is a different story (see Barnard 2008: 241–3, and 2011: 193–41).

Another way to envisage these models – Allen's, Knight's and Freud's alike – is in terms of social contract theory. Like Hobbes (1991 [1651]), John Locke (1988 [1690]: 265–428) and J. J. Rousseau (1997b [1762]: 39–152), they envisage an 'original' society from which all societies are descended. They create their imagined original societies through a Western mythological event, perhaps one they believe literally occurred at some point in time, perhaps not. Yet, there are clear differences. For example, for Hobbes, the 'Sovereign' (either a king or a parliament) remains necessary to maintain order; for Freud, this 'primal father' is no longer necessary. The Freudian social contract, among the band of brothers, is precisely that which does away with this figure of authority. Freud and Knight are similar in many ways, but Freud's vision is male-centred, whereas Knight's is female-centred. Allen's concern and Knight's too are with the generation of primal structures, and they share this goal too with Lévi-Strauss. If the latter was not quite a social contract theorist, it is because his concern was always with the structures themselves rather than with the agents of their creation.

Rock art in religion, religion in rock art

Rock art is the first form of symbolic representation easily recognizable as such, and as art, by any human today. Theories of rock art proliferate, and I shall not discuss them here, except for one: that known as the 'symbolic approach'. This approach emerged in an interesting way, namely through statistical analysis. The archaeologist Patricia Vinnicombe grew up on a farm near the Drakensberg Mountains and their numerous rock art sites. She noticed that the incidence of one species, the eland, vastly exceeded the occurrence of that species in the area. She then, in the 1960s, began recording the attributes, twenty in all, of rock art figures in the area: subject (human or animal), style (monochrome, biochrome, etc.), scene (hunting, dancing, etc.), and so on. Rejecting both the 'art for art's sake' view and the 'sympathetic magic' view, Vinnicombe (1972) concluded that religious significance was the factor most important in rock art. Another key player here, and the one most relevant to our concerns, is the South African archaeologist David Lewis-Williams. In his magnificent *Believing and seeing* (1981), and in later more popular works, Lewis-Williams puts his rock art research together with Ju/'hoan ethnography and /Xam (southern San) mythology to offer insightful explanations based on the premise that at least southern African rock art has symbolic action in its roots.

Essentially, Lewis-Williams' approach emphasizes spiritual and ritual associations of the art, either observed within the paintings and engravings themselves, or assumed from context to have been present in the minds of the artists. The religion involved here is shamanism, splendidly defined in one introduction (Stutley 2003: 2) as including three things: (1) belief in the existence of spirits, often taking the form of animals; (2) trance performance on the part of a medicine man or shaman, generally accompanied by music and dancing that help to induce the trance state; and (3) ceremonial curing rituals practised by the shaman while in trance. Among the numerous books and articles Lewis-Williams has written on the subject, I would pick out three for comment here. In *Deciphering ancient minds*, Lewis-Williams and his collaborator Sam Challis trace San belief in the art, in the ethnography and through the work and changing theories of generations of Western scholars and the indigenous believers who have helped them interpret the art. Lewis-Williams and Challis (2011: 153–77) make the point that the examples of San art were not put on the rock as finished pieces, but blended, one painting with another, in the form of narratives. These are closely related to San mythology, as well as to shamanic belief and practice. Shamans (or 'medicine people', as they are called in several San languages) are depicted in the art, and they often take the form of therianthropes. The art comes in both 'realistic' and 'trance-based' fragments. The former include images of trance performers bleeding from the nose, bending at the waste and using dance rattles, and images of women clapping and singing. The latter include rather more mysterious things: images of the spirit leaving the body when in trance (depicted by lines emerging from the head), of the performer entering the spirit world through holes in the rock face or being transformed into animals, or of the 'threads of light' that signify the trance state. San shamans, both those in nineteenth-century South Africa and Lesotho where the rock art was painted and farther north today in Botswana and Namibia, claim to see these when in trance. San religion is essentially monotheistic and characterized by rituals of initiation into adulthood and rain making, as well as of trance performance. Although San explanations differ as to whether the spiritual entity present is the High God or some other spirit, the rituals are basically the same across southern Africa.

The two other texts relevant here are *The mind in the cave* (Lewis-Williams 2002) and *Conceiving God* (2010). Both step beyond the usual artistic and technical interpretations of rock art to explain shamanic belief as a step in human consciousness. In the former, Lewis-Williams argues that a higher order of consciousness was acquired by *Homo sapiens*, both in Africa and in Europe, and that this enabled our ancestors to produce the art they did on these two continents and elsewhere. He argues further that although Neanderthals could learn the tool techniques of their Cro-Magnon neighbours, they could not learn to appreciate or to create their art. The mind in the cave, whether in the Drakensberg or at Lascaux, was a creative mind and one that believed in a cosmos beyond nature as we (and the Neanderthals) knew it. It was also a cosmos situated beyond human society. In *Conceiving God*, Lewis-Williams takes his argument a step or two further. He touches on the neurological basis for religious belief, and explores the foundation of consciousness in the brain and the logical consequences of belief and consciousness. These are art, religious ritual and the altered states of consciousness that give rise to the specific forms found in San or Bushman religion and art.

There are many forms of rock art: engraving and painting, and, importantly here, abstract (usually engraving) or representational (including engraving and painting). There are several possibilities for the evolution of rock art. Either there is simple evolution from one form to another, for example from abstract to representational art (or the other way around), or there is parallel evolution, where diverse cultural traditions maintain diverse artistic traditions too, or there is a more complex form of evolution, such as co-evolution. In the last instance, two artistic forms evolve together, influence each other, or perhaps have different roles, for example, one sacred and the other secular.

A related matter is: which came first, indexical meanings or purely symbolic (arbitrary) ones? Here the answer seems to be more obvious, and I agree with Frederick Coolidge and Thomas Wynn (2011: 381) in their assumption that index logically comes first. For Coolidge and Wynn, this view forms part of their objection to the precise theory proposed by Christopher Henshilwood and Benoît Dubreuil (2011) for the cognitive mechanisms implied in Middle Stone Age material culture. The acceptability of that theory does not concern me here, one way or the other. Rather, let me simply note Coolidge and Wynn's example: the Christian cross stands for the resurrection not in an arbitrary way, but rather through a symbolic meaning that plays upon the indexical relation between cross and crucifixion. And so it was between the Blombos beads (d'Errico *et al.* 2005) and their meaning – whatever that might have been. Human symbolic thought, preceding or evolving along with complex language, was undoubtedly about linking things together. Meanings must have been shared and collectively understood before they could become truly arbitrary.

Did Neanderthals have symbolic culture? Recent research suggests possibly they did. More specifically, the extensive review of the evidence by João Zilhão (2007) notes that while in southern Africa there were personal ornaments by 75,000 BP, in Europe they occurred (or have been found only in sites dated to) shortly after 45,000 BP. Yet, there were no anatomically modern Europeans in Europe at the time! In fact, these earliest European cases are in Neanderthal contexts. The earliest figurative art occurs after 32,000 BP, several millennia later than the period of first known contact between

Neanderthals and moderns. Zilhão's (2007: 35–41) conclusion is that 'behavioural modernity' was triggered by social and demographic occurrences and was not species-specific. If this is true, then to me the implication must be that Neanderthals were cognitively capable of 'art' and all that one does with it, and that art was either very early (invented by the common ancestors of *Homo sapiens* and *H. neanderthalensis*) or that it somehow crossed the species boundary. I do not necessarily believe in the necessity to demarcate the species in this way in any case, but merely do so because the alternative (referring constantly to *H. sapiens sapiens* and *H. sapiens neanderthalensis*) is more cumbersome.

Whether Neanderthals had art or not, rock art is found on every continent except Antarctica, and at least represents one form, or diversity of forms, that can not only be dated but analysed for content with some degree of sophistication. Earliest dates for rock art on each continent are: South America, 10,000 BP; North America, 11,500 BP (although this date is contested); Asia, 14,000 BP; Australia, 28,000 BP; Africa, 26,000 or 28,000 BP; and Europe, 32,000 BP (Bednarik 2003). The African example is a painting of an animal on a stone slab from Apollo 11 Cave in Namibia, and the European ones are those of caves in France and Spain that date from 32,000 to 10,500 BP. We also have sculpture, notably an animal head from Tolbaga, Russia, dated at 35,000 BP, and ostrich egg shell beads from several sites in India dated at between 40,000 and 25,000 BP (2003: 91), and, of course, Barham's evidence of pigment use in Zambia much earlier. We have several, more dubious, suggestions of engraved stones, cupules and so on, still much earlier. For me, these more dubious claims raise another question, and one also implied by the etched red ochre from Blombos: is it art, or is it (just) symbolic thought? In short, does symbolic thought have to be art, or can it exist in material form without being art?

Structuralism or interpretivism?

In *History and theory in anthropology* (Barnard 2000: 122–3, 160–1), I contrasted structuralism with interpretivism and argued that both see society or culture as analogous to language, though they see this metaphor quite differently.

Essentially, structuralism holds that society or culture has a kind of 'grammar'. The duty of a structural anthropologist is to work out that grammar. For a structuralist, therefore, the 'meaning' of something has no meaning except within a cultural context, effectively a 'language', a *system of meanings*. The colour green, for example, takes on meaning according to whether it is in a traffic light (where it means 'go'), on a politician's rosette (where in the UK it signifies the Green Party) or on a football jersey or scarf (where in Scotland it might represent either Celtic Football Club or Hibernian, both teams with Irish connections). In each case, there is an implied contrast to other colours, which likewise take on their meanings within such cultural (or national) systems. A cultural system is like a language, and its grammar tells us the meaning.

Interpretivism assumes that culture requires 'translation'. In order to understand an alien culture, one must first learn to use its symbols as one learns to use its words. But then one needs to 'translate' them into those of a different culture – that of one's listeners or readers. The problem of cultural translation for an anthropologist is much the same as in linguistic translation for an interpreter: does one go for a literal translation or an idiomatic one? Translate too literally and the translator loses her readers; no one except the 'native' will understand what she is saying. Translate too idiomatically, and he will fail to render fully the deeper meaning of the original. The 'native's' thought becomes merely that of the translator's alien listener.

In reality, the opposition between structuralism and interpretivism is complicated by the fact that these are logical extremes. All anthropological analysis makes use of both translation in some sense, and interpretation through a knowledge of linguistic and cultural structures. Pure interpretivism and pure structuralism are therefore equally unlikely, because the interpretive and the structural *go together*. The difference can simply be a matter of emphasis. The distinction can be nuanced and dependent too on another variable: how we treat the speaker or actor in our analysis. The chief interpretive anthropologist in the United States, Clifford Geertz (1966), famously described religion as a 'cultural system', specifically a system of symbols through which people communicate. While his essay 'Religion as a cultural system' may be but one example of his work on the path towards an explicit interpretive anthropology (Geertz 1973 and 1983), nevertheless, it illustrates well the fact that structure and interpretation are both part of a wider system of local and anthropological knowledge. For Geertz, the individual actor's manipulation of symbols within a cultural system is crucial to anthropological analysis, but seeing the mutual dependence of structure and interpretation would work equally well in less actor-centred approaches too, such as those of the self-confessed structuralist Claude Lévi-Strauss, or the interpretivist (as I have classified him) Sir Edward Evans-Pritchard.

Lévi-Strauss' most indicative texts are perhaps *The savage mind* (1966 [1962]) and the four volumes of the 'Mythologiques', beginning with *The raw and the cooked* (1969a [1964]). The former does indeed involve the actor, through the figure of the *bricoleur* – a handyman whose craft of *bricolage*, putting together bits of this and that, creates through 'devious means'. Lévi-Strauss explains that the result when metaphorically applied to myth is the intellectual *bricolage* that defines mythical thought (1969a: 16–17). Yet Lévi-Strauss' emphasis is not on the *bricoleur* but on the *bricolage* which results in, and which contains in its essence, not randomness, but structure. Myth is highly structured, as are the markings on the Blombos ochre: they occur with regularity and in geometrical patterns. So too, of course, are music and language. It is not without meaning that *The raw and the cooked*, a book about South American mythology, is constructed almost entirely in musical metaphor. It begins with an 'overture', contains themes and variations, the odd solo, song and coda, canon, toccata and fugue, a chromatic piece, a rondo, a cantata, symphonies and a bird chorus. In it, the author recreates the patterns that are actually there, in the myths and in the subconscious thoughts of the myth makers and myth tellers. Again, agency is far less important than the collective mind, but the latter is by no means devoid of creativity.

Evans-Pritchard is perhaps less significant here, but his attempts to wrestle with the religious meaning of alien concepts, rendered meaningful through translation in familiar idiom, is revealing both of Nuer (Naath) thought and of Evans-Pritchard's own. Both manipulate symbols, and much of the discussion, particularly in the most relevant work,

Nuer religion (1956), concerns concepts like *kwoth* (God, spirit, breath, etc.) as well as equivalences and differences between Evans-Pritchard's notions of sacrifice, soul and ghost and those of his South Sudanese informants. For me, this lends support to this relativist view that all 'cultures' are equal, and, more to the point, that seeking the sophistication that is buried in symbolic thought, rather than assuming its primitiveness, yields greater insight into its origins.

5 The flowering of language

Language is the key. There were relevant changes in the brain that enabled greater cognitive skills, and relevant too are current debates and recent discoveries, most famously the discovery of a mutation on the FOXP2 (forkhead box P2) gene which governs aspects of both speech and language (Enard *et al.* 2002). Thus (full) language appears to be relatively recent in hominin evolution and equally appears to have a biological basis. There have been suggestions that Neanderthals, as well as *Homo sapiens* (or *Homo sapiens sapiens*), underwent the required mutation for the development of full language (e.g., Krause *et al.* 2007). These genetic findings in FOXP2 are supported also by archaeological evidence from Kebra Cave in Israel in which a 60,000-year-old Neanderthal skeleton was found to possess a hyoid bone similar to modern humans, suggesting that they 'may have been capable of complex speech' (Wells 2011: 100).

Such findings raise profound questions, particularly if John Shea is correct in his interpretation of recent FOXP2 results. He points out that we now have DNA from Neanderthal skeletal material which suggests that the Neanderthals had the right genetic makeup for language. Pointing to 'strong selective pressure for spoken language', and therefore 'prior selective pressure for symbolic communication', he argues that *Homo sapiens* was probably not the only species to use symbols (Shea 2011: 25). Rather, *H. sapiens* is simply the only one still to survive.

I accept an earlier origin of symbolic thought than most, but the richness of language as we know it still needs to be explained. This chapter considers the relation between the evolution of syntax, and the representation of symbolic thought in mythology, ritual, poetry, art and society. I have developed two complementary theories of the evolution of language (Barnard 2009 and 2010a). Many other anthropologists, archaeologists, linguists and neuroscientists have theories too, including theories which are relevant to the origins of symbolism, art and music, and this chapter will touch on some of these.

Inquisitive meerkat invents recursion

Recursion is the embedding of an element of linguistic expression within another of the same kind, for example a prepositional phrase within another prepositional phrase. Commonly, the term refers to embedding sentences within other sentences: 'The dog who chased the cat who caught the mouse went into his doghouse.' 'Full language' depends on recursion, and (at least in most languages) it depends on intricate morphology: changes in the form of words often by use of prefixes, suffixes and so on. I have argued (e.g., Barnard 2010a and 2011: 93) that these are not necessary for ordinary communication, but are necessary within narrative, and in particular within myth. Therefore, at a certain level, 'language' is not about communication. It is about thought processes which relate to belief. In other words, it betokens Noam Chomsky's notion of I-language (language's internal aspect), not his E-language (its external aspect) (see Chomsky 1986: 19–50; Isac and Reiss 2008). Loosely, I-language may be characterized as language in the guise of cognitive science, and E-language as language in communication (with data sets from actual examples of such). Theoretically, there is a third possibility too, P-language (where 'P' stands for Platonic): language in existence independently of any people (Isac and Reiss 2008: 71–2). Of course, what, say, 'English' might consist of here is but a philosophical problem: do Chaucer and Shakespeare belong to the same P-language? And recursion may be 'infinite', but *only* in P-language.

My earlier argument on language as belief (Barnard 2010a), part of I-language, used as its example a /Xam myth. In particular, it used a single, very intricate sentence, which is in fact five sentences embedded within each other, with a quotation within a quotation, with a unique narrative-form verb, with mythological characters who are not human but act as if humans, who deceive, who display characteristic moral and social properties and which (the story as a whole) is based on a metaphor. I shall omit the /Xam sentence here: let me give here simply the English translation, or actually my slightly more literal rewording of Lucy Lloyd's (Bleek and Lloyd 1911: 33) translation: 'Then /Kuamman-a said: "I desire thee to say to grandfather, Why is it that grandfather continues to go among people who are different?"' The unidentified character /Kuamman-a is probably a meerkat, and this sentence he utters gives the grammatical complexity required by the story. It is five or six sentences, or implied sentences, in one.

There are many other such sentences within the texts recorded by Wilhelm Bleek and Lucy Lloyd in the late nineteenth century, and they come from different informants. The one just quoted comes from /Han≠kass'o. Here is an example from another informant, Dia!kwain: 'And, our grandfather, speaking, said: "Ye must come and stand around, that I may be cutting off from the Ostrich's lungs, that I may be giving them to you, that ye may be swallowing them down"' (Bleek and Lloyd 1911: 133–5). And here is a slightly longer piece of narrative from Bleek and Lloyd's third main informant, and best known, //Kabbo:

> Thou knowest that I sit waiting for the moon to turn back for me, that I may return to my place. That I may listen to all the people's stories, when I visit them; that I may listen to their stories that which they tell; they listen to the Flat Bushmen's stories from the other side of the place. They are those which they thus tell, they are listening to them; while the other *!xoe-ssho-!kui* (the sun) becomes a little warm, that I may sit in the sun; that I may sitting, listen to the stories which come from a distance. Then, I shall get ahold of a story from them, because they (the stories) float out from a distance; while the sun feels a little warm; while I feel that I must altogether visit; that I may be talking with them, my fellow men. (Bleek and Lloyd 1911: 299–301)

The ability to create such discourse lies within the language, and, of course, is not exclusive to mythology or to any other kind of narrative. //Kabbo's sentences here do lie within a narrative, though quite a different kind from myth: not a fictional, folkloristic or mythological story, but his relation of where stories come from. My point here is that narrative requires such sentences, whereas ordinary discourse generally does not. Many of the most eminent writers on the origin of language (e.g., Tomasello 2008; Corballis 2011) seem to jump rather too easily from chimpanzee communication to full language without a 'bridge theory' to account for the theoretical inferences in such a jump (see Botha 2009: 107–11). My theory to bridge this enormous gap is that language is not communication. It is founded in myth. Noam Chomsky has said something quite similar about language as *not* communication many times in his public pronouncements, although he grounds the substance of language in its internal aspect, that is, in thought *as opposed to* communication. Or, as Frederick Newmeyer (1983: 100) once suggested: 'Language is used for thought, for problem solving ... and possibly to fulfil an instinctive need for symbolic behavior.' He adds that there is no evidence to suggest that language came into being for the purpose of communication. The crucial point is that either *need* did not come into play at all, or the need which language fulfils is not one of communication. It is something else.

My own opening sentence a couple of paragraphs ago ('My earlier argument on language as belief ... ') is another example of a form of recursion, but it is in a sense a 'scientific' one (the science of language). And science is an extension of myth. It is also another example of recursion, at a semantic level: it is a sentence which is itself a sentence about another sentence. Talk of hunting and gathering, making tools and shelters, parenthood and childbearing, or whatever, do not require such syntactic complexity. Myth and science do. For this reason, it is best take seriously Chomsky's distinction and to give priority to I-language, rather than E-language, when we think of what language is. Of course, symbolism communicates too, but it communicates 'internally' through sets of symbols that are ordered consciously and culturally. Symbolism is not in itself language, but it is analogous to language in what it can do, and, to some extent, how it does it. It is not, however, recursive.

Just taken for granted: implications of language

Ritual and myth

'Society cannot exist without symbolism', wrote Lévi-Strauss (1945: 518). His notion, expressed just after this statement, that the genesis of symbolic thought must just be taken 'for granted', was echoed by

Chomsky in his longstanding refusal to consider such a question with reference to the genesis of language. Nevertheless, Chomsky's earlier position has been overthrown, at least by passing references in recent work (e.g., Chomsky 2006: 175–6) and in his famous paper with Marc Hauser and Tecumseh Fitch (Hauser *et al.* 2002). Lévi-Strauss (e.g., 1963: 31–54) was fond of pointing out the relations between culture and language and between anthropology and linguistics. Indeed, language and culture are similar in many ways, as are the two disciplines, but in fact society is dependent on neither. Society precedes culture, and it long precedes any form of what might realistically be understood as language. As I have suggested above, language is not mere communication, but something quite different. Society, or sociality, as it is found among *Homo sapiens sapiens* is in its essence about symbolism. Language and culture of the kind found here, as opposed to forms of culture found among earlier hominin species or among chimpanzees, inevitably express symbolic thought. It is for that very reason that social anthropology should seek with renewed vigour the genesis of symbolic thought. Symbolic thought is precisely the domain of this discipline, even more than it is of linguistics.

This thesis is not incompatible at all with my suggestion that mythology is central to true language, or at least to complex grammar, or that it is central to symbolic thought. Both myth and other expressions of symbolic thought, namely ritual, express the symbolic in similar ways. Both ritual and myth employ symbolism to show contradictions in society, or use disorder or inversions of social norms to emphasize the transition to new states of order. Famous examples include, in the ethnography of Gregory Bateson (1936), the *naven* ritual of the Iatmul, and in that of Victor Turner (1967), various ritual practices, such as circumcision and hunting ritual, of the Ndembu of Zambia. The *naven* ritual marks the Iatmul transition to adulthood by means of formalized mock sexual acts and gender reversals: men acting and dressing as women, and vice versa. Ndembu rituals are similar in their emphasis on liminality: when human action is not quite normal, but is between one thing and another (for example, between youth and initiated adult). Mythology is similar, except it expresses contradiction not through reversal but through complex linguistic expression in the form of narrative.

Virtually every mythological system in the world, if not every myth, plays on the idea of contradiction. Like ritual, myth enacts contradictions, and in particular taboo. Ritual and myth re-enforce normative behaviour through the process of exposing the nature and consequences of the violation of taboos, whatever they might be, in different cultural traditions. The Oedipus myth, for example, contains a plethora of contradictions, most obviously Oedipus' dilemma upon realizing he has committed incest, because Jocasta is both his wife and his mother. Other taboos include the burial of close kin, as well as parricide and fratricide (see, e.g., Lévi-Strauss 1963 [1955]: 213–18). The Indologist Wendy Doniger, writing of Lévi-Straussian analyses of myth, expresses this when she says that myths exist in order to *solve* some unsolvable paradox. The point is that the myth *cannot* solve the paradox. Instead, it transforms paradox into a narrative that expresses the contradictions, 'two human truths that are simultaneously true and mutually opposed' (Doniger 2009: 206). She is concerned with myths as stories and with the literary values of tension and suspense. In anthropology, we tend to look instead for weightier, more philosophical problems hidden in the myths and to the cultural meanings that lie within them. The two approaches, however, are not incompatible, and here yield the same conclusions.

Plainly, myth does require very great linguistic sophistication, whereas ritual is, in a sense, the opposite. Ritual requires no speech, no language at all. It can express paradox through action alone, but this is nevertheless action which itself contains contradiction, and it uses only this to make the same point. There is also the possibility that myth and ritual are related. In the nineteenth century, William Robertson Smith (2002 [1894]: 17–20) argued that the function of myth is to explain rites whose original meaning is lost. For him, myth is early in religious thought, and replaced by dogma in later religious systems. While I would not argue precisely that, it is worth in any case considering such social as well as linguistic origins for mythology itself. Or at least, considering ethnographic cases of the correspondence between ritual and myth with a view to defining which arose first in specific instances.

Why not communication?

Evolutionary psychologist Robin Dunbar (e.g., 1996) argues that language was necessary, given the probable size of 'archaic' *Homo sapiens* groups. At a maximal size of nearly 150, more in the case of Neanderthals (if Dunbar's theory of the correlation between brain size and group size is correct), communication required language across distances, between families and between bands of the same group. In addition, there were requirements for 'language' of some sort to have taken over from grooming earlier in hominin evolution. In Dunbar's (2003: 173–5) view, language would be required when grooming reached 30 per cent of one's waking hours, which would imply a group size of about 110 and fall within the presumed *H. erectus* stage. With *H. sapiens* and a group size of 150, without language it should be taking up 43 per cent of individuals' time. Ethologist I. Eibl-Eibesfeldt (1979: 122–87) goes further in suggesting natural tendencies both for larger groups and for inter-group aggression. His hypothesis is based primarily on hunter-gatherer ethnography, and it has at its basis the notion that humans are territorial. For Eibl-Eibesfeldt, inter-group aggression is a necessary consequence of competition for territory, even between small groups in sparsely populated areas.

There is, though, a problem with this reasoning, both in the writings of Dunbar and those of Eibl-Eibesfeldt. We learn here that on the one hand language is about communication. We learn that on the other, it is a replacement for grooming and exists because, without it, grooming would take up too much time. Implicitly, too, there is a tendency for groups to be bigger and perhaps for language to be of greater use the larger the group. These different but related scenarios might ring true. They might, in fact, explain different aspects of language. However, they do not explain at all why language exists *in the form that it does*. In other words, neither the scenario of Dunbar nor that of Eibl-Eibesfeldt explains linguistic complexity. My view is that language, or, more accurately, complex language, is much more than a form of communication. This means that it must be explained in its own right. Language is complex because complexity is required for meaning, for example, in narrative. Stories about the past, and mythology in particular, require it. Some linguists work in related areas, notably the development of grammar, and future collaboration between linguists and anthropologists in the area might be fruitful.

Explanations for the origins of language are diverse, but not only that, they actually represent 'explanations' of rather different things: the development of grammar, the biological improvements in cognition and psychological implications for self-awareness, changes in how communication works, the increasing complexity of social structures and so on. In his 'anthropological perspective' on the origins of grammar, Martin Edwardes (2010) puts several of such phenomena together. He emphasizes social aspects of the evolution of grammar, especially the modelling, through language(s), of the 'self' in interactions with the 'other'. This can be taken as either a cognitive (I-language) issue or a communicative (E-language) one. He usefully distinguishes four types of social usage of language (Edwardes 2010: 12–13), or to put it another way, four levels or stages in the evolution of linguistic sociality. The first is the phatic stage: the use of gestures or sounds to acknowledge relations between people, or indeed animals. The second is direction, which involves the utilization of imperatives, for example, to enable people or animals to get things done. The third is more sophisticated: negotiation. This requires a slightly richer linguistic understanding: the use of nouns and verbs, and denotation (pointing things out, either verbally or otherwise) if not yet tense. His final type, or phase, is that of information sharing. This, he argues, does require linguistic tense, or, as he see it, temporal relationships between things and individuals, including third parties.

In an earlier attempt at reconstructing the evolution of grammar, Mary LeCron Foster (1999: 771–2) summarizes her comparative linguistic findings through a speculative scheme of seven stages. First, there was australopithecine communication through imitation. Then, there was early *Homo* communication through visual-vocal signs, with semantic correlations like inward, enclosing, female, etc. (and possibly home base, mothering, eating, receiving, etc.), on the one hand, and outward, thrusting, male, etc. (and distance, male erection, butchering, bringing, etc.), on the other hand. She postulates the 'phememes' *M for the former and *T for the latter. After this, there came social changes which required an increase in communication over distances, and consequently, *p (going, killing, etc.), *t (butchering, tool-making, etc.), *m (mouth, vagina, eating, etc.), *n (pregnancy, blood, hearth, etc.). With hafting came sequences of consonants and vowels. In the fifth and final hunter-gatherer phase, there might have been an expansion of the phonemic inventory. Foster (1999: 722) then proposes two final phases, with a 'birth of grammar' within the Neolithic, between 10,000 and 5,000 BP, and 'language as we know it' in the Bronze Age, from 5,000 BP. However, to my mind, the dating of her two final phases is, I am afraid, rather nonsensical in that it suggests that true language is post-hunter-gatherer. Presumably, the dates themselves might be remotely possible, but to imply that hunter-gatherers only have 'language as we know it' if they borrowed it from Bronze Age cultivators will never work. There was never a Bronze Age in southern Africa. Grammar is not needed in order to grow crops, build megaliths or mix copper with tin, but it is needed in order to tell a good myth. Equally problematic is Foster's assumption of a relation between sophistication in metaphor, advances in mythological explanation and the invention of deities as metaphors for social classes. The last may indeed be associated with the Bronze Age; metaphors for other things, especially in mythology, are prominent too among hunter-gatherers. It is worth reflecting on the fact that from early *Homo* onwards, her scheme does assume there is some sort of metaphor at the very root of language.

The Neolithic and Bronze Age issues aside, my question is still why? Why should sharing information require what, in fact, language can offer? We have unnecessary things like agreement between subject and verb, we have noun classes, we have agglutination and we have phenomenal vocabularies to play with and elegant grammatical constructions with which to do the same. The /Xam language had all these things, and it had no fewer than fourteen ways in which to make a noun plural. By my count, it also seems to have had about thirty verbal particles, placed before the verb to indicate mood and tense, and a smaller number of suffixes, placed at the end of the verb, to indicate duration of action, completion of action, repetition of action, imperative mood and what have you (see Bleek 1928/9 and 1929/30).

And beyond myth, there is poetry, and the ability to create simile and metaphor. We have the 'how'; what is the Darwinian 'why'? Very simply, language in the form we have it must exist for some purpose other than mere communication, and communication itself is enhanced because of our potential to go beyond it.

Language, symbolism and art

Simile and metaphor: A red, red rose

O, my luve's like a red, red rose,
That's newly sprung in June;
O, my luve's like the melodie,
That's sweetly play'd in tune.   (Robert Burns)

In the West, poetry has rhythm and often repetition, frequently rhymes, uses simile or metaphor, has slightly unusual syntax and occasionally appears in archaic or dialect forms that are not those of the hearer or even the speaker. We see this in the Burns poem or song 'Red, red rose', written in 1794 from a traditional source. Although at least arguably in the eighteenth-century Ayrshire dialect of the Lowland Scots language, every word of the first verse is readily intelligible, written or spoken, to almost every literate English-speaker today. (Later verses are perhaps more obscure.) In Bushman myths (in some Bushman languages), similar conventions are employed. Bleek and Lloyd (1911) deliberately translated from /Xam mythology with archaic English forms, evoking poetic imagery as Burns' Lowland Scots represents to speakers of English. Bushman myths may have rhythm and repetition, metaphor, archaic syntax and supposed 'animal speech'. All these contribute to its poetic effect, and they set it apart from ordinary speech. We saw this above in the English versions of /Xam myths I have briefly quoted. Typically, /Xam myths are between 1,000 and 4,000 words long.

There are nearly as many *theories* of language origins as there are *theorists* of language origins, and not all these are incompatible. One I am increasingly finding favour with is the one known as the 'Scheherezade effect' (e.g., Miller 2000: 341–91). It is indeed compatible with my theory (if theory it be) that we should be looking less to language as communication and more, at least in its later stages of development, to language as that which is necessary for narrative. The 'Scheherezade effect' suggests that complex language came about due to the ability of protagonists to attract potential mates and keep them verbally entertained. In other words, narrative, including myth and poetry, became part of sexual allure, and became a focal point of natural selection. Geoffrey Miller (2000: 353) argues that after an initial stage of language evolution, humans probably used their acquired language abilities for courting potential mates. 'Well-articulated thoughts' aided Darwinian fitness, and sexual selection. Miller (2000: 369) also emphasizes vocabulary size. He notes that the average English-speaker has a vocabulary of 60,000 words. I know a linguist who claims an English vocabulary more than three times that, plus tens of thousands of words in other languages too. Yet an intelligent bonobo has a lexicon of just 200 visual symbols. A typical primate, in comparison, has only between five and twenty discrete calls. Who is going to be successful at finding a mate will be the one who can keep him entertained. With the genders inverted, there is, of course, a 'Cyrano effect' too. As Burns taught us, where sexual selection is at issue, language is as good for men as it is good for women.

Simile and metaphor make up language as much as literal expression. Poetry is perhaps in the eye of the beholder, but I vividly remember when Naro semi-hunter-gatherers with whom I worked, in the western Kalahari, made up clever allusions, plays on words and other linguistic games I never understood. Obviously, these things are not just for urban English-speaking teenagers, but part of the fullness of full language itself. In his inaugural lecture as Professor of Language Evolution at Edinburgh, Simon Kirby (2011) made the point that not only have humans evolved the capacity for language, but language itself evolves. He and his team have shown this both experimentally with human subjects and more theoretically with computer models. This has profound implications not only for philosophers but for linguists and anthropologists too. One could argue that this thing we call language seems to have 'a mind of its own'. Of course, I mean this metaphorically, but then what is metaphor but a different way of expressing reality?

What else is language for?

We must not forget that language, once in existence, can be put to many uses. Some may have existed in the earliest stages of symbolic culture. I presume kinship was there at the beginning and that it evolved to or towards its final stages of hunter-gatherer kinship inclusiveness (universal kin categorization), as well as for making a distinction between 'joking partners' and 'avoidance partners' at that time (Barnard 2008).

In a number of short entries in *An encyclopedia of /Gui and //Gana culture and society* (Tanaka and Sugawara 2010), Kazuyoshi Sugawara comments on /Gui and //Gana discourse and occasionally too on Western theories of discourse analysis. In the latter, there is something called the 'turn-taking system', which presumably applies as the norm within Western conversation. Each person in turn produces a 'projection of possible completion' which comes to be realized through an immediate response by the other in a 'transition relevance place'. For example, I ask a question and you answer it. /Gui conversation, Sugawara tells us (Tanaka and Sugawara 2010: 20–1), has this too. However, /Gui conversation also takes other forms. For example, there is prolonged simultaneous discourse, and there is overlapping discourse. Sometimes, speakers engage in harmonious conversational monologues in which they each say much the same thing, in their own words and at the same time. Sometimes they argue, similarly, at the same time. They can also engage in parallel conversations, often with more than two participants, each engaging in a different choice 'conversation' and with comments on each other's. I witnessed this last form almost hourly, it now seems, in my own fieldwork with the closely related Naro – except that, out of politeness, they usually tried to stop if I wanted to get a word in. Of course, this was related to my own inadequacies with the language, but it was also a recognition that there exist different ways to converse, according to social circumstances.

Another example from the /Gui–//Gana encyclopedia is that of formalized 'prolonged talk', such as one case witnessed by Sugawara, between a man and a woman whose son and daughter had married each other (Tanaka and Sugawara 2010: 84). Their conversations took two forms. In the first, one party would talk for perhaps ten minutes, while the other simply repeated the end of each sentence, laughed at appropriate points or muttered polite agreement. In the other form, characteristic of 'avoidance relationships' in the kinship system, long monologues simply alternated between the speakers. There was no 'projection of possible completion' or 'transition relevance place' here.

In these latter examples, language may or may not involve the sharing of information, but certainly it does involve the sharing of status-recognition. In the West, status is relatively unimportant. In Japan, status is relatively more important and is hierarchical. Among the /Gui and //Gana, while hierarchy is even less important than in the West, what is important is the distinction between 'joking partners' (who may sit close to each other, touch, tease, tell rude jokes and so on) and 'avoidance partners' (who, on the contrary, must behave with the utmost respect). The former include, for example, same-sex siblings, cross-cousins and grandparents/grandchildren, while the latter include opposite-sex siblings, parents/children and especially in-laws. Unlike most other kinship systems, /Gui and //Gana make an absolute distinction between 'joking' (or non-avoidance) and 'avoidance' relatives. Even many Australian systems have finer gradations. For example, among the Mardudjara of Australia's Western Desert there are 'avoidance', 'restraint', 'moderation', 'lack of restraint' and 'joking' as a gradation from formal towards less formal behaviour patterns defined by kin category (Tonkinson 1978: 48). In all this, I am simplifying, but my main point is that language, and here discourse, is about much more than sharing information, and certainly more than sharing factual information.

In short, language entails sophisticated systems of meaning. Like hunter-gatherers of the twentieth and twenty-first centuries, those living 500 centuries ago must have been technically skilled and deeply familiar with their environments. I believe that we should stop treating them like our early *Homo erectus* ancestors, who lived not a mere 500 centuries back but more than 20,000 centuries ago. There may be no evidence of poetry in the archaeological record, but certainly there is evidence of symbolic behaviour and the suggestion of, for example, body decoration (Watts 1999; Barham 2002). As for beautifully constructed kinship systems, there is plenty of evidence too, not prehistoric evidence perhaps, but through ethnographic comparison on a global scale. Unfortunately, when the idea of 'global comparison' was in vogue, it all too often took the form of looking for correlations in data on diversity (e.g., Murdock 1949), whereas much more could be learned also from an exploration of human cultural universals. That might still leave open the question of whether the source is traceable to migration, to diffusion or to independent invention, a topic which is itself worthy of exploration.

As the existence of poetry reminds us, there is still a world that is difficult for language to touch. The poet and writer on Aboriginal religion James G. Cowan (1992: 69) has described myth and legend as 'perfect vehicles for the exploration of non-material realities that defy the logic of language and rational thought'. I would not deny myth, legend or poetry the expression of rationality, but his point is well made. Symbolic humanity represents a stage of thought that lies beyond the material. It is not entirely beyond language though, but rather uses language to its full. Cowan (1992: 69) continues with the suggestion that myth allows us to 'extract from disparate material in nature a workable hypothesis for understanding the world'. I would add, or, rather, emphasize, that without myth there can be no hypothesis. Mythological systems are what philosophers of science would call paradigms expressed in language, and through these paradigms, symbolic thought approaches a theoretical understanding of the universe.

In the collection *Kalahari hunter-gatherers*, the juxtaposition of Megan Biesele's (1976) chapter on folklore and Nicolas Blurton Jones and Melvin Konner's (1976) chapter on Ju/'hoan objective knowledge of animal behaviour is an interesting one. It is no accident that stories accompany meat distribution among the Ju/'hoansi, as in a picture provided for Biesele's (1976: 305) account, and perhaps odd that Blurton Jones and Konner (1976: 338) feel they need to explain that stories are told (at Ju/'hoan gatherings they organized in order to discuss animal behaviour) 'because people are gathered around a fire'.

Fire, or rather the hearth, is supremely important in many hunter-gatherer societies, especially desert ones. As Job Morris, a contemporary Naro San from Botswana, has put it: 'The fire circle at night is where we expose our souls and where we reach out to the fears and joys of one another' (Morris 2011: 7). As he explains, the fire is the place of both healing and story-telling and for him is the 'symbol' of the collective wisdom of his society. It is fitting too that the Argentine lawyer and amateur ethnographer Carlos Valiente Noailles called the Spanish edition of his Kua ethnography *El circulo y el fuego: sociedad y derecho de los kúa* (The circle and the fire: society and right [law] of the Kua) (Valiente Noailles 1988). Kua is a generic term for San or Bushmen, and refers to San in general, but also especially to the /Gui and //Gana of the southern part of the Central Kalahari Game Reserve who use this term. The circle of people who congregate around the fire embody both language and symbol, and both 'culture' (collective wisdom) and 'society' (law).

Finally here, let me return briefly to the Book of Genesis. Genesis 11:1–9 tells the story of the Tower of Babel, a mythical tower built after the Flood. At the time, 'the whole earth was of one language, and of one speech', but God apparently did not approve of humans getting together, building this tower, which reached into the heavens. So he destroyed the tower, confounded the language and forced its speakers to scatter. Similar myths are found throughout the world: Frazer records many of them, scattered throughout the three volumes of his *Folk-lore in the Old Testament* (1919). Whether these myths are related, as diffusionist theory would have it, is a reasonable question. Also reasonable is the notion that they are similar because they reflect fundamental principles in the mind, or because similar thoughts and responses occur among differing peoples in similar circumstances. Diffusionism assumes humans are uninventive: things are invented once and then spread; and evolutionism assumes we are inventive: the same thing is invented many times over, because humans the world over think alike (see Barnard 2000: 47). Whether there was once a language we could call proto-World, after Toba if not after Babel, is a serious question. The relation of one myth to another is equally serious, as Lévi-Strauss knew well, and as both he and Frazer spent most of long lives trying to decipher.

And just how many languages?

At the many conferences on the 'origin of language' we blithely talk a lot about language in the abstract. Yes, the world speaks many languages, and these are (according to some linguists) diverse in structure, even if they are all ultimately from the same source tens of thousands of years ago. We know from comparative studies that languages change at reasonably constant rates, and however controversial the details may be, we can say for certain that Italian and French are not the same language, and that the Latin of ancient Rome, from which they are derived, was different from both Italian and French today.

My social anthropological interest is related, but a little different: how many languages did a Middle Stone Age ancestor of yours and mine speak? Were the children of Blombos multilingual? Certainly, today's hunter-gatherer inhabitants of southern Africa are far more multilingual than I am. I have known illiterate hunter-gatherers who are fluent in five or six languages, in three or more different language families. Even the precise numbers of these languages are problematic because it depends how we count them. For example, are /Gui and //Gana to be counted as different languages? Certainly, they are closer than French and Italian. What about Naro, which is quite different but with some mutual intelligibility?

Is Khoisan one language family, or several: Ju or !Kung, Khoe-Kwadi, Tuu, etc.? I know people who can speak both Khoe and Tuu languages, or both Khoe and Ju languages, plus Setswana and Sekgalagadi (Bantu languages) and Afrikaans (an Indo-European language). These are not 'simple' languages either. As we learned in Chapter 1, Naro (along with all other Khoe languages) has an absurdly large number of person-gender-number markers. Nouns and pronouns have three genders (masculine, feminine and common) and three numbers (singular, dual and plural). Forms change according to both case function and place in a sentence. Other Khoisan languages have their own peculiarities, and Khoisan, if it is a single language family, is far more diverse in structure and more ancient in time depth than, for example, Indo-European. Although they share some vocabulary, Naro is in fact more distant from the neighbouring Ju/'hoan or !Kung language than English is from Hindi. Some linguists believe that Naro and Ju/'hoan are not even related at all, having merely merged together through thousands of years of geographical and consequent linguistic contact (e.g., Güldemann 1998).

Australia is far more diverse than the Kalahari in the languages of its earliest inhabitants, and we find similar multilingualism there too. At the time of European colonization, some 200 languages and 600 dialects were spoken in Australia, and even today many Aborigines speak several Aboriginal languages. Linguists still disagree profoundly about how they are all related, and these differences seem to be increasing the more linguists learn about the languages (see also Dixon 2002; Bowern and Koch 2004). Before 1788, a 'tribe' (the traditional term in Aboriginal ethnography for a linguistic group) typically numbered between 300 and 1,000 people, with land-owning units just 15 or up to 70 (Peterson 1999: 318–19). In linguistic ability, almost any San or Aborigine will put an English-speaker to shame.

Therefore, I see no reason to assume that individual hunter-gatherers living at the time Blombos was inhabited spoke fewer languages, although their languages may have been more closely related. Of course, some individuals may have spoken fewer languages, especially if groups lived in greater isolation. Languages will have been more closely related if complex migrations, such as those of Bantu-speakers and Indo-European-speakers, had not occurred. If we project the situation in Australia or the Kalahari back in time, we can envisage bands consisting of a few dozen individuals, some closely related and some not, some people from within the linguistic unit, but perhaps several they are in contact with coming from quite different linguistic backgrounds. In other words, not only might the inhabitants of Blombos have possessed 'language', they might also have known of and even *have known* several languages.

Symbolism and art

It is important to establish, in our minds, the complexity of language. Most linguists who write on the issue assume we are talking about 'true language' or 'full language', which is why I wanted to dispel completely the notion that language is merely some advanced form of primate communication.

So, we know that language is very late in human evolution. But when did symbolism arise? According to Derek Bickerton (2003: 81), symbolism may be some 2,000,000 years earlier than syntax. Writing in the same volume, Iain Davidson (2003: 141) seems to suggest that Bickerton is saying just the opposite. William Noble and Iain Davidson (1996) had earlier argued at length in favour of symbolic beginnings: symbolism preceded language. Terrence Deacon (1997) pushed at about the same time for the co-evolution, not just of language and the brain, but of symbolic thought and the brain. His more recent work pursues this problem: language is dependent on symbolic thought, and vice versa. All their positions are rather more subtle than these simple statements imply, and nuanced speculations proliferate. This does not mean that the problem is beyond solution, nor even that there is any fundamental disagreement about the basics of human evolution or what might constitute syntax, language or symbolism in a material sense. What it does mean is that symbolic thought (and not just its origin) cannot be taken for granted at all. Furthermore, the writers I cite here are only the tip of an iceberg, and their positions do change from publication to publication.

Putting all this together, it is useful to visualize the temporal relations between language, symbolism, rock art and so on, and to see this in the context of human biological evolution. Figure 5.1 illustrates a time line for the genus *Homo*. Through it, several points are brought to mind. First is the great longevity of *Homo erectus*, as compared to *H. sapiens*. Then, there is the fact of the short duration of the Neolithic and all that followed. 'Natural' humanity, if there is such a thing, long predates the domestication of animals and plants, although there is plenty of evidence for 'domestication light' among today's hunter-gatherers (by analogy with light or 'lite' cola, as opposed to the real thing). In part, this is due to the fact that hunter-gatherers relate to their environments differently from non-hunter-gatherers (Ingold 2000: 61–76). Therefore, some form of management of resources (domestication light), rather than the strict harnessing of them (domestication proper), is reasonable to assume for hunter-gatherers of the past as well as in the present. David Harris (1989), among others, has made this point for Africa and other parts of the world, where burning vegetation is a common precursor to the 'natural' regeneration of wild food plants in the archaeological record. It occurs several steps before domestication, from

Language, symbolism and art

```
2.4 mya                                                          present

tools    fire    symbolic thought?    music, ritual, art?    language, myth
|─────────────────────────────────────────────────────────────────────────|
|                           the genus Homo                                |

    ----─────────────────────────────────────────────── - - - - - -
                          Homo erectus

                                                       - - ──────────|
                                              Homo sapiens sapiens

                                                                    ──|
                                    Homo sapiens sapiens with domestication
```

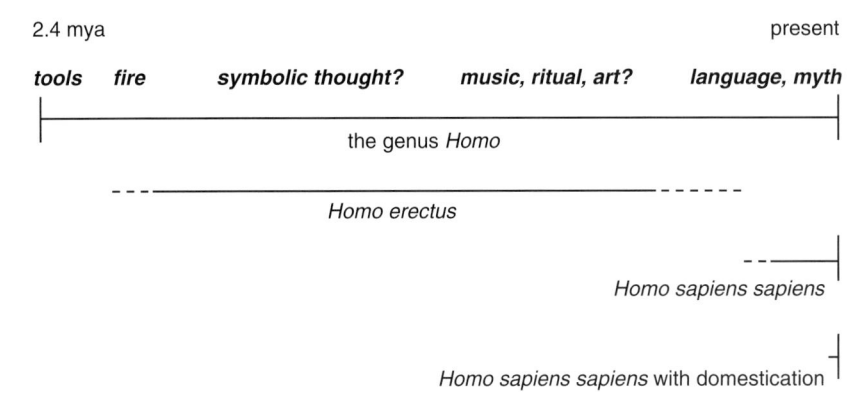

Figure 5.1. Time line for the genus *Homo*

procurement after regeneration in a burnt-off area, to production through replacement planting or transplanting, to mass harvesting, to soil clearance, to the cultivation and propagation of desired varieties, and the storage of the produce.

For reasons of both simplicity and vividness, Figure 5.1 omits all cultural invention apart from domestication. It is worthwhile though to imagine the time frame of these as well. It is noteworthy in this regard that fire is so early in human evolution, certainly among *Homo erectus*. Cooking has been dated possibly to 790,000 BP (Goren-Inbar *et al.* 2004), and there are numerous examples of the use of a hearth, and the hearth as a source of warmth and sociality may predate its use in cooking (see, e.g., James 1989). The hearth and cooking have even been suggested as possible origins for marriage, gift-giving and exchange, as well as for the relative sexual equality of males and females (the latter doing the cooking) among *H. sapiens*, and, I would presume possibly also, *H. heidelbergensis* hunter-gatherers. This is true whether we compare them to their predecessors or to very late *H. sapiens sapiens* non-hunter-gatherers (Wrangham 2009: 147–77). It is commonly assumed that a form of communication existed long before full language, and it is reasonable to assume that fire created a place in camp for people to gather around, either in family groups or for the camp as a whole. The evidence of modern hunter-gatherers shows these two forms of fire as social settings to be virtually universal. And what do people do around a communal fire? They perform rituals. Australian corroborees, southern African medicine dances, Arctic and South American shamanic performances, various North American ritual activities and so on, all occur around the fire. Dance and music are virtually universal in these, and the association of these three things – dance, music and ritual – is, arguably, what makes us human. Decoration, art and myth follow from these elements of symbolic behaviour. Symbolic behaviour, in turn, reflects symbolic thought. Depending on how we define it, symbolic thought too seems a possibility, in some form, even for *H. erectus* or *H. heidelbergensis* as well as for *H. sapiens*.

Aural and visual arts, and religion, too, are in our 'blood'. Even since the symbolic revolution, biology has fed into human development, though not in the simplistic way one may think. The relation between biology and cultural tradition does not work through Darwinian natural selection in a crude sense, but is manifest in something much richer. Commenting on the invention of computers, televisions and radios, ethnomusicologist John Blacking (1976: 114) once said that inventions are but 'purposeful discoveries'. As ideas, they exist already and develop through greater consciousness of the world. In culture history, they come into being through biological processes and social interaction. Fundamentally, then, culture builds on biology, and the two are not entirely separate; nor is the division between them entirely obvious.

Tim Ingold argued something similar through a number of the twenty-three essays in his book *The perception of the environment* (Ingold 2000). Indeed, he goes further. I am less interested here in his technological and more narrowly ecological examples, and more interested in his provocative notion of the 'illusion of origins'. This comes out clearly in his essay 'Speech, writing and the modern origins of "language origins"' (Ingold 2000: 392–405). Because Ingold rejects the notion of (the capacity for) 'language', he must therefore reject the notion of its origin. For Ingold, language only exists in speech, which itself is a continuing evolutionary process: that of speaking. The illusion that 'language' can have an origin stems, in his view, from the bias produced through our perception of language through writing. Instead, Ingold uses the analogy of violin-playing. The art is in the playing, not in the acquisition of an abstract skill. Music and language, he says, should both be defined according to such a principle. And taking John Blacking's statement into account, we could say that the same is true of culture.

However, let us not get carried away. There has long been a fashion to poke holes in the commonplace assumptions of Noam Chomsky (1965: 3–14, and 1986: 19–50) or Ferdinand de Saussure (1974 [1916]: 9–15), and Boasian anthropology too. Yet modern linguistics is founded on distinctions such as I-language and E-language (or competence and performance) or those of *langue* and *parole*. Anthropology assumes that 'nature' and 'culture' exist at least as (fairly universal) cultural constructs, and that biology is different from culture. There is a wealth of environmental perception in Ingold's book, but the fact that biology in some interesting sense feeds into culture, or that skill alone does not create art in the abstract, but requires performance, merely shows that each commonplace distinction both requires the other and merges with it. It does not show that the other is not there at all.

Of course, language has an origin, and, of course, that origin entails speaking (or signing) and the *development* of a capacity for linguistic expression from a lesser capacity to a greater one. And some things may even be clearer in point of origin: etched red ochre, perceived as symbolic, instantly becomes symbolic. The discovery of such things as etched red ochre at Blombos ranks among archaeology's greatest contributions to the study of early symbolic thought, but it will not be the last.

6 Conquering the globe

Only four years after the discovery of Neanderthal, three grand questions were said to be under discussion in 'the higher branches of ethnology'. In a lecture presented at the Mechanics' Institution, Liverpool, the nineteenth-century polymath R. G. Latham (1851: 49) defined these as:

1. The unity or non-unity of the species.
2. Its antiquity.
3. Its geographical origin.

Other writers today have pointed back to this text too, and it still guides research and speculation in the field of human origins.

From findings in genetics we now know that all living branches of humanity are descended from a small population of southern or eastern Africans. Even arguments for the contribution of non-African genetic material to modern humanity remain sparse and a minority view (for a brief review of the evidence, see Stoneking 2006). Although much of the globe had previously been colonized by *Homo erectus* and later species, all humanity in Asia, Australia, Europe and the Americas came much later, from eastern Africa. The population bottleneck of early *H. sapiens sapiens* may have numbered as few as 2,000 (Wells 2007: 140). Because of the effects of the Toba volcanic explosion around 74,000 BP (or sometime between 77,000 and 69,000 BP), we can date the start of the main *H. sapiens sapiens* human global migrations: perhaps 60,000 BP, but not much earlier. Supporters of the Toba theory (e.g., Ambrose 1998) hold that such arguments account for data in many fields, although it is also possible that there were one or more migrations before Toba and that this produced surviving populations that mixed with the migrants of 60,000 years ago (see Oppenheimer 2004: 166–84).

In fact, human evolution had for more than two million years been one of evolution of material culture, repeated changes in climate and migrations, at first within Africa and later to other continents, and, of course, evolution of the brain. The notion that the brain evolved first is 'a negation of the principles of natural selection' (Oppenheimer 2007: 98). It evolved because it had to evolve, and continued doing so through the adoption of meat eating and all the cultural baggage that comes with that. *Homo erectus* had already spread through Asia and beyond. Then, around 350,000 years ago, an ice age hit the world (as it had done before), and by 300,000 years ago some group of *Homo* evolved in Africa to become 'archaic' *Homo sapiens* or *Homo helmei*. Their material culture became the Middle Palaeolithic. Some spread into Asia and Europe in a warm period around 250,000 years ago. The great ice age of 200,000 BP marks a severe bottleneck of the human population group from whom we modern humans are all descended. Toba marks another. Some population groups left in the interglacial of around 120,000 BP but later died out. By that time, we were fully human and evolving symbolic thought. Whether we had language is another question. Stephen Oppenheimer (2007: 109) traces the theory of gradual development to Étienne Bonnot de Condillac in the eighteenth century (who like Michael Corballis today looked to gesture as its origin). The more common view at present is a 'big bang' event between 50,000 and 35,000 years ago, giving us an explosion of language as we know it. There may be some linguistic evidence for this, from existing languages (one might say 'remaining' languages), but for me, this is too recent. I am inclined here to side with Oppenheimer (2007: 110), a geneticist, who suggests a date before 80,000 BP – when in his view the major Out of Africa migration occurred.

Oppenheimer's (2009) most recent assessment of relevant dates, based on both genetic and more specifically phylogeographic evidence, suggests some fine-tuning, and his paper is quite precise. That said, as he notes (2009: 3), the genetic approach in phylogeography (literally, the geography of the gene-tree) is very good at identifying migration routes, but not as accurate in defining precise dates. *Homo sapiens sapiens* emerged in Africa at least by 150,000 BP. Some went north through Egypt and then Israel and Palestine around 120,000 BP but died out around 90,000 BP. The group from whom all non-Africans today are descended travelled through the southern part of the Arabian Peninsula and then to India about 85,000 BP. Some moved to Southeast Asia and to China about 75,000 BP, and from Timor to Australia around 65,000 BP. Between 50,000 and 46,000 BP *H. sapiens sapiens* entered Europe, and most of today's Europeans can trace their mtDNA lines either to these people or, in any case, to lines which appeared between 50,000 and 13,000 BP. Meanwhile, in Asia, by around 40,000 BP some groups went north up the Indus into Central Asia and between 30,000 and 20,000 BP dispersed both west towards Europe and east into eastern Siberia. From the east, others migrated along what became the Silk Road towards the dispersal point of these Central Asian groups. That migration also took place around 40,000 years ago. Oppenheimer (2009) dates the crossing of the (then-existing) Bering Land Bridge at between 25,000 and 22,000 BP. Artefacts from Pennsylvania dated at between 19,000 and 15,000 BP suggest pre-Ice Age entry to the Americas, and there is archaeological evidence too of coastal migration by 12,500 BP as far south as Monte Verde in Chile.

The dates make sense in archaeology more broadly too, for example, in interpreting the material culture of Blombos and other sites in Africa as well as India and Australia (India and Australia being among Stephen Oppenheimer's main concerns). As Christopher Henshilwood and Curtis Marean (2003) contend, and without that much opposition, symbolic culture emerged well before 50,000 years ago, and reflected changes in social behaviour, including the storage and the exchange of artefacts. Therefore, it cannot be understood merely through a (Euro-centric) list of features based on technological complexity alone. It is more complicated than that, and the metaphorical 'archaeology' of symbolic thought more intuitive (see also Henshilwood and Marean 2006).

This chapter describes what we know of the great global migrations, and what the great dispersal means for understanding the common global culture shared by all humanity. Issues touched on will be the universals of hunter-gatherer populations, in things like kinship and myth, as well as how we might to some extent explain their origins. Such 'culture circle' notions may have been 'discredited' since the tail end of diffusionism and rise of functionalism in the 1920s and 1930s. Yet with huge developments in related disciplines, the time is right for social anthropology again to engage in debate with our sister subjects. Ironically, Edward Evans-Pritchard took up diffusionism late in life (he died in 1973), but the time was not right for it. 'Out of Africa' was not yet the accepted theory that it later became (see Evans-Pritchard 1973).

Till a' the seas gang dry

Global migration, whenever it was, tends to be characterized by small migrant groups spreading along coastlines, occasionally taking boats, though more often than not making use of land bridges. For example, there were land bridges between Africa itself and what is now the Arabian Peninsula, and ultimately across other ancient land masses now submerged to Australia and to the Americas. Figure 6.1 illustrates the approximate global migration routes and their dates.

Over the last decade or so, genetic studies have produced some interesting conclusions. Zhivotovsky, Rosenberg and Feldman (2003) suggest that the ancestral population of humankind numbered only a few thousand, with a divergence of African hunter-gatherer groups between 142,000 and 71,000 years ago. Around this time, a migrant population group diverging from the remaining ancestors of African farmers became the ancestors of the non-African population of the world. The ancestors of the farmers (long before they adopted farming) will have numbered fewer than 2,000. More precisely Zhivotovsky and his colleagues' figures give a calculation of effective population size, prior to growth, of 2,609 for the hunter-gatherers and 1,883 for the others. Science writer Gary Stix (2008) suggests that from these others, as few as 150 to 1,000 may have crossed the Red Sea. Given present-day population sizes, such figures may sound counter-intuitive, but they do perhaps make clearer to non-geneticists the fact that there is far greater genetic diversity among the small number of living African hunter-gatherer populations than among the rest of the population of the planet today. The rather complex dating of divergences aside, in simple terms African hunter-gatherers are descended from a hypothetical 2,609 people, other Africans from a yet smaller number, and Eurasians, East Asians, Oceanians and Americans combined from fewer still.

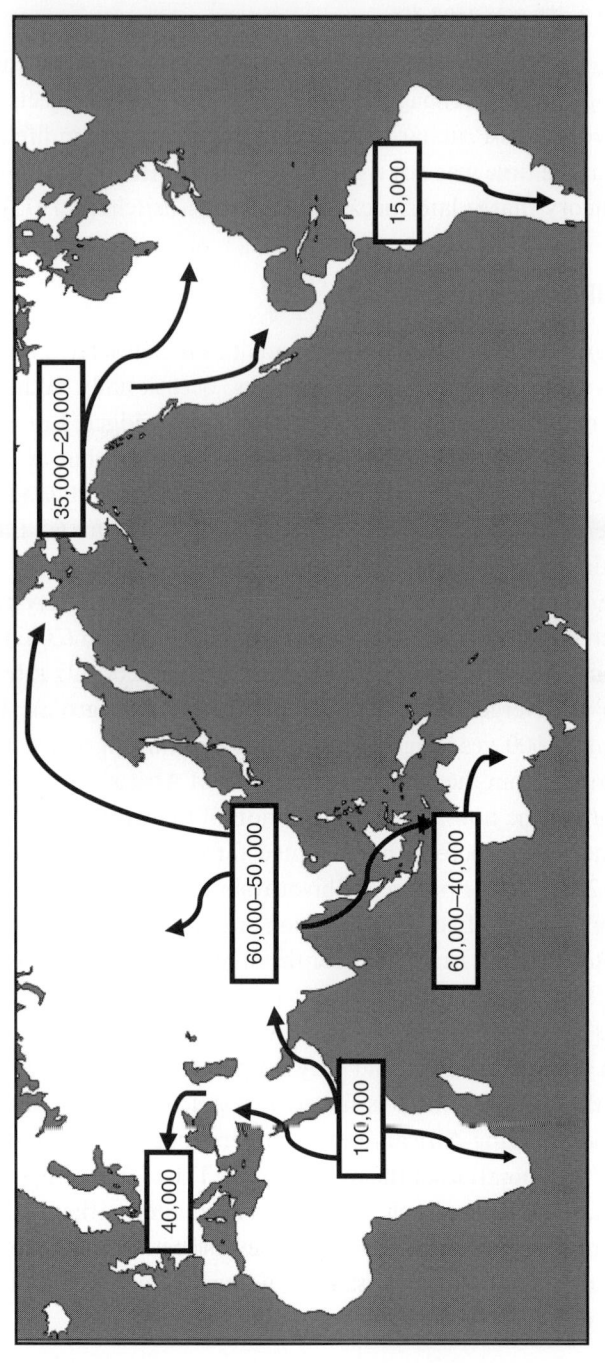

Figure 6.1. Major prehistoric human migrations, with approximate dates BP (*Source*: Barnard 2011: 42)

A related problem concerns common ancestry. Genetic models to date Mitochondrial Eve classically give dates between 200,000 and 100,000 BP. Y-chromosomal Adam is perhaps 50,000 BP. Mathematical models devised to yield a figure for the most recent common ancestor of all humans alive today give figures as recent as just a few thousand years ago, and certainly within the age of written history (e.g., Rohde *et al.* 2004). Such mathematical models generally assume random mating and leave aside problems raised by known migrations and the probable isolation of given populations. Yet the gist is clear: with everyone descended through many lines from the same sets of individuals, humanity is more closely related, biologically, than many might tend to think. The next logical problem concerns how we might all be related, culturally. That problem was certainly not alien to the ethnology of Friedrich Ratzel (1896–8 [1885–8]) or Fritz Graebner (1911). While English anthropologists of the later nineteenth century assumed that humankind was inventive (humans everywhere thinking up the same things over and over), German anthropologists assumed a lack of invention. The former, evolutionist approach gave us a trajectory from simple to complex, primitive to advanced, whereas the latter gave us 'culture circles' of ever-expanding influences from common geographical points of origin.

The genetic divergence of Khoisan populations from the remainder of the world's groups has been variously estimated at between 130,000 and 100,000 years ago, and the Andamanese split at 70,000 (Bancel *et al.* 2006: 11). The latest suggestion is 130,000 BP (or between 157,000 and 108,000 BP), with an Out of Africa date of 50,000 BP (or between 64,000 and 38,000 BP). That estimate, by Heng Li and Richard Durbin (2011), relies on mathematics beyond my comprehension, but it bears an uncanny similarity to my earlier but more intuitive suggestion, based simply on the known or (in some cases) likely sequence of events, that symbolic culture was in place around 130,000 years ago. The difference between 'thought' and 'culture' is by no means clear either in anthropological literature or in my own mind, but nevertheless earlier rather than later dates for either would seem to be the best bet. As for the origin of language only 50,000 years ago, that would seem to be less plausible than it was in the past. New evidence is not necessarily correct just because it is new, but to my mind everything does seem to point to a symbolic revolution as well as at least the ability to create symbolic explanation through language before a population bottleneck, global migration and the material remains assumed by archaeologists to be symbolic. Also, the dates invariably seem to be getting earlier, never later. That is one reason I like the assumption of a date around 130,000 BP.

What of the migrations? The date of the population split for the Andaman Islanders, of course, is not necessarily the date of geographical occupation of the islands: they may have migrated to the islands later. Nevertheless, occupation not long after 70,000 BP is plausible. We know that Australia was inhabited by perhaps 45,000 BP, although evidence of earlier habitation is more difficult to ascertain. Recently, it has been argued that the evidence of earlier Sahul (Australia and New Guinea) sites is poor and that the arguments for earlier dates are not well supported (O'Connell and Allen 2004). Paul Mellars (2006: 9385–6) pinpoints the southern coastal area of Asia as a weak point in the archaeological record, and focuses attention on that area as the place where more research is needed in order to establish the details of Out of Africa migration.

One team of geneticists (Macaulay *et al.* 2005) has determined that in spite of a lack of archaeological data on the original Out of Africa migration, they can nevertheless infer a good deal from genetics on this migration. Their conclusions, based mainly on analyses of Southeast Asian populations, are that there was one single migration rather than several, that this was along the Indian Ocean coast. Furthermore, it was rapid. As the team points out, over the last ten years or so arguments for an earlier rather than a later migration (after Toba or even before) have been gaining ground, and 75,000 BP is the date they suggest. Then there was a dispersal from India to Australia from about 65,000 BP. They suggest an 'arrival time' in India of 66,000 BP and in Australia of 63,000 BP. Other dates they cite are 200,000 BP for the most recent common ancestor of all humans, 125,000 BP for human occupation in Eritrea and the use of marine resources there (from archaeological evidence), 84,000 BP for the split of non-African from African populations and possibly from 70,000 or definitively from 40,000 BP for continuous occupation of Southeast Asia by hunter-gatherers (again, from archaeological evidence). All these dates are approximate, of course, but they are typical of the revelation that findings in genetics do tend to yield earlier dates than relevant archaeological sites yet discovered. Vincent Macaulay and his team, citing the gradualist, 'non-revolution' view of the important paper by Sally McBrearty and Alison Brooks (2000), suggest in their interpretation that: 'the subsequent Upper Paleolithic "revolution" in western Eurasia was one regional indication of the emergence of modern humans, rather than a radical break with the past' (2005: 1036). However, to my mind the alternative is equally possible: the dates indicate what archaeologists have found thus far, not what they might possibly find and certainly not the dates of non-material culture required for symbolism in material remains.

So, recent or early, symbolically sophisticated or still slowly evolving culturally, who were these migrants? And can a social anthropologist say anything at all about their likely customs or social structure? Or about the makeup of their, decidedly small, population? One recent article (Keinan *et al.* 2008) suggests that early Out of Africa migrants tended to be mainly male. This may contradict other interpretations, and certainly contradicts the premises on which some mtDNA studies are based. Whether it is true or not, it nevertheless conjures an image worth thinking about: relatively sedentary females living with their parents, while males wander in from elsewhere. And they keep wandering: more males than females, literally to the ends of the earth. This has obvious implications for social organization and kinship structures. We would have *de facto* uxorilocality and possibly even matriliny, but perhaps with significant numbers of absent fathers. The image that this might imply to many anthropologists is, most likely, not one of matrilineal clans or phratries, but rather one of Nayar-style *sambandham* partners. Before the twentieth century, this South Indian people had a system in which a high-status man would perform part of the normal Hindu marriage ceremony (the tying of the marriage emblem known as the *tali*), and other men, known as *sambandham* partners, either in sequence or permanently, would stay with the women and impregnate them. Thus for Nayars of the past, 'marriage' is in two parts: the 'husband' (who ties the *tali*) never sleeps with his wife, and the other 'husbands' never perform this marriage ritual (see, e.g., Fuller 1976: 99–122). In the Out of Africa case, we can envisage wandering impregnators of women populating (in more than one sense) much of the globe, with the women perhaps protected by other, more stationary, bands of brothers whose attachment to the group would imply rules of incest avoidance and ultimately perhaps exogamy.

The question of human universals, once prominent in anthropology, deserves to be revisited too. In particular, the boundary between the natural and the culturally universal invites exploration. For example, disposal of corpses might be taken as a natural given for humans, or at least a cultural universal with natural implications. Yet, we also have cultural phenomena that are very widespread, if not universal, such as a reluctance to *speak the name* of a dead person. Frazer notes that custom is found across the globe, among

> peoples so widely separated from each other as the Samoyeds of Siberia and the Todas of Southern India; the Mongols of Tartary and the Tuaregs of the Sahara; the Ainos of Japan and the Akamba and Nandi of Eastern Africa; the Tinguianes of the Philippines and the inhabitants of the Nicobar Islands, of Borneo, of Madagascar, and of Tasmania. (Frazer 1922: 252)

Of course, this custom is not universal, but it does seem to reflect similar beliefs in different parts of the world, and these could be similar either because of evolution or because of diffusion. In this case, Frazer suggests a fear of the ghost or soul of the deceased as the common origin. He notes too related customs, such as the *temporary* taboo of using the name of the deceased, the fear of naming someone after another person or changing the name of a deceased person's namesake, either temporarily or permanently. He mentions dozens of such customs, across the globe. This leads me to the question: is it meaningful to revisit too the theory of diffusion in light of the now widely accepted notion of global migration? Frazer was an evolutionist, and this begs the question: common point of origin, or common mind of humanity? The latter would be the preferred evolutionist option, and that of any non-diffusionist proponents of the doctrine of psychic unity. We shall explore that in the next chapter.

At the other extreme, the definition of 'death' is cultural, and diverse beliefs include a range from 'brain death' to the idea that the corpse is not fully 'dead' until a reburial ritual is performed – sometimes a year after the occurrence of biological death. Such customs are found, for example, quite extensively in Madagascar (e.g., M. Bloch 1971), as well as in Southeast Asia, Aboriginal Australia and elsewhere. In the first case, reburial has to do with the incorporation of the deceased into the patrilineage – something that never quite happens in life. In the case of Aboriginal Australia, there is also evidence of post-cremation smashing of the bones of the 'earliest' of Australians, one of the Lake Mungo skeletons (Bowler *et al.* 1970).

Simplifying theory: three ages of archaeology and social anthropology

In the third edition of the *New science*, Giambattista Vico (1982 [1744]: 250–8) outlined what later became known as a 'three-age theory'. His vision was of 'three natures', divine (poetic), heroic and human; and from these, three sorts of customs; three kinds of natural law. Likewise, there were three kinds of government: theocratic, heroic (aristocratic) and egalitarian, and three kinds of language: divine (cognition without communication), heroic (through military emblems or symbols) and through speech. And there were three kinds of jurisprudence and three kinds of authority. Vico's notion of three ages – those of gods, of heroes and of humans – was reminiscent of archaeology's three-age theory, developed in the early nineteenth century and still in use today: whether Stone Age, Bronze Age and Iron Age, or Palaeolithic, Mesolithic and Neolithic (Rowley-Conwy 2007).

In another sense, it is informative to think of archaeology itself in this way. Earlier archaeology employed a culture-historical approach, seeing the discipline as an extension of history backwards in time, and a method to determine historical developments through material remains. The second major approach is processual archaeology, otherwise known as the 'new archaeology'. This approach was developed in the 1960s by Lewis Binford and his followers, mainly in North America. Binford, a prolific writer, published several volumes of his collected works, but perhaps the most readable of his books is *In pursuit of the past* (Binford 2002 [1983]), which outlines his project through a series of lectures and seminars from his European tour in 1980 to 1981. Binford's approach is evolutionist and employs ideas from cultural ecology, systems theory, philosophy of science. It is also heavily influenced by ethnographic analogy and the milieu of four-field anthropology in North America, where archaeology and cultural anthropology are closely allied. The third approach here is post-processualism. In the 1980s and since, Ian Hodder and other post-processual archaeologists have challenged the scientific assumptions of the discipline. Archaeology, they argue, can never recreate the past. Recent trends within this broad approach have incorporated elements of structuralist, post-structuralist, Marxist and feminist theory, along with interests from recent decades in social anthropology: the body, power, agency, cognition and meaning (Hodder and Hutson 2003). However, one recent introduction to archaeological theory characterizes that discipline a little differently. Matthew Johnson, both in his text (2010: 216–35) and quite vividly in accompanying diagrams, shows archaeological thought through recent decades as three very different scenarios. Let me summarize these here:

1988. A battle in the centre between processualists and post-processualists, with classical archaeological interests maintaining a disinterested peripheral position.

1998. No core of the discipline, but many fragments, and those who battled it out before then retreating to their own specialized interests in feminism, neo-Darwinism, classical interests, heritage management or whatever.

2008. A new battle, in the mind of every archaeologist, between the material and the ideas. In the former, there are sites, layers, cultures, described through site reports, public lectures and so on. In the latter, there are big theorists like Latour, Foucault or Darwin, with expression through everything from assessed writings to policy documents.

In social anthropology, things are not quite so clear-cut, but one can nevertheless characterize periods within the history of the discipline as having dominant themes (cf. Kuper 1996; Barnard 2000; Kuper 2005). The first was the time of diachronic approaches, evolutionism and diffusionism; this dominated the nineteenth century, for example the work of the evolutionist Lewis Henry Morgan (e.g., 1877) or the diffusionist Wilhelm Schmidt (e.g., 1931). From 1922, we have the second: the age of synchronic approaches, initially the functionalism and structural-functionalism of the British tradition and the early relativism, in its various forms, of the American school of Franz Boas. Later, the British tradition adopted structuralist ideas: both functionalism and structuralism see the world through pattern whether in society (in functionalism) or in culture (in structuralism). Then we would have a third phase, with interpretivist and late relativist (postmodernist) approaches. And, as apparently Vico imagined, the three ages represent cyclical trends. After interpretivism and late relativism, what next: evolutionism and diffusionism again?

There is no doubt in my mind that diachronic approaches are on the ascendancy again. This is a good thing, as it heralds the return of the 'gods' on whom much of anthropology defines itself when thinking big things: Durkheim, Frazer or earlier thinkers. The 'heroes' of the discipline, unquestionably, are people like the founders of academic traditions of anthropology such as Franz Boas in America, or Bronislaw Malinowski in Britain. It also shows the potential for the reunification of anthropological sciences, if once again theoretical ideas in archaeology and social anthropology are in alignment.

From Dziebel's theory of kinship back to Lévi-Strauss

Until the 1980s, there were two competing theories of human origins: Multiregional Continuity and Out of Africa. From the time of the decisive paper by Rebecca Cann, Mark Stoneking and Allan Wilson (1987), the Out of Africa model became almost universally accepted among geneticists and was taken up almost as universally among archaeologists as well. A few of the latter held on to, or even still hold on to, various modified versions of the region development model. Yet, the consensus is that, because of genetic diversity in Africa, we can assume all living humans are descended from a southern or eastern or African population.

However, a new and controversial theory has now appeared. In 2007, German Dziebel published a large, detailed and closely argued book, *The genius of kinship*, and this takes the opposite position: not out of Africa, but out of the Americas (and into Africa). Because of cultural diversity in

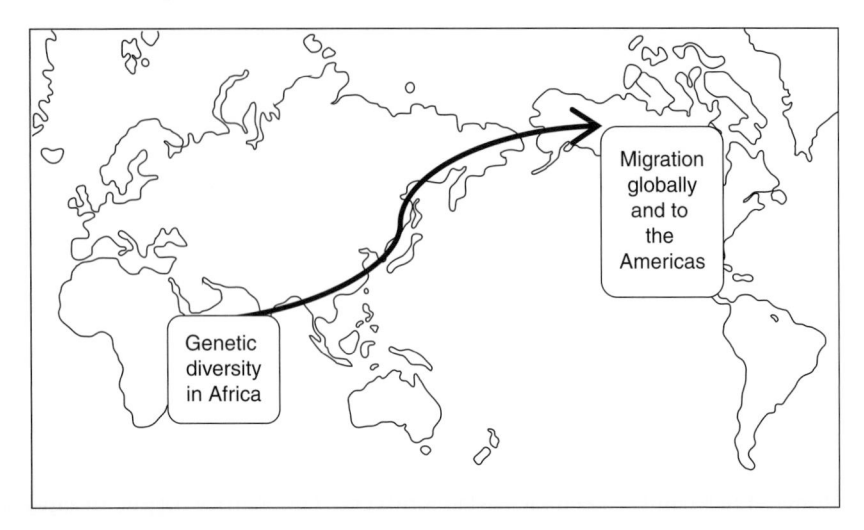

Figure 6.2. The consensus view: African genetic diversity and global migration

the Americas, and in Dziebel's view also because of inconsistencies in the genetic evidence, we could reverse the consensus position and see a North American and South American origin for symbolic culture, and, in particular, kinship systems. Dziebel rejects the common understanding that humanity's common global symbolic heritage must be African. He cites Daniel Kaufman's (2002) controversial claim that an unknown species is the source of modern human biological and cultural heritage, and that it need not be African.

A simple representation of the consensus view of global migration is shown in Figure 6.2. Dziebel's contrasting position is illustrated in Figure 6.3.

For me, all this still leaves open the question of: where and when? I do not agree with Dziebel, but even if he is right about the origins of kinship structures being more in South American than in African forms, these need not have their origins in South America itself. Dziebel (2007: 346) tells us that in the Americas today we can find very ancient linguistic and kinship structures which have been entirely lost on other continents. In the Old World, he says, there are 'only ghosts'. Yet, he does note that one could well envisage the origins of South American-type systems in

From Dziebel back to Lévi-Strauss 117

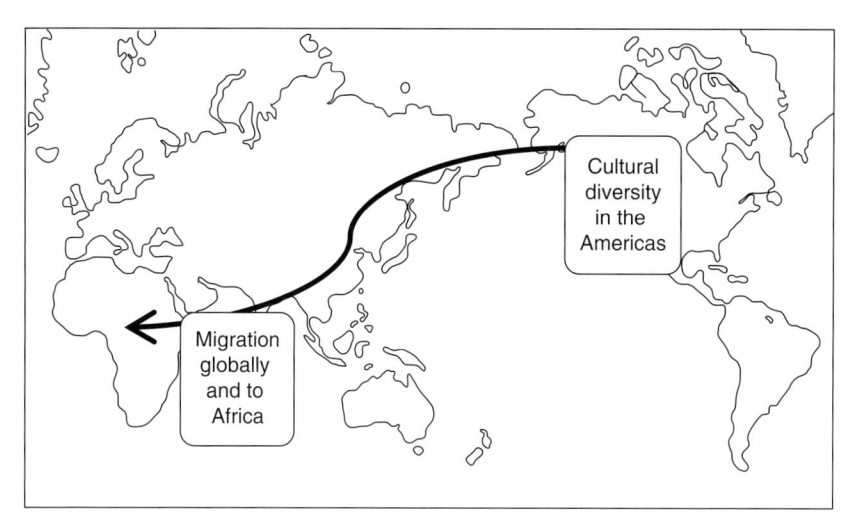

Figure 6.3. Dziebel's view: American cultural diversity and global migration

Africa, and then being found today, as Wissler's theory might have it, being still present on the periphery. That is, having travelled from Africa to South America, the systems being lost in the African 'centre' while still found in the later-developing 'periphery' (see also Chapter 3). The same could in theory also be true with Allen's models, and what works for kinship structures here may be equally applicable to art, symbolism, ritual, myth and symbolic thought generally. Some of the myths Lévi-Strauss recorded and analysed from South America, and also myths he analysed from North America, are similar to myths found in every part of the world (see Lévi-Strauss 1978: 113–268). In short, artefacts of non-material culture could have originated in Africa, or they could be South American in origin.

To emphasize once again, I accept neither Dziebel's theory of kinship origins nor a Wisslerian view of a South American system originating in Africa and migrating or diffusing to the Americas – because I do not believe South American (or Australian) kinship structures are primal. However, the Wisslerian notion of origin and spread might well make sense of some other aspects of symbolic systems, such as ritual, myth and so on. In this realm, of course, it may be difficult to separate primal thought reinvented time and time again in the human mind, from myths or rituals that travelled the globe with human expansion. In Lévi-Strauss' view, even certain logical relations among players exist in inseparable and constraining structures: myths are communications from gods to humans, and rites are communications from humans to gods (Lévi-Strauss 1978: 66). When myths change through time and in migration through geographical space, we have a 'conservation of mythical material'. He also tells us that new myths can emerge from earlier myths (1978: 256). As Lévi-Strauss knew better than anyone, mythology lies deep in the human mind, and deciphering the prehistory of mythology systems could prove as complex as it is interesting.

The latest spanners in the works

Among the latest spanners in the works is a discovery only made in 2008 and announced in 2010: a small fragment of finger-bone from someone called the X-woman. Through further excavations, and with work carried out by geneticists in 2010 (Krause *et al.* 2010), it is now possible to state firmly that this woman and her kind are more different from modern humans as are Neanderthals, and that in fact these three species interbred.

Partly because there is little in the way of anatomical evidence, the species has not yet been named and therefore is absent from my Table 2.1. No skull fragments or large bones have been found, but there are now several teeth and finger and toe bones. The 'people' are known as the Denisovans (see Stringer 2011: 195–7). They lived at Denisova Cave in the Altai Mountains of southern Siberia. They diverged from the modern human line after *Homo erectus* (and therefore are not part of a *H. erectus* migration 1,900,000 years ago), probably migrated from a *H. heidelbergensis* line in Africa, or came later but before the Neanderthal population.

Since 2008, several comparative studies at the Max Planck Institute for Evolutionary Anthropology in Leipzig, and elsewhere, have shown genetic affinities with a number of modern European and Asian peoples and particularly with modern Melanesians. The European and Asian affinities are thought to imply a wide distribution for the Denisovans, and affinities with modern Melanesians are said to suggest contact on the Melanesians' own ancestral journey from Africa *en route* to the Pacific (see, e.g., Reich *et al.* 2010). What intrigues me most in all this, even more than the biological interbreeding, is the possibility of cultural borrowing. Ornaments, including a bracelet, have been found in the cave and seem not unlikely (although the evidence is not definitive) to be associated with bones of the Denisovans (Derevianko *et al.* 2008). Their dates are around 40,000 BP, the same time as the attested period of interbreeding. Could even the Denisovans, descended from African *Homo heidelbergensis* (as are both Neanderthals and *H. sapiens*), but separated by half a million years until they met up, have had decorative arts? Personal adornment? Symbolic culture?

Another recent twist is the suggestion of not one, but two migrations across the southern regions of Asia, one to Australia, branching off from the rest of humanity (in Africa) between 75,000 and 60,000 BP, and the other between 40,000 and 25,000 BP (see, e.g., Gibbons 2011). The dates are based on genetic evidence from a lock of Aboriginal hair collected in 1923 by the anthropologist A. C. Haddon: before admixture with Europeans and Asians. The former date, between 75,000 and 60,000 BP, implies migration into Australia earlier than thought, and more specifically by 50,000 years ago. However, the latter dates (by molecular clock) are too recent for archaeologists, since they could be taken as implying migration to Europe later than known archaeological sites. What they do suggest, though, is a relatively recent date of divergence of Asians and Europeans. Most intriguing here, though, is the presence of Denisovan DNA in Australia. Everything, except archaeology, seems to point to the wide dispersal of Denisovans across Asia, and, of course, to the presence of their genes in many non-Africans alive today. As one eminent geneticist has put it, it looks as though Asia is but a 'checkerboard of populations', some having Denisovan material and some not having it (Mark Stoneking, quoted in Gibbons 2011: 1691).

One more recent twist has been revealed in a re-study of skeletal material from western Africa (Harvati *et al.* 2011). At Iwo Eleru, in Nigeria, lies a rock-shelter burial site excavated in 1965. It has been re-dated to 11,700 years ago, but the skull found in it looks like no one found in Africa today: in form and feature, it looks much older. In short, the skull is *Homo sapiens* but has archaic as well as modern features. This implies not only interbreeding but also (since *H. sapiens* is by definition symbolic and highly 'cultural') both greater genetic diversity than exists in the world today and cultural borrowing between genetically diverse branches of humanity. Could cultural borrowing have occurred in both directions? The material culture found in association with the site is easily recognizable as (African) Later Stone Age, although we have no evidence of decorative arts, nor ritual, nor, of course, myth.

To reiterate my earlier point, like Evans-Pritchard (1973), I too wonder if the time is not right to take diffusionism seriously again. The evidence is again indicative. If we admit to the quest for diachronic explanation, the testing of diffusionist hypotheses, along with evolutionist ones, is the logical consequence. The new genetic evidence also calls into question the notion of 'modernity', both in a biological sense and in a cultural one too.

The prehistory of symbolic thought

In the nineteenth century, it was common to speculate on the prehistory of society, kinship, religion and so on. Not so today, but let me suggest a plausible historical scheme. What concerns me most is the date of 50,000 BP for the origin of language, so ubiquitous in the literature that, like the genesis of symbolic thought, it is just taken for granted. In my view, though, there is no reason to assume it, especially in the face of recent FOXP2 and other findings in genetics, the possibility of language death (along with 'species' extinction in the case of Neanderthals and Denisovans), *Homo sapiens* bottlenecks and the very time depth involved. Language in fact could have evolved much earlier, even if we allow for a subsequent origin of the languages existing today. The recent FOXP2 and related findings I refer to are those presenting evidence of the very early mutation of language genes, possibly as early as 260,000 or 200,000 years ago, possibly even earlier – in substitutions shared between Neanderthals and modern humans (e.g., Krause *et al.* 2007; Ptak *et al.* 2009). The earliest 'true' language, after all, may be older than symbolic thought, and 'behavioural modernity' may indeed coincide with 'anatomical modernity'.

Here is my suggestion of the order in which human evolution took place (or might have taken place):

1. Anatomical modernity.
2. The FOXP2 mutation.
3. Language.
4. Symbolic thought.
5. The flowering of language, through mythology.
6. Genetic divergence of San, Aborigines, etc.
7. Toba volcanic winter and a subsequent population bottleneck.
8. Out of Africa migrations.
9. Remaining human dispersals.
10. Development of advanced hunter-gatherer thought throughout the world.

The evolution of kinship systems, rules of hunter-gatherer sociality, religious ideas, and so on, undoubtedly had complex origins and evolutionary sequences. These may have touchstones, for example, to the earliest symbolic thought as well as to the development of advanced hunter-gatherer thought. Crucial in the evolution of symbolic forms will have been shamanistic and totemic ideas, as well as theistic ones, though I would rather not speculate in detail on these. Of course, many nineteenth-century theorists did, but the data available today are rather more complicated. What I would claim is that *narrative* is so embedded in the advance of language, and vice versa, that these must have preceded the *Homo sapiens* Out of Africa migrations. Mythology is world heritage writ very large indeed, as indeed is religion itself.

All that followed is inconsequential in comparison, but it is nevertheless the subject of the next chapter. With the Neolithic came pastoralism, agriculture, the division of labour, social hierarchy and the state. 'Natural humanity' in all its glory and its complexity is what was left behind for most of us. While the rise of property, increased standards of living, improvements in medicine, technological developments and advances in knowledge itself are all worthwhile, they are nevertheless not the essence of human nature.

7 After symbolic thought: the Neolithic

The Neolithic is relevant precisely because with it, so much changed. I have written many times before, for example, about the loss of universal kinship classification (in which all members of a small-scale society are called by specific kinship terms). These systems are found almost everywhere among hunter-gatherers, but hardly anywhere among non-hunter-gatherers. I have written too about changes in economic ideology, and many other social anthropologists have written on these as well. We do not all agree on the details, and we disagree quite strongly on which elements of economic ideology are the most significant. Yet, the collective formulation by hunter-gatherer specialists does hint at ways in which the Neolithic did move us away from what we, all humanity, once shared. We anthropologists can recover something of what is lost among non-hunter-gatherers simply by treating seriously hunter-gatherer universals in light of archaeological material. I believe we can also recover something of earlier times through the comparative exploration of hunter-gatherer difference. This includes things like myth, moon symbolism and so on.

'Neolithic revolution' or 'Neolithic transition'?

The word 'Neolithic' was invented by Sir John Lubbock (1865: 1–2) to describe a stone tool tradition in contrast to the Palaeolithic. Mesolithic soon came into use, though first to mean something akin to what is now called Upper Palaeolithic, and only rather later accepted as a description of a phase between the Palaeolithic and the Neolithic. Today, the Palaeolithic of the Near East and Europe is recognized as the long set of traditions from the first pre-*Homo sapiens* settlers and earliest stone tools to remnant populations living about 10,000 BP. The Mesolithic is recognized as lasting from about 22,000 to 5900 BP, the Neolithic lasted perhaps from 12,700 or 11,500 BP in the Near East to the Bronze Age, about 5300 BP. The dates are a matter of debate, and the end point (especially in northern Europe) is invariably both more difficult to identify and less significant in the minds of archaeologists. Asian and West African tool traditions are similarly labelled, whereas since the 1920s southern and eastern Africa have had their own regionally specific labelling. The African Middle Stone Age is not the Mesolithic but an earlier phase coinciding partly with the European Upper Palaeolithic and partly with the European Middle Palaeolithic (see Table 2.2).

So which is the Neolithic: a revolution or a transition? In my view, it is both, and I employ each label to represent something slightly different. For Gordon Childe (1936: 66–104), the 'Neolithic revolution' marked a revolutionary stage of human evolution when agriculture was introduced, the division of labour and social hierarchy began and cities became possible. More recent commentators (see, e.g., Whittle and Cummings 2007) have emphasized instead the diversity and slow evolution of the Neolithic (which Childe had also recognized). These writers prefer to describe the Neolithic as a 'transition'. For me, 'Neolithic revolution' is a useful label for the revolutionary changes which occurred towards the end of the long Neolithic transition, whereas I use the word 'transition' to describe the longer period. Changes that Childe understood as coming at the end were largely material ones, such as incipient urbanization, whereas for me they are ideological: what I have called the *accumulation mode of thought*, as opposed to the *foraging* or *hunter-gatherer mode of thought* (e.g., Barnard 2002). Figure 7.1 illustrates this widespread cultural practice, and its longstanding hunter-gatherer alternative. Hunter-gatherers value sharing, and therefore tend to favour immediate consumption and the redistribution of material goods, food and other goods, rather than their accumulation. Non-hunter-gatherers tend to favour the accumulation of things: saving is good for the family, and therefore good for society. It is not that hunter-gatherers are just 'nice people' because they share, but that sharing and its mechanism of immediate consumption are necessary factors both in their lifestyles and in their ways of thinking.

Hunter-gatherer ideology

Accumulation	Anti-social – equated with not sharing
Immediate consumption	Social – equated with sharing

Neolithic and post-Neolithic ideology

Accumulation	Social – equated with saving
Immediate consumption	Anti-social – equated with not saving

Figure 7.1. Hunter-gatherer versus Neolithic ideologies

Long before the Neolithic, Middle Stone Age and Later Stone Age hunter-gatherers were developing sophistication in stone tool technology, in symbolic representation and social organization. The last includes exchange mechanisms, perhaps mutual systems of 'permission-giving' for the mutual exploitation of resources, and climatic adaptations in several successive stages at least over the last 20,000 years (Kusimba 2003: 188–200). One form of 'modernity', as I would define it, begins with the Neolithic, or at least not long after – in spite of the retention of sharing ideology among part-time hunter-gatherers across the globe. Of course, we who can read and write are fortunate to have all that the Neolithic and later developments have brought to us. However, we Neolithic and post-Neolithic peoples have nevertheless lost much: our ability to recite myths, to know our fellow humans literally as kin (that is, to classify everyone we meet as belonging to specific kin categories), to acquire a deep knowledge of the environments we inhabit, to know how to use our spare time or indeed to have any spare time at all.

Childe (1936) noted two logical developments of the Neolithic, namely two further revolutions: the *urban revolution* already implied above (and which required new forms of social organization, including social hierarchy) and the consequent *revolution in human knowledge* (including literacy and numeracy, which resulted from the practical needs of urbanization). The latter is not quite the same thing as my notion of two different modes of thought in pre-Neolithic and Neolithic times. Mine is purely ideological, and indeed perhaps I should have used that label: ideologies, as opposed to modes of thought. If one form of modernity begins with the Neolithic, then another form of modernity, which we also inherit, begins at the dawn of symbolic culture. Richard Lee (1976: 17) puts this rather well when he writes: 'The similarity of their [Ju/'hoan] thinking to our own suggests that the logico-deductive model of science may be very ancient, and may in fact have originated with the first fully human hunter-gatherers in the Pleistocene.' Totemism and mythology imply, not just some sort of symbolism, but a search for symbolic order in the universe.

I referred in Chapter 2, in passing, to the problem of 'behavioural modernity'. John Shea objects to the idea, partly because he favours a research agenda directed much more at behavioural variability and as well as a long trajectory for (Palaeolithic) comparisons – from proto-humans to humans, as well as within the human species. Yet, the idea of 'modernity' more broadly is indeed broad enough to render it meaningless without further qualification. The problem is that we often need to define either a revolutionary change, or a distinction between what is now and what was before. For me, the Neolithic is precisely both of these things: revolutionary (if too slow a revolution to merit the term 'revolution' in archaeology) and modern. It is 'modern' in that it gives us the hierarchical social structures, and the grand worldviews (in religion, science and political thought) that we have today. The historian and political philosopher Francis Fukuyama (2011: 90–4) wonders why Africa did not develop states (his definition of modernity) until recent centuries. His answer is that 'political order' depends on population density, and he sees such order in the form of centralization. This, he says (2011: 104–24), first occurred in China, during the Eastern Zhou Dynasty of 770–256 BCE. China in this dynasty had both the required population density and adjunct of control over territory in the hands of authority (through standing armies within several Eastern Zhou states). One could see this pattern of state formation, along with Childe's more Near Eastern concerns with urbanization and the growth of knowledge (which would apply in China too), as a logical consequence of Neolithization. We may have acquired bronze or iron tools since then, but in this mode of definition we are still living in the Neolithic.

As for the postmodern, that term was coined by the philosopher Jean-François Lyotard in 1979. In Lyotard's (1984 [1979]: xxiv) terms, it refers to 'incredulity toward metanarratives', in other words a rejection of the propositions of big theory, particularly in science, but also in grand philosophies such as Marxism. For Lyotard, the eighteenth-century Enlightenment and what followed was the 'modern', and developments in European thought since the Second World War are the 'postmodern'. I am not a postmodernist, but if I were I would argue that not only does modernism begin earlier, but so too does postmodernism. If postmodernism is about the recognition of a plurality of cultural traditions, then we have this within Bushman or San religion, where diverse views are tolerated and even contradictory views held by the same individual. Mathias Guenther (1979) and I (Barnard 1988) recorded this phenomenon independently, among quite different population groups of Naro San in the 1970s. No one knows how long that tradition has been in existence, but it is reasonable to suppose that a pluralistic sense of religious belief might be found in hunter-gatherers both recent and long ago. It is also reasonable to imagine the opposite: that a system of thought more 'modern', or more all-pervasive than that of Western science, might be found among hunter-gatherers too. Such a view has been argued for Aboriginal Australia, when contrasted to more flexible Canadian Subarctic thought and society (Turner 1985). In another sense, anthropology itself is postmodern in its very recognition and discussion of cultural diversity, and particularly the relativist traditions within the discipline (see Barnard 2000: 99–119).

Nature and culture? Us and them?

Perceptions of the environment are cultural. We can learn a great deal through comparison with broad strokes. What is different about hunter-gatherers and non-hunter-gatherers? And where there are differences, can we assume that the hunter-gatherer lifestyle is the earlier?

However, we must not be too quick to impute an 'us'/'them' dichotomy in respect of cognition. Quite the opposite. We should seek the universals in human thought that govern not only all societies today, but also human culture as it existed in the distant *Homo sapiens* past. Jack Goody has devoted much of his long career to the comparison of East and West, Africa and Asia, literate and preliterate and so on. In his early but perhaps still most important work, *The domestication of the savage mind*, Goody (1977: 1–35) argues that although the acquisition of literacy may alter cognitive processes, nevertheless we find in any (modern human) society individual creative activity and even intellectuals. Dan Sperber's (1985: 70–3) commentary on the mistranslation of the title of *La pensée sauvage* is relevant here too. Lévi-Strauss explicitly did not give it the title *La pensée des sauvages* (literally, 'the thinking of savages'), but rather intended the meaning 'untamed thinking'. The anonymous translator for the English edition rendered it *The savage mind* (Lévi-Strauss 1966 [1962]), thus connoting 'the thinking of savages'. While their specific positions on relativism in anthropology or literacy in modern society may not accord, Goody, Lévi-Strauss and Sperber all agree. 'Untamed thought' is prevalent in the human condition. What particularly both Lévi-Strauss and Sperber mean by it is the natural, creative human understanding that comes from almost any intellectual activity, apart from 'science' in a narrow sense. As Sperber prefers to put it, in Saussurian terms there is no 'signified'; there are only 'signifiers' (cf. Saussure 1974 [1916]: 65–78). Any one thing can mean or imply any number of other things, and in this way mythological thought, for example, is free to be both structured and poetic at the same time.

It is commonplace today to think of the sequence *romance, companionship, sexual passion and the upbringing of children* either as 'natural' or as characteristic of 'modern, Western, middle-class culture'. But is either view really true? On the one hand, these elements fit together so well for many 'moderns' that it is difficult even to conceive that they are not natural, or at least that they are not all aspects of an ideal (if fictitious) natural order. On the other hand, historians remind us that before the late eighteenth century, there was not much of a middle class either in Europe or even in the European-colonized Americas, and romance and marital bliss were not only unrelated but virtually opposites. Medieval troubadours expressed a different sort of 'love', and all was allegorical and not to be taken very literally (Bloch 1991). Women for centuries represented some mystical thing which today academics would say they 'embodied'. And sociologists tell us that later, especially in the 1950s, sexual 'right' and 'wrong' depended on boys and girls correctly playing the game, until in the 1960s the rules somehow changed (and women became 'liberated') (Giddens 1993).

In his posthumous *Ritual and religion in the making of humanity*, Papua New Guinea ethnographer Roy Rappaport (1999) argued beautifully and at length that religion is not only ecologically adaptive but even central to human evolution. He had anticipated his mature work in earlier papers, especially in 'The sacred in human evolution'. There he made (Rappaport 1971: 29–30) a more specific point, namely that religion and language co-evolved. This view touches on evolutionary psychology's then-emerging concerns with the capacity for lying. Religion keeps lies in check through differentiating the sacred from other realms (he did not use the word 'profane'). Faith, expressed collectively, unites believers in social and communicative linguistic unity. For Rappaport, ritual is also collective communication, and this is the case as much for ritual as for verbal forms such as in myth or prayer. After the emergence of agriculture and its consequent forms of social hierarchy, he tells us, language and religion itself were transformed, as the capacity for lying increased and theocracy came into being. Through archaeological research in Mexico, Joyce Marcus and Kent Flannery (2004) take this argument one step further. They explore changes in the use of ritual space in the Valley of Oaxaca over a 7,000-year period, from a hunter-gatherer phase (10,000 to around 4000 BP) to a settled, egalitarian, maize-cultivation phase (3450 to 3100 BP) to a larger, hierarchical society with a ruling elite (3100 to 2450 BP) to the archaic Zapotec state (which emerged from around 2450 BP). The earliest phase was that of dancing in an open space, and Marcus and Flannery assume similar ritual practice as among contemporary hunter-gatherers. With maize cultivation came men's houses oriented according to the path of the sun (and the presumption, by the archaeologists, of rituals fixed in time). Then came elaborate ritual practice, with evidence of bloodletting, human self-sacrifice and cannibalism. Then, finally, there was an emergence of elaborate temples and a priestly caste. Thus religion, like language, seems to be with us as a human universal, but as Durkheim (1915 [1912]) said long ago, its form echoes that of the society in which it is situated. If there is a 'natural religion', it is that expressed through the myth and ritual practice of the egalitarian hunter-gatherers, who have lived far longer on earth than their pastoralist and agricultural neighbours. *Exactly* which form this might be is, obviously, open to debate.

Settlement and migration: sloppy stereotypes

There are two common, and downright wrong, stereotypes about the differences between hunter-gatherers and farmers. Let us dispense with the *first* quickly, since at least among professional anthropologists it has come to be so widely known to be false. This is the notion that hunter-gatherers have always lived difficult lives since subsistence is so much more troublesome for them than for farmers. As detailed ethnographic studies of real hunter-gatherer subsistence activities have shown, especially since the 1960s (e.g., Lee 1969), hunter-gatherer lifestyles do not depend on high work effort. Hunter-gatherers in general value free time more than they value accumulation of property. This became well known after 1968 through various spoken and published versions of Marshall Sahlins' (1974: 1–39) 'original affluent society' thesis. Of course, hunter-gatherers are dependent on environmental conditions and annual cycles, but not as much as farmers are. In times of drought or other natural disaster, hunter-gatherers can change their habits rather more easily than pastoralists or agricultural peoples can.

The second stereotype about hunter-gatherers is that they are 'nomadic', while agricultural peoples are 'settled'. In fact, as Hugh Brody (2000: 7, 87–90) so forcefully argued, the reverse is true. Individual agricultural communities are, in a sense, settled. Of course, *Homo erectus* hunter-gatherers migrated across (and settled) most of the Old World. *Homo sapiens sapiens* hunter-gatherers migrated through (and settled) every continent except Antarctica. But so too did farmers. The farmers also conquered Asia, Europe, Africa and the Americas with their grains and other crops. Agriculture may have been invented independently seven times, as some say, but it was not invented 700 times. The Bantu-speaking agro-pastoralists swept across Africa, and a plethora of agricultural peoples migrated across Asia and Europe and down through the Americas. The hunter-gatherers they encountered either took up agriculture or resisted, but on the whole hunter-gatherers, then and now, have tended to remain on lands that they recognize as their own. Even in Europe, advanced Mesolithic hunter-gatherers lived in settlements previously assumed to have been Neolithic, there was great diversity in how, why and what kind of agriculture was taken up and the Neolithic is certainly no longer seen as quite as monolithic as once it was (see Price 2000; Whittle and Cummings 2007).

The migrations and consequent occupation of southern Africa by pastoralist and agro-pastoralist peoples, both black and white, has been thoroughly documented (e.g., Mitchell 2002: 227–412). Yet even in southern Africa, popular perceptions of hunter-gatherers assume that they were the migrants. We know from linguistic as well as archaeological evidence that Kalahari hunter-gatherers have been in their present locations for millennia (Barnard 1992: 28–36). The Bantu-speaking peoples certainly have not. If hunter-gatherers appear to be nomadic, in fact, the world over, they tend rather to be transhumant and their groups prone to seasonal aggregations and dispersals. In other words, groups move only within their territories, not between one territory and another, and individuals move within territories they 'own' or to territories to which they have recognized claims. That principle is well established, especially in Canadian Subarctic ethnography, but also throughout the world in ethnography from Africa, Asia and Australia (e.g., Lee and DeVore 1968b; Damas 1969), in spite of enormous diversity in hunter-gatherer lifeways (Kelly 1995).

That said, it is still wise to make the distinction between sedentary, food-storing hunter-gatherers and those we think of as more itinerant (generally transhumant) and lacking the incentive to accumulate goods or store food for the future. Alain Testart (1982a: 59–111, and 1982b) has argued that it is among the former that we find the origins of inequality. His examples include Northwest Coast peoples, the indigenous inhabitants of California and those of southeastern Siberia and the island of Hokkaido. James Woodburn (1982) has made similar claims. With regard to his distinction between *immediate-* and *delayed-return* economies, he, in a sense, draws the line between pre-Neolithic and Neolithic rather 'earlier' than others: egalitarian hunter-gatherers consume immediately and in the process share the produce of the land rather than storing (or hoarding) it. In contrast, delayed-return hunter-gatherers, like Neolithic and post-Neolithic peoples, have already made the transition to a kind of economic modernity. They invest for the future through making complex hunting equipment, such as nets among Mbuti Pygmies, and they invest through saving for themselves rather than immediately sharing what they acquire. Their incipient inegalitarianism is anathema to the ideologies of many hunting-and-gathering peoples, and places them alongside most peoples of the world in their preference for economic maximization over sharing. It is worth remembering too that Lévi-Strauss always regarded the very foundation of anthropology to be the origin of inequality, or more specifically Rousseau's famous discourse on inequality (1997a [1755]: 111–231) on that subject.

One has to be careful here of endlessly circular arguments, but Alasdair Whittle (2003: 70–106), drawing on social anthropologists for both theory and ethnography to enlighten his understanding of the Neolithic, shows too that the Neolithic created new ways of thinking. This is especially true in thinking about animals and about myth. I say 'be careful here', because it would be all too easy for me to see the Neolithic through Whittle's archaeological reading of social anthropology, rather than through my social anthropological reading of Whittle's archaeology! That said, Whittle is quite right: African agro-pastoralists do see animals differently from their hunter-gatherer neighbours. Hunter-gatherers often make little distinction between animals and people, and in their myths animals and people are either indistinguishable or represent each other. San mythological beings may be mammals, or they may be insects, deities or insect-deities, but they possess the characteristics of human beings. The built environment of the Neolithic too was very different from what had been before, as were religion, social hierarchy and gender relations, as David Lewis-Williams and David Pearce (2005: 102–48) explain through their comparisons between the Kalahari fringe in the nineteenth century (representing what was before) and Çatalhöyük after around 7500 (representing the Neolithic). The Çatalhöyük cosmos, as interpreted by Lewis-Williams and Pearce and by many who wrote before them, may represent a phase of transition between hunter-gatherer and agro-pastoralist existence, with shamanistic journeys and the veneration of domestic animals and mother goddesses all present in the Çatalhöyük Neolithic though not necessarily at exactly the same time.

Controversial claims

Two very different, even opposite, sets of ideas are relevant at this point: one from nineteenth-century German anthropology (Adolf Bastian) and the other from twenty-first-century American genetics (Gregory Cochran and Henry Harpending). The Neolithic evokes images of us/them dichotomies, and of either primitivism or evolutionist triumphalism. Even so, it is important not to reject strange ideas out of hand, but to think them through and apply evidence to assertions. As is well known, hunter-gatherers represent to many anthropologists neither an unsophisticated branch of humanity that could not adapt to agriculture, nor a culturally impoverished branch. Typically, as I have implied above, hunter-gatherers have better diets, are healthier and work fewer hours than their agro-pastoralist neighbours (see, e.g., Lee 1969 and 1979: 250–80). The adoption of agriculture led to reduced intake of vitamins and minerals and increased intake of carbohydrates, and therefore tooth decay, anaemia and diabetes, shortened stature, increased infant mortality and so on, although there was, as is now known, great variation around the world (see Pinhasi and Stock 2011).

Although hunter-gatherer ways of thinking can be quite different from those of settled, agricultural and pastoralist peoples, nevertheless these variations may also be seen simply as part of human cultural diversity. The point is that cultural diversity is just that: it is *cultural* and lies within a mode of thought that is universal among 'anatomically modern' human beings – presumably those of 200,000 years ago, as well as all those living today.

Adolf Bastian

While there may be many claims to being the worst writer in the history of anthropology, Adolf Bastian probably has the strongest. For this reason, although his work was significant, it has always remained largely untranslated apart from short snippets (but see Koepping 2005 [1983]: 155–228). Yet it had great influence both in the German anthropology of the day and in other traditions, including the British tradition, through Edward Tylor, and the American tradition, which was derived directly from the German one. Bastian's most significant idea was that of the 'psychic unity of humankind' (*psychische Einheit des Menschen*): the notion that all *Homo sapiens sapiens* think in the same way. He proposed this through his distinction between 'elementary ideas' (*Elementargedanken*) and 'folk ideas' (*Völkergedanken*).

Elementary ideas, or patterns of thought, lie deep: in what later would be called the subconscious. They are not made explicit within the folk ideas of particular peoples, but we can, according to Bastian, gain access to them through comparing folk ideas. Folk ideas reside within the collective consciousness of the world's ethnic groups, and each such group has a collective, folk idea and a consequent different symbolic representation for each elementary idea. For example, he talks of the laws of nature being disguised in 'myth images' such as those implying a supernatural understanding of thunderbolts or hailstones (Bastian 2005 [1893–4]: 173). Although the prose may be impenetrable when read word by word, the gist of Bastian's analogy and examples are reasonably clear. Humans in any cultural tradition share certain elementary ideas, here those derived from meteorology, but differ in their culturally specific folk thoughts. Bastian refers to their 'symbolic guise', which is not quite an accurate description, but one which nevertheless is telling here. It is not just that folk thoughts are on the surface, transparent or clear, and elementary thoughts are deep and hidden. Rather, symbolic thought is also often in its own way deep, that is, hidden to those whose elementary thoughts may be the same but whose own symbolic system differs because of differences in 'culture'.

While the doctrine of psychic unity conformed to the nineteenth-century anthropology, Bastian articulated it. He gave it a name and a mechanism, through elementary and folk ideas. Whatever we might call the doctrine, it underlies all social anthropology as we know it. In particular, the assumption of psychic unity, along with monogenesis (a single origin for all humankind), was held by nineteenth-century evolutionists and twentieth-century relativists alike, and by adherents to all subsequent paradigms of social and cultural anthropology.

If we look at Neolithic and post-Neolithic times in this way, we can discern a common ideological substratum which differs from that of hunter-gatherers. Non-hunter-gatherers think differently not because they have greater cognitive capacity, but because in a certain sense they have less. They, or we who can read this book, have lost part of our ability to think symbolically, just as we perceive differently relations between land and people, between society and the individual, between kin and non-kin and between sharing and accumulation (Barnard 2002 and 2007b). Biological forms are lost in time. So too are cultural forms (see Figure 7.2). Or, rather, things like attitudes to land or relations among people differ because they are transformed through the adoption of an *accumulation*, as opposed to a *sharing*, ideology. Agro-pastoralists and urban dwellers see land in terms of sovereignty (Barnard 2007b: 11–12). They look to semi-sacred doctrines like 'the monarch', 'the nation', 'democracy', 'freedom' and so on, which they see as associated with political authority, with people belonging, for example as subjects or citizens, to some larger unit. Hunter-gatherers see the reverse. The land is sacrosanct and associated with primordial possession, but the people are sovereign, as free individuals and families. Even the supernatural world operates differently (2007b: 13). In agro-pastoralist societies, magic is more common and it is practised by individuals independently, and it is often for evil and focused on in-laws or on enemies. In hunter-gatherer societies, magic tends to be communal and performed for good: for example, the healing dance found among all the Kalahari San groups, which benefits all present, San or non-San alike (e.g., Marshall 1999: 63–90).

Controversial claims 135

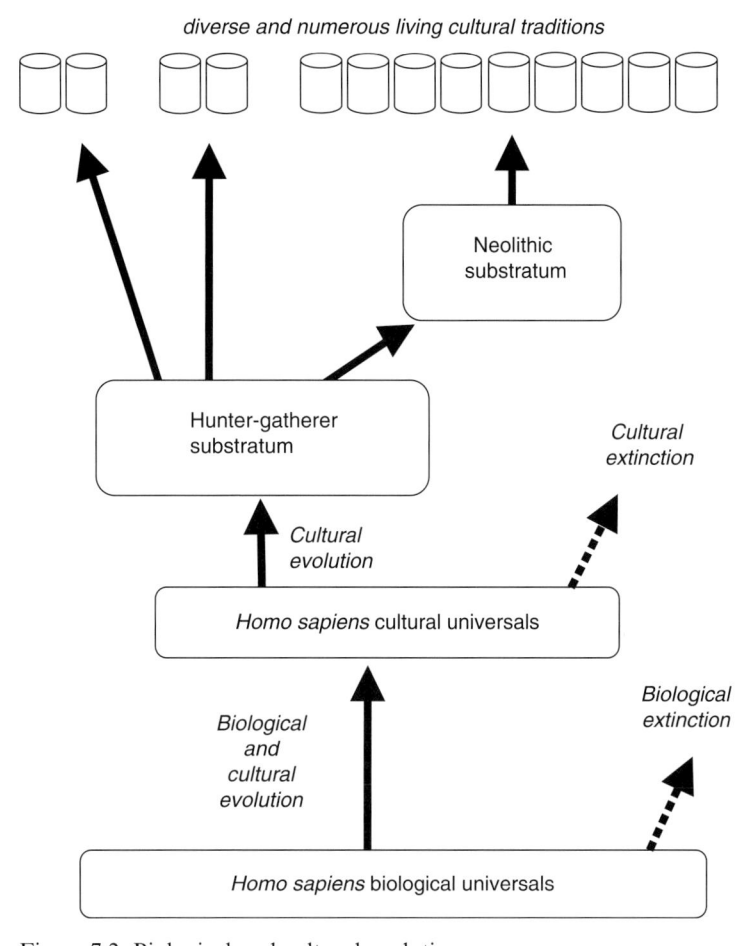

Figure 7.2. Biological and cultural evolution

Such attributes of hunter-gatherers are dependent on ideology, or mode of thought, but not absolutely so. In earlier papers, I have remarked on the slow transition to an accumulation ideology. It is not that hunter-gatherers are 'slow' to think, but quite the contrary. Their values stress *sharing* and all the cultural traditions and egalitarian social relations that go with it. Living 'hunter-gatherers' have chosen to retain these traditions in spite of enormous pressures of the Neolithic and subsequent periods which are all around them, and in spite of the fact that most now simply retain the ideology and occasional hunting-and-gathering pursuits. Most hunter-gatherers today have acquired non-hunter-gatherer means of subsistence and practise a mixed economy if not a mixed way of thinking.

Cochran and Harpending

The second set of ideas, from twenty-first-century American genetics, concerns the suggestion that evolution did not end with the symbolic revolution. In the view of Gregory Cochran and Henry Harpending (2009), not only did it not end then, but it continues to this day. Cochran and Harpending (2009: 31–2) argue that specifically in the Eemian interglacial period, at about 125,000 BP, humans were biologically different than they were in the Holocene interglacial period, at around 10,000 BP. They point out that around the latter period, agriculture was independently invented seven times. It was, of course, not invented at all in 125,000 BP. Richard Klein (2002: 270) argues much the same, although he puts this down to a single genetic mutation, whereas Cochran and Harpending suggest there were many such mutations. Either way, the implication is that humans were not capable of agriculture at the earlier date, and that technology such as sewing skins for garments and making atlatls, and bows and arrows, were beyond their reach. Painting, it is argued, was as yet not within their consciousness. Klein, Cochran and Harpending do admit, however, that all these activities are well within the capabilities of modern hunter-gatherers.

The great leap forward, Cochran and Harpending argue, was some 40,000 or 50,000 years ago, after which 'qualitatively different' forms of artwork began to appear. They dismiss the etched ochre pieces from Blombos Cave as inferior to (later) European art, such as the sculptures in mammoth ivory dating from around 30,000 BP. They liken Neanderthal burials, in comparison to *Homo sapiens*, to 'flushing a goldfish down the toilet' (Cochran and Harpending 2009: 34–5). Even more controversially, Cochran and Harpending (2009: 187–224) argue that Ashkenazi Jews have gained in intelligence because occupational restrictions in the Middle Ages and since then led to genetic drift towards greater intelligence (bankers and merchants need to be brighter than farmers do). They argue further that

Ashkenazi Jews are brighter than their distant cousins, the Jewish population of North Africa and the Middle East (who, on average, occupy lower economic positions). Their more general point, which I do *not* share, is that it is time for researchers to reject the notion of psychic unity (2009: 227).

While I accept Cochran and Harpending's arguments concerning the likelihood of changes within the human genome over the last several tens of thousands of years, nevertheless I cannot accept either their assumptions of significant differences in intelligence or cognition or their views on prehistoric art. The importance of the ochre from Blombos is not simply that it is incised, but that it was transported and stored carefully. Presumably it was used not simply as the art itself, but in the production of further art, such as body decoration. Of course, we do not know this for certain, but analogy to the use of ochre among hunter-gatherers elsewhere, indeed across the globe, would suggest this (Wadley 2006). Whether bankers do or do not need to be brighter than farmers, it is very *unlikely* that bankers need to be more knowledgeable of their environments than hunter-gatherers. Whatever the inhabitants of Blombos were doing with their ochre, it undoubtedly required cognitive abilities as great as those of European ivory carvers 45,000 years later. It sounds trite to say it, but it probably involved ritual, and that probably involved a reasonably sophisticated belief system, which in turn assumes some kind of language. These early modern humans were probably at least conversing about art and cosmology along lines that we, reading this book, would understand.

Through comparative ethnographic evidence, Marshall Sahlins showed back in the 1960s that hunter-gatherers work fewer, not longer hours, than agricultural peoples, and biological anthropologist Lawrence Angel showed that Mediterranean Palaeolithic and Mesolithic hunter-gatherers (30,000 to 8,000 BCE) lived longer lives and had greater average stature than either early or late Neolithic farmers (7000 to 3000 BCE). Median life span did not recover until the Bronze Age or possibly the Iron Age (i.e., sometime after 3000 BCE), and average stature has still not recovered. It was 177 cm for men and 167 cm for women in the Mediterranean Upper Palaeolithic. By the late Neolithic, it had fallen to 161 for men and 154 for women (Wells 2011: 22–4). Of course, there is more than one Darwinian explanation of this. Possibly, shorter people are better at farming than they are at hunting and gathering. Or taller people make better hunters, but if you become a farmer your stature does not matter. Or short, sexy farmers are more desirable than tall food-gatherers. Or even, the local taller tribes happened to have died out, and the local shorter tribes happened to have taken up farming.

What these two examples taken together show, Bastian on the one hand and Cochran and Harpending on the other, is that the human sciences are complicated. The history of these sciences is thus not simply a matter of ever-more progressive traditions developing from closed-minded ones. Of course, all anthropologists accept the notion of the psychic unity of humankind, as controversial in Bastian's day as some of Cochran and Harpending's assertions may be today. But what is 'humankind'? Does this include the Neanderthals? And what does it mean that humankind is still evolving through natural selection? I am primarily interested in the dawn of symbolic thought, and, happily, less so in the complexity of more recent times. The presumption of psychic unity today is at least a good beginning for cross-cultural reflections on what symbolic thought may have been in the past.

The end of an era

For me, the Neolithic is the end of an era, and not just the beginning of a new one. In spite of Cochran and Harpending's assertions about recent genetic changes or about changes in human intelligence among non-hunter-gatherers, the best way to understand relatively recent human cultural change, that is the changes of the last 10,000 or 12,000 years, and in some parts of the world much more recently, is in light of longer-term developments.

In Table 7.1, I list the major developments, both biological and socio-cultural, of humankind over the last 500,000 years. The starting point is not entirely arbitrary but represents a reasonable date within the *Homo heidelbergensis* time span (880,000 to 250,000 BP) for us to imagine the earliest possible manifestations of symbolic thought. The splitting of *H. neanderthalensis* and *H. sapiens* (both from *H. heidelbergensis*) was around 400,000 or 300,000 BP. The table shows the earliest developments at the bottom (as in an archaeological site), but it can be read

Table 7.1. *Humankind: the most recent 500,000 years*

12,700 BP to present	Neolithic and post-Neolithic periods
18,000 BP	*H. floresiensis* on Flores
25,000 BP	cave painting
35,000 or 20,000 BP	modern humans in the Americas
35,000 BP	possible domestication of the dog
35,000 BP	evolution of modern human brain (according to Stringer)
39,000 BP	Campi Flegrei eruption, Italy
40,000 to 35,000 BP	figurines and beadwork near Danube
40,000 BP	ritual burial and cremation in Australia
40,000 BP	modern humans in Europe (Cro-Magnon)
50,000 BP	'Neanderthal flute'
50,000 BP	behavioural modernity (according to Klein)
55,000 BP	pressure flaking techniques
60,000 or 40,000 BP	modern humans in Australia
65,000 BP	Neanderthal burial at Kebara, Israel
66,000 to 59,000 BP	Howiesons Poort industry
70,000 to 60,000 BP	possible Out of Africa migrations
70,000 BP	possible carved rock cave entrance, Botswana
74,000 BP	Toba eruption (approximate)
77,000 to 72,000 BP	Still Bay industry
77,000 BP	ochre use in South Africa (Blombos Cave)
80,000 to 60,000 BP	behavioural modernity (according to Mellars)
83,000 BP	possible engraved ostrich egg shell in Namibia
100,000 to 80,000 BP	shell beads in Algeria
100,000 BP	modern humans in Middle East
120,000 BP	Sahara covered by rivers and lakes
160,000 BP	Herto site, Ethiopia (*Homo sapiens idaltu*)
200,000 to 130,000 BP	evolution of modern humans in Africa
250,000 to 100,000 BP	behavioural modernity (according to McBrearty and Brooks)
260,000 BP	hafted spears in Zambia
270,000 or 170,000 BP	possible ochre use in Zambia
300,000 to 125,000 BP	*H. heidelbergensis rhodesiensis*
320,000 BP	possible ritual burial in Spain
400,000 or 300,000 BP	early wooden spears (Germany and England)
400,000 to 300,000 BP	split of Neanderthals and *H. sapiens* (according to Stringer)
500,000 BP	heyday of *Homo heidelbergensis*

either bottom up or top down. Importantly, where there are reasonable alternatives, I have tried not to show prejudice of one theory over another or one date over another, but rather to illustrate all theories and dates as possibilities. Thus, for example, Paul Mellars' (2006) date of 80,000 to 60,000 BP and Richard Klein's (2008) of 50,000 BP are both given: the reader may choose between them, or indeed choose instead the slow period of transition, from 250,000 to 100,000 BP, suggested by Sally McBrearty and Alison Brooks (2000).

The sources are, of course, numerous. They represent material discussed throughout this book. However, I would single out one reference for comment here. This is Chris Stringer's *The origin of our species* (2011). Throughout his book, too, there is commentary on many of these theories and dates, and I have drawn on his expert interpretations in putting this table together. In that book, Stringer seems partial to *H. heidelbergensis* too. It is significant in part because its African representative 'Rhodesian Man' (sometimes classified *H. rhodesiensis*) was the earliest 'early man' find in Africa, in 1921. And that African representative is especially significant too perhaps because of its completeness as a fossil, its mixture of primitiveness and modernity, its beauty (sizeable, and with very prominent brow ridges), its mysterious lack of context (found in a mine, and with its archaeological association obscured) and for Stringer, no doubt, because the type find inhabits a safe near his office at the Natural History Museum in London. Stringer was among the first to argue for the classification of that fossil as *H. heidelbergensis* (along with the jaw found at Heidelberg in 1907). I do not disagree with that assignment (and as a social anthropologist lack any relevant expertise with which to do so), though for clarity I do refer where appropriate to the traditional designation of the African fossil as *H. rhodesiensis*. Whatever we call it, we can trace our origins, biologically and perhaps culturally too, to the fossil from Kabwe and his or her relatives elsewhere on the continent of Africa.

At the other end of pre-Neolithic symbolic culture, remnants are still with us. We have the mythologies of many peoples, including both the South American and North American mythologies recorded by Lévi-Strauss (e.g., 1969a [1964]) in the 'Mythologiques'. These are found either among non-hunter-gatherers or in small-scale horticultural communities often with rich symbolic systems. We have Australian Aboriginal, Southeast Asian and South Asian hunter-gatherer belief systems which preserve ideas that are strange to Europeans. But they are often equally strange to Africans too, even African hunter-gatherers – who tend to be *not* animistic or totemic at all, but traditionally monotheistic. It is as important to recognize diversity in the belief systems of hunter-gatherers as it is to recognize their common resilience. Yet, what interests me even more is the possibility of detecting very long periods of continuity in the archaeological record, for example in Aboriginal Australia and southern Africa. This is most obvious in rock art, but other avenues of exploration, sometimes with the odd conjecture thrown in, can be equally fruitful. At Sehonghong (a rock shelter in the Drakensberg Mountains of Lesotho), for example, the archaeologist Peter Mitchell (2010) has argued a 57,000-year period of continuity that runs right up to the present, from the Middle Stone Age to Later Stone Age Bushmen and the cattle-keepers who replaced them as recently as the nineteenth century. The longest continuities are perhaps the record of plant remains, and this reflects many changes in the surrounding climate. There is material culture as well, and rock art, including paintings of eland (invariably interpreted as symbolic) and paintings of the coming of the Iron Age cattle-keepers and their weapons. The Bantu-speakers apparently arrived at the site in the 1870s, which was also the time of Qing, a Bushman who famously interpreted the local rock art through mythology for the antiquarian J. M. Orpen. Interestingly, too, this happened to be a time when archaeologists of sorts (George Stow), philologists (W. H. I. Bleek and Lucy Lloyd) and ethnologists (Andrew Lang) were sharing ideas on some of these very issues (Barnard 2007a: 34–6).

8 Conclusion

In the closing lines of *Social anthropology and human origins* (Barnard 2011: 151), I argued that social anthropology ought to be involved in trying to understand prehistory. A branch of social anthropology specializing in human origins is possible. Although one reviewer seemed to think I was arguing that it should swallow up the whole of human origins studies, that was not my intention. Rather, social anthropology should make its contribution where it best can: and there is a great deal it can say about the genesis and spread of symbolic thought, much more than can be said about social life in any other period of prehistory except for the Neolithic and since. This short chapter will summarize what I have argued. More importantly, I want to look forward to other areas of engagement with archaeology and linguistics, especially with regard to the time frame of symbolic thought and culture.

Disciplinary boundaries

At the risk of getting raked over the coals, I would like each of us in the study of human origins to think about our bread-and-butter occupations and to reflect on how these relate to the bigger questions of the wider anthropology. Who is likely to have the most insight into human origins? Someone who . . .?

- dissects brains
- measures fossil femurs
- scrapes dirt off cave floors
- coaxes strangers to spit into plastic vials
- observes chimps and collects their dung

Disciplinary boundaries 143

- gets students to play 'Chinese whispers'
- befriends foreigners and asks them silly questions

There is, of course, no correct answer. We all have things to contribute, but our contributions will be quite different and our understanding will be as well. I happen to come from the discipline, or sub-discipline, that befriends strangers and asks them silly questions – sometimes for years at a time. I believe that this discipline has as much to offer human origins as most of the others. On the specific question of the origin of symbolic thought and behaviour, we must have at least as much as any of the others. We observe symbolic behaviour, ask our questions about it *ad infinitum*, usually in the language of those practising it, we see it in comparative perspective and try to explain it every day of our working lives.

Yet, interestingly, of the fourteen contributors to a book called *What makes us human?* (Pasternak 2007), not one was a social anthropologist. Biological anthropology, evolutionary psychology, archaeology, genetics, theology and other fields were all represented, but not social anthropology. Likewise, in the same year when a team of social anthropologists got together to explore the 'big, comparative questions' of our discipline, *Questions of anthropology* (Astuti *et al.* 2007), no one even touched on either human origins or symbolic thought – except peripherally and only in the latter case (through discussions of ritual, religion and truth). Admittedly, *Questions of anthropology* aims to reach out to 'ordinary people' rather than neighbouring disciplines, but its publication in the series London School of Economics Monographs on Social Anthropology means that it can only do so from within the discipline. Yet when prospective students or other 'ordinary people' ask me what anthropology is for, I can assure my colleagues that human origins and symbolic thought are both in the frame.

Adam Kuper and Jonathan Marks (2011: 168), respectively a leading British social anthropologist and a leading American biological one, argue that the time is right for different kinds of anthropologists to join together: 'to read each other's papers, to attend each other's conferences and to debate concrete cases and specific hypotheses'. They date the division to the 1980s, but to some extent it is older than that. Ironically, symbolic culture is of traditional concern in virtually all permutations of social and cultural anthropology: evolutionism, diffusionism, functionalism, structuralism, interpretivism and even postmodernism (which was a major force in the 1980s). And symbolic culture is also now a driving force in prehistoric archaeology, in various forms of biological anthropology and in the study of language origins. However, only the latter disciplines seem concerned about its origins. Social and cultural anthropologists seem to have lost interest, in favour of growth areas like the anthropology of medicinal knowledge, political action, the body, landscape, relatedness and a host of others. I would not argue that social anthropologists should take over territory from either archaeology or biological anthropology, but simply that we ought to start asking questions again about origins. We do not even have to stop asking questions about structures or meaning. In one sense, diachronic questions are separate from synchronic ones, and in other senses they depend upon them. The study of origins rests on a good foundation of social anthropological concerns.

Twentieth-century ethnographers referred to nineteenth-century theorists as 'armchair anthropologists'. In the nineteenth century, few who did theory also did ethnography, and vice versa. In this century, all of us involved in the study of human origins are, in some sense, laptop prehistorians. That is because our studies are now so intertwined that we can never be expert in all the fields we need to take into account: archaeology, genetics and so on. The part that social anthropology can play is significant in many areas, none more obvious than in the study of early evidence of symbolic thought.

Summary

Throughout this book I have argued, by example, that (contrary to Lévi-Strauss' casual observation) working out the genesis of symbolic thought is possible. It was not possible in the 1940s, when he was writing, nor at the dawn of the twentieth century, when Durkheim (who believed that it was possible) was writing. With the aid of discoveries in the latter half of the twentieth century, and particularly its last fifteen years and in the time since the twenty-first century began, the potential for

Summary

deciphering such things has become entirely different. Yet, the data come only partly from within social anthropology: in comparative ethnography and especially in the comparative study of modern hunter-gatherer societies and the application of anthropological theory developed in the field of hunter-gatherer studies. The relevant discoveries and data come as much, perhaps rather more in fact, from genetics, neuroscience, evolutionary psychology and archaeology.

In Chapters 1 and 2, I outlined the fossil record and highlighted those archaeological discoveries of greatest relevance to the subject. These latter include mainly research in southern Africa over the last few decades, and this work is still going on with great intensity. New discoveries of great significance are sure to emerge in the very near future. Thus our work is surely not complete.

Chapter 3 concerned an area more clearly in social anthropology's recognized domain: the evolution of sociality, and especially of kinship structures in their relation to cosmological structures. The structural study of kinship is far less prominent now than it once was, and alternative theories (those emphasizing 'relatedness' and the deep cultural and indeed symbolic meanings of kinship) are now both more prominent and persuasive within ethnography. However, the earlier interests in structures of descent and marriage, and of the relation of these to society in the abstract, remain important in the very different realm of prehistory. They also provide a touchstone to meaning, in the sense that symbolic structures are by their nature grounded in social structure or (as Frazer might have preferred to see it) vice versa. A fundamental problem for prehistory is whether the earliest social systems were ordered, with symbolic behaviour closely linked to kinship in every respect, or whether flexible arrangements were likely in the beginning. I favour the latter view, but many others favour the former.

In Chapter 4 we looked at ritual and religion. This is an area of much interest in the social anthropology of prehistory over the last quarter century, and one which will certainly remain significant, as social anthropologists as well as archaeologists continue to work on the problem. In archaeology, rock art studies have long fed into the understanding of religion before ethnography was possible. Rock art goes back to the earliest painters and engravers, while ethnography is, by definition, only possible for scholars able to interview and write down the ideas of their contemporaries. Questions of relations between ritual, belief and society are as old as anthropology, and the earliest anthropologists were indulging in armchair-based theoretical speculation half a century before their intellectual descendants (in the early twentieth century) combined the two as the basis of the new professional anthropology that followed.

Chapter 5 dealt with language. Theories of the origin and evolution of language seem to proliferate, and the field is these days a driving force of research in archaeology, psychology, primatology and many other disciplines. Everyone seems to have a theory, and often these complement each other, in explaining different things about language. I myself have two, complementary, theories. The crucial thing is the relation between language and other aspects of symbolic thought, and here I think an important future direction must be in the relation between symbolic and linguistic complexity. That is why my own focus at present is on mythology, which requires language to a much greater extent than do simple matters of basic communication.

Humans, or rather some of us, spread to vast areas of the globe – after we developed sophisticated tool use, symbolism and language. Of course, our *Homo erectus* ancestors, or rather some of them, did that long before as well. Indeed, we are not descended from them, but from those *H. erectus* or *H. ergaster* who remained in Africa, and from the much more recent *H. heidelbergensis* or *H. rhodesiensis* who were possibly thinking symbolic thoughts half a million years ago. More to the point, thanks to genetic bottlenecks since then, we are really descended from a rather small group of Africans in very recent times: only a few tens of thousands of years ago. Recent findings such as these make the global history of humanity far more interesting than it was only a few decades ago, especially now in light of great archaeological discoveries of material representations of the symbolic now being made in southern and eastern Africa. All this is touched on in Chapter 6.

Chapter 7 turned briefly to life since symbolic culture. I am sceptical of prehistory's emphasis on the Neolithic, not because it was not

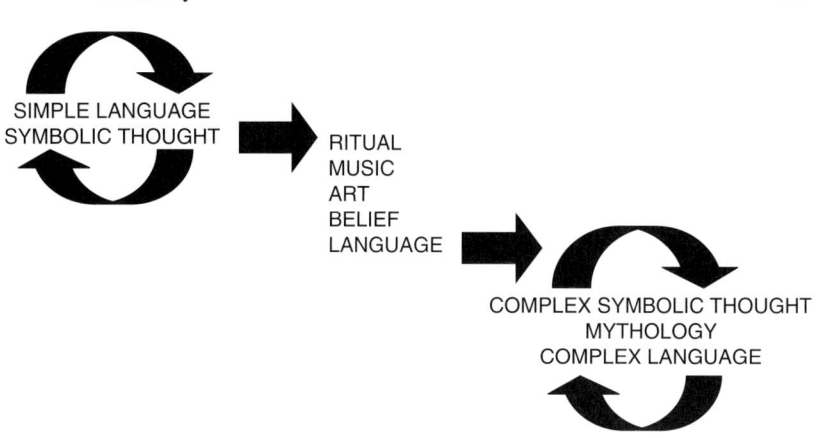

```
    SIMPLE LANGUAGE
    SYMBOLIC THOUGHT  ⟹   RITUAL
                          MUSIC
                          ART
                          BELIEF
                          LANGUAGE  ⟹   COMPLEX SYMBOLIC THOUGHT
                                        MYTHOLOGY
                                        COMPLEX LANGUAGE
```

Figure 8.1. Genesis of symbolic thought

important for most of humanity, but rather because it can be seen as a step backwards from the thrust of human evolution, which is towards ever-more symbolic and spiritual understandings of the relation between (hunter-gatherer) humanity and nature. Of course, I do not imagine that we can ever return to hunter-gatherer subsistence, but that is what is in our 'blood'.

Figure 8.1 is my attempt to put a summary of events since the earliest occurrences of symbolic thought into diagrammatic form. Once symbolic thought occurs, it influences language, and ritual, music, art and belief, and a fuller development of language will follow. And from these cultural forms will eventually spring the linguistic complexity that is required for mythological thought, that is, for the further development, through myth, of greater and greater permutations of symbolic thought. Mythological thought entails the necessity for more and more complex language, which in turn may well yield more and more complex mythological and symbolic thought. Much of this seems to have disappeared in recent millennia, it is said, in favour of some kind of 'modern' or 'scientific' thinking. And while it is commonplace to mark the boundary between Lévi-Strauss' (1966 [1962]: 1–33) 'science of the concrete' and what we might call the 'science of the abstract' somewhere at the 'modern', I would prefer to mark it at least for some purposes between the golden age of hunter-gatherer symbolism and the Neolithic.

The Lévi-Straussian science of the concrete, as found among hunter-gatherers, is *creative* if not abstract, theoretical or methodical. The creativity it entails is of necessity both symbolic and, as Mathias Guenther (1999: 133–40) has characterized it, *playful*, as well as adaptive and part of a foraging way of thinking. It is precisely this playfulness which is responsible for numerous forms of adaptation in hunter-gatherer behaviour, from flexibility in settlement patterns to the ability to alter subsistence according to the availability of resources. Non-hunter-gatherers lack that ability to adapt: San hunter-gatherers know the names, uses, locations and seasonality of literally hundreds of plants. Their agro-pastoralist neighbours do not. The playfulness that Guenther describes in the creation and recreation in retelling of stories is analogous to the 'foraging mode of thought', and Guenther describes it in this way. I would never suggest that any of us who have crossed that boundary should go back to that hunter-gatherer lifestyle, but I would suggest that we understand it and celebrate it. That lifestyle is what made us human in the first place.

The limits of our reach?

Social anthropologists disagree on many things, and probably the overwhelming majority will disagree with me if they see primitivism in my comments above. Yet, whether we see the discipline as comprising 'society', or as embracing 'culture', we are in broad agreement about the discipline's unity and its importance. Whether we look mainly to what unites humankind, or more to differences among diverse cultural traditions, nevertheless we all broadly agree on a number of fundamentals. These include maintaining an interest both in ethnographic detail and in comparison, and accepting that social and cultural life differ from place to place, while still collectively embodying human universals. Social anthropology is a discipline very conscious of its history, and we take guidance from our intellectual ancestors as well as stimulation from the debates of our present time. I hope I have shown that engagement with issues such as the genesis of symbolic thought can be beneficial for and interesting to social anthropology itself, as well of possible benefit to practitioners of related disciplines.

Perhaps in its search for narrower degrees of specialization, social anthropology in recent years has lost some of its impetus as a generalizing science. Yet the pursuit of big questions, such as the genesis of symbolic thought, has the potential not only to make the discipline more visible to those in other disciplines, but also to aid in the unification of social anthropology itself. This does not mean anthropologists have to come to agreement even on epistemological fundamentals. We are a diverse discipline, in spite of unity in our concerns with understanding humanity through looking at its own diversity. That is not a problem. The problem would be if we failed to ask the best questions.

In his memoirs, the founding father of prehistory reminded us: 'When [Mungo] Park asked the Arabs what became of the sun at night, ... they replied that such a question was foolish, being entirely beyond the reach of human investigation' (Avebury 1911: 231). Avebury's argument was that the truly foolish thing is to lay down limits at all on what is and what is not beyond such reach. Social anthropology laid down such limits long ago when it ceased any further involvement in prehistory. Yet as I have recently argued at length (Barnard 2011), this will not do. We social anthropologists have at least as much legitimacy as practitioners of other disciplines to examine prehistoric society, and increasingly we are developing the means with which to do it. Much of that development is, of course, not our own, and we are indebted to geneticists, archaeologists and others for doing the necessary background work.

'Forty per cent of Neanderthals believe in ghosts.' While writing this book, I woke up one morning with that line ringing in my head, and believing I had read it somewhere. I determined to get up and find the reference, but, of course, it would be unlikely I would. More likely, I had dreamed the line – particularly since, I think, it had occurred in the present tense. There are, of course, limits on what we can explain. Neither archaeology, nor sociology or anthropology, can find much of an answer to the detail of Neanderthal beliefs. Indeed, the precise questions we ask can be different too. A sociologist would likely want to know who these 40 per cent are: is the percentage evenly distributed across Neanderthal populations, or otherwise? Is it say 30 per cent ghost believers among German Neanderthals, and 50 per cent among Spanish

Neanderthals, or vice versa? And why? A social anthropologist would more likely want to know: *what exactly* do Neanderthal believers believe about their ghosts?

When in 1945 Lévi-Strauss wrote that the genesis of symbolic thought cannot be explained, he was wrong. I like to think that later in life he would have agreed with me: unlike Neanderthal beliefs about ghosts, the genesis of symbolic thought is, after all, worthy of investigation and open to some kind of explanation. I hope that here I have at least started to explain it, not only in archaeology but also through analogy, comparison and an appreciation of the significance of linguistic and cultural universals. Even if I have explained very little in this book, that is not the point. The point is that such investigations *and explanations* ought to be possible, and in the future social anthropology will find better and better ways in which to pursue such interesting questions.

Glossary

Aboriginal   Relating to the original population of Australia. First settlement is commonly dated between 60,000 and 40,000 BP.

accumulation mode of thought   My term for an ideology emphasizing the acquisition of property. This ideology is Neolithic and post-Neolithic. The opposite is the **foraging mode of thought**.

Acheulean   A Mode 2 stone tool industry of the Lower Palaeolithic, beginning as early as 1,650,000 BP and lasting until as late as 100,000 BP. Named after St Acheul, a suburb of Amiens in France.

affinal relative   A relative by marriage. Cf. **consanguineal relative**.

age-area hypothesis   Clark Wissler's hypothesis that older culture traits tend to be those on the periphery of a culture area, rather than in the centre. This hypothesis is based on the idea that things are invented in the centre and diffuse outwards.

allegorical   Narrative in the form of extended metaphor in which characters symbolize ideas.

alliance   Relations in marriage, between individuals or groups. From the French *alliance* (meaning 'marriage').

Altamira   A cave in northern Spain famous for its Magdalenian (Upper Palaeolithic) rock art, the earliest dated to about 18,000 BP.

anatomically modern human (AMH)   The species *Homo sapiens* in fully modern form, from about 200,000 BP, including *H. sapiens* before the (presumed) appearance of symbolic culture.

Andaman Islands   Islands in the Bay of Bengal between Burma and mainland India.

animism   Belief that natural objects, such as rocks and trees, have a spiritual existence.

anthropology   The study of humankind. In North America it includes the 'four fields' of cultural anthropology, physical anthropology, anthropological linguistics and prehistoric archaeology. Elsewhere, the term is often used more narrowly, and is synonymous with either cultural anthropology (social anthropology) or physical anthropology (biological anthropology).

Apollo 11   A cave in southern Namibia, and the site of early beadwork and rock art. The latter includes portable paintings more than 25,000 years old. Its name comes from the space mission which was in the news in 1969, when excavations began.

archaeology   The study of the past through its physical remains.

Ardipithecus   A probably bipedal hominin genus with ape-like teeth. It lived in East Africa roughly 4,500,000 to 4,000,000 BP.

Aurignacian   Upper Palaeolithic period, roughly from 45,000 to 35,000 BP. Includes the early figurative art, especially figurines of animals, humans and therianthropes, like the famous Lion Man of the Hohlenstein Stadel. See **'lion man'**.

australopithecines (*Australopithecus*)   The genus which includes 'gracile' forms such as *A. africanus* and 'robust' forms such as *A. robustus* (*Paranthropus robustus*). Australopithecines lived in eastern and southern Africa from about 5,000,000 to about 1,000,000 years ago.

Australopithecus afarensis   Species dating roughly from 3,600,000 to 3,200,000 BP and found in eastern Africa. The earliest find was 'Lucy', discovered in 1973 by Donald Johanson.

Australopithecus africanus   Species found in eastern and southern Africa from 3,000,000 to 2,300,000 BP. The earliest find was 'Dart's child', discovered in 1924 by Raymond Dart.

Australopithecus garhi   A gracile australopithecine found in Ethiopia. Said by some to be the first tool user. See also **Oldowan**.

Australopithecus sediba   Recently discovered species of australopithecine, with *Homo*-like features. Lived in South Africa around 2,000,000 years ago.

autochthonous   Relating to the relation between land and people. Cf. **indigenous**.

avoidance relationship   A kin relationship with required deference and respect, for example commonly between in-laws. The opposite is a **joking relationship**.

band   A hunter-gatherer residential group: smaller than a band cluster, but larger than a family.

band cluster   A unit of hunter-gatherer social organization comprised of several bands, which might aggregate seasonally or simply share a common identity.

Bantu-speaking   Adjective used to describe peoples who speak Bantu languages. These languages are found throughout the southern half of the African continent, and those who speak them brought agriculture and iron technology on their migrations southwards from Cameroon, beginning about 3,000 years ago.

Glossary

BCE   The abbreviation for Before the Common Era, a secular equivalent to BC (Before Christ).

behavioural modernity   The set of cultural and behavioural traits common to modern humans but not to earlier ancestors. These traits include, among others, language, mythology, religion and art. See also **modernity**.

bilateral descent   A descent system which possesses neither patrilineal nor matrilineal kin groups, or descent through non-lineal relatives in a patrilineal or matrilineal system. Also known as cognatic descent.

biological anthropology   Modern term for what was once called physical anthropology, used in recognition of the fact that biological studies now include genetics and other sciences, rather than simply the physical properties or dimensions of fossils and living beings.

Blombos Cave   South African Indian Ocean coastal site excavated by Chris Henshilwood, Francesco d'Errico and others. Important for etched pieces of red ochre (dating from 77,000 BP) and for very early beadwork.

bonding   Friendship and co-operation among men, between spouses, etc.

bonobo   The 'pygmy chimp', *Pan paniscus*.

BP   The abbreviation for 'Before Present'. When used as a precise dating measure, it is taken to mean the year 1950 (when radiocarbon dating became practicable).

Broken Hill   The site of 'Rhodesian Man', the *Homo heidelbergensis* fossil discovered in a mine in then Northern Rhodesia in 1921. The name is derived from a similar mine in Australia, and the Zambian town is now called Kabwe.

Bronze Age   The age of copper and its alloy bronze, used in tool- and weapon-making in the Near East from about 3300 BCE. Bronze is easier to produce than iron, but its components are rarer, and therefore its use had different geographical and social implications.

Bushmen   Southern African hunter-gatherers, including Ju/'hoansi (!Kung), /Gui, //Gana, Naro, /Xam and other groups. Also known collectively as San.

Campi Flegrei   An underwater volcano near Naples. It has been argued that its eruption in about 39,000 BP led to the extinction of the Neanderthals.

carbon-14   A dating method used by archaeologists to estimate the age of carbon-containing material such as bones, artefacts or charcoal. It is based on the rate of decay of the radioactive isotope of carbon of that name, found in minute quantities along with non-radioactive carbon isotopes.

Çatalhöyük   A Neolithic archaeological site in Anatolia, southern Turkey famed for its excellent preservation of domestic buildings, murals and figurines. It was a large settlement, with as many as 10,000 people, and occupied from about 7500 to 5700 BCE.

Glossary

ceramics Inorganic, non-metallic materials such as pottery and glass, produced by a process of heating and cooling.

chimpanzee Species of the genus Pan, in the wide sense including both *Pan paniscus* (the common chimp) and *Pan pygmaeus* (the bonobo).

Chomskyan Relating to the linguistic work of Noam Chomsky (b. 1928), specifically his work on universal grammar (the structures that all languages share) and the deep structures of particular languages.

chromosome A cellular structure of DNA.

clan A large kin group, composed of several lineages and formed through either patrilineal or matrilineal descent.

cognatic descent A descent system which possesses neither patrilineal nor matrilineal kin groups, or descent through non-lineal relatives in a patrilineal or matrilineal system. Also known as bilateral descent. In a sense, the opposite of **double** (duolineal) **descent**.

cognition The process of knowing, through perception and reasoning.

collateral relative A consanguineal relative related through a brother or sister link.

collective consciousness (collective representation) Any of the collective understandings which people in a given community or society share. The term is derived from Durkheimian sociology.

communication The process of conveying information between individual humans or animals.

community A group of people who live together or share common values. It is smaller than a society, but of no precise size.

competence Noam Chomsky's earlier term for the idealized aspect of language: the ability to speak a language and to determine the grammaticality of an utterance. Cf. **performance**.

complex system Claude Lévi-Strauss' term for a kinship structure which has negative marriage rules. For example, one is not allowed to marry a brother or a sister. The opposite is an **elementary system**. See also **Crow-Omaha system**.

consanguineal relative A relative by 'blood'. Cf. **affinal relative**.

core In archaeology, a stone from which flakes are removed to produce a tool.

cranial capacity The volume of the cranium.

cranium That part of the skull which covers the brain.

Cro-Magnon Early modern humans of Europe, from a site in southern France excavated in 1868.

cross-cousin Father's sister's child or mother's brother's child. Cf. **parallel cousin**.

cross-relative   A collateral relative related through an opposite-sex sibling link.

Crow-Omaha system   Claude Lévi-Strauss' term for a kinship structure which has either a 'Crow' or an 'Omaha' terminology (i.e., one in which given kin terms are applied to entire lineages, matrilineal for 'Crow' or patrilineal for 'Omaha'), and in which the marriage prohibitions extended through such lineages are so extensive that the 'complex' structure comes to resemble an 'elementary' one.

cultural anthropology   The branch of anthropology that studies cultural phenomena. The term is common in some traditions and countries (e.g., in the United States, in Japan) but less so in others (e.g., in the United Kingdom).

cultural tradition   A. R. Radcliffe-Brown's preferred term for customs held in common among a group of people. Cf. **culture**.

culture   That which is not natural but learned. One may speak of culture in the abstract, or of cultures (plural), though the latter is often regarded as contentious.

culture area   A geographical region comprising peoples of similar culture.

culture circle   A cluster of related culture traits, or the geographical area where they are found. The idea is fundamental to German-Austrian diffusionists, who saw these circles as spreading progressively over earlier culture circles. From the German *Kulturkreis*. See also **Kulturkreis**.

culture-historical archaeology   Traditional archaeological theory that defines ethnic groups through their material culture. Largely superseded by processual archaeology in the 1960s.

cupule   In rock art studies, a small cup-shaped indentation presumed to have been made by a rock held in human hands.

'Dart's child'   The nickname of the first *Australopithecus* find, a juvenile skull discovered by Raymond Dart in 1924 and described in *Nature* in 1925.

Darwinian   Referring to the ideas of Charles Darwin (1809–82). Specifically, the notion that evolution is through natural selection. cf. **Lamarckian**.

delayed-return   James Woodburn's term for the economic and social system of 'advanced' hunter-gatherers and non-hunter-gatherers, where time *is* invested in planning ahead in subsistence activity. The opposite of **immediate-return**.

Denisova Cave   A cave in the Altai Mountains of southern Siberia, home to the **Denisovans**. It was occupied from about 50,000 to 30,000 BP. It is presently being excavated.

Denisovans   A recently discovered hominin species, as yet unnamed, that are descended from *Homo heidelbergensis*. There is evidence of interbreeding with Neanderthals and *H. sapiens* about 40,000 years ago.

descent   Relations between the generations in terms of group membership. There are four basic types: patrilineal, matrilineal, double (duolineal) and cognatic (bilateral).

diachronic Literally 'through time'. The opposite is **synchronic**.

diffusionism The diachronic theoretical perspective that stresses migration and diffusion of cultural ideas, rather than evolution. Cf. **evolutionism**.

discourse In linguistics, a unit of speech longer than a sentence. In the social sciences, the term often refers to a body of knowledge or the use of that knowledge, such as in structures of power.

DNA Deoxyribonucleic acid, the substance which contains genetic information.

double descent A descent system which possesses both patrilineal and matrilineal kin groups. Also known as duolineal descent. In a sense, the opposite of **cognatic** (bilateral) **descent**.

Dreamtime In Australian Aboriginal belief, the Dreamtime or Dreaming is a mythological time that is both the point of creation and eternal. It also represents both the world of spirit and that of the structure of society and the universe.

Early Stone Age (ESA) Southern African designation of the Palaeolithic, usually assumed to be prior to the invention of art, ritual, language, etc. (the Middle Stone Age). Also called the Earlier Stone Age.

ecology The relationship between organisms and their natural environment.

egocentric category A category of kin defined through a given individual. Cf. **socio-centric category**.

E-language Noam Chomsky's term for the external or spoken aspect of language. Cf. **I-language** and **P-language**.

elementary ideas Adolf Bastian's notion of ideas or thoughts common to all humankind. From the German *Elementargedanken*. Cf. **folk ideas**.

elementary system Claude Lévi-Strauss' term for a kinship structure which has positive marriage rules. For example, one is obliged to marry into the category that includes the cross-cousin. The opposite is a **complex system**. See also **Crow-Omaha system**.

Eoanthropus dawsoni The supposed fossil 'discovered' in Kent, southeastern England, in 1912. See **'Piltdown Man'**.

Eolithic A former name for the presumed 'Dawn Stone Age'. It has been replaced by the term **Palaeolithic**.

'Eskimo' A kinship terminology structure which distinguishes siblings from cousins but not parallel cousins from cross-cousins. The terminology structure of English and several other languages spoken in Europe is 'Eskimo'.

ethnicity The characterization of groups by presumed, and/or self-defined, biological or cultural similarity.

ethnology Loosely, a synonym for social and cultural anthropology, but often more specifically referring to points of view that emphasize culture history, and especially diffusionism.

ethos The distinctive character of an event or a cultural tradition. The opposite is the eidos, which represents its form or structure.

evolutionary psychology The field that studies the relationship between natural selection and brain size, cognition and behaviour.

evolutionism In biology, the theory that 'higher' organisms evolve from 'lower' forms. In social anthropology, the diachronic perspective that stresses change for the better or advancement from simple to complex. In contrast to a 'revolutionist' perspective, the term can also refer to slow as opposed to rapid change of this kind. Cf. **diffusionism**.

exogamy Marriage outside of a group. (Marriage within a group is known as *endogamy*, and a rule permitting marriage either inside or outside a group is called *agamy*.)

fetishism The worship of fetishes, or objects that are thought to have supernatural power.

five modes Grahame Clark's set of five forms of lithic technology from simple choppers to complex (combining stone with wood and leather or grass) artefacts. Because it is more precise, some archaeologists use this classification in preference to traditional periods or geographical names such as Lower Palaeolithic or Oldowan. See **Modes 1, 2, 3, 4, 5**.

flaked tool A tool made by striking it from a prepared core.

folk ideas Adolf Bastian's notion of ideas or thoughts peculiar to a specific culture. From the German *Völkergedanken*. Cf. **elementary ideas**.

foraging mode of thought My term for an ideology emphasizing *not* the acquisition of property, but foraging and sharing. This ideology is common among hunter-gatherers. The opposite is the **accumulation mode of thought**.

fossil record Prehistory, as determined through accumulation of the remains of plants, animals and artefacts. In biological anthropology, it tends to refer to prehistory deciphered from the fossilized bones of human ancestors.

FOXP2 A gene that controls brain and lung development. In humans it also controls speech, and the ability of the brain to formulate complex rules of grammar. A FOXP2 mutation during the evolution of *Homo* is believed to be partly responsible for the development of humankind's linguistic abilities.

functionalism The synchronic theoretical perspective that emphasizes the purpose of institutions or customs, or how things work in relation to each other. Often the term is employed as a synonym for **structural-functionalism**.

genealogical level Technically, a term used in preference to 'generation' to refer to a set of closely related people whose 'level' is determined in relation to their parents and children.

generation A vague term for a set of people born about the same time, as distinct from the generation of their parents or children.

genetics The science of heredity.

genome The sum of the genetic information encoded in the genes, chromosomes, etc., of an individual.

gesture Non-verbal forms of communication, i.e., communication through finger, hand, arm or body movement.

global comparison Comparison on a worldwide basis in the search for universal cross-cultural generalizations or predictions.

great apes Orang-utans, gorillas, chimpanzees and bonobos.

grid-group analysis Mary Douglas' term for a method to differentiate societies or groups within society according to relative constraints of insulation (grid) and those of collective behaviour (group). The cross-cutting of these axes creates four boxes, in which individuals, groups or societies are classified.

grooming Maintaining bodily cleanliness and appearance, especially the appearance of others (called 'social grooming'). Among primates, social grooming maintains social relations and serves as a form of communication.

'group marriage' The hypothetical system in which a set of people are 'married' to each other. Belief in group marriage as the original form of marriage was common among nineteenth-century evolutionists.

Hadar An archaeological site in Ethiopia where the fossil 'Lucy' (*Australopithecus afarensis*) was discovered in 1973.

hafting The attachment of stone to wood artefacts, for example by tying a spear point to a spear handle with leather straps or by inserting it in a slit in the handle.

Herto An early *Homo sapiens* (*H. sapiens idaltu*) site in Ethiopia.

Holocene The present geological epoch. It followed the Pleistocene, about 10,000 years ago.

hominids (Hominidae) In present usage, the Linnaean family that includes great apes and humans. In earlier usage, it was employed for *Homo* and immediate ancestors.

hominins (Hominini) The Linnaean tribe that includes humans and human ancestors. In present usage, it includes australopithecines, but used to be defined more narrowly.

Homo antecessor A human species living in Africa and Europe from about 1,200,000 to 800,000 BP. It is believed to be ancestral to *H. heidelbergensis* and ultimately to *H. sapiens*.

Homo erectus The species living in East Africa and later Asia and Europe from about 2,000,000 to 300,000 BP. *H. erectus* tamed fire, developed techniques for

Glossary

working stone tools and travelled outside Africa to the Far East and to Europe. Sometimes the term is used specifically for the species that migrated to Asia and Africa, with the term *H. ergaster* being employed for the earlier species that evolved in Africa.

Homo ergaster African *H. erectus* or the species which diverged and spread throughout the Old World. (See ***Homo erectus***.)

Homo floresiensis The species of *Homo* recently discovered on Flores, in Indonesia, and dated to about 18,000 BP. This species is sometimes called 'the hobbit', and resembles *H. erectus* but is much smaller.

Homo gautengensis Recently discovered fossil from South Africa, believed to have lived from about 2,000,000 to 600,000 BP. Small-brained, with large teeth, it was largely vegetarian, used stone tools and possibly possessed fire.

Homo habilis The earliest member of the genus *Homo*, living 2,300,000 to 1,400,000 BP. The species that developed the use of Oldowan stone tools around 1,700,000 BP.

Homo heidelbergensis Species of *Homo* that lived in Africa and Europe from 600,000 to 250,000 BP and is possibly ancestral to both Neanderthals and modern humans.

Homo helmei African *H. heidelbergensis* when classified as a separate species. More modern than European *H. heidelbergensis*.

Homo neanderthalensis*, *H. sapiens neanderthalensis The Neanderthals. The type find was from the Neander valley (*thal*, or in modern spelling *tal*), in 1857.

Homo rudolfensis Similar to *H. habilis*, and dated at 1,900,000 BP ('Skull 1470').

Homo sapiens The only remaining species of *Homo*. Often includes near relatives, namely 'Archaic' *H. sapiens* (*H. sapiens neanderthalensis* and *H. sapiens heidelbergensis*).

Homo sapiens sapiens Fully modern, linguistic *Homo sapiens* (excluding near relatives such as Neanderthals).

horde In Australian ethnography, the ususal word for a 'band'.

Howiesons Poort An advanced Middle Stone Age cultural tradition that includes hafted microlithic artefacts and the use of ochre, roughly 66,000 to 59,000 BP.

human Referring to the genus *Homo*, or more specifically *H. sapiens*.

human origins Broadly, the study of prehistoric humanity and its precursors.

human revolution The term employed in 1964 by Charles Hockett and Robert Ascher for the revolutionary set of biological and technological advances that gave rise to humanity, as distinct from the apes. The term is sometimes used today for more recent advances, such as the 'symbolic revolution'.

hunter-gatherers Peoples who subsist by hunting, gathering and/or fishing, and do not practise food production (pastoralism or agriculture). More loosely, peoples who have an insignificant amount of food production and subsist mainly by hunting, gathering and/or fishing.

I-language Noam Chomsky's term for the internal or cognitive aspect of language. Cf. **E-language** and **P-language**.

immediate-return James Woodburn's term for the economic and social system of small-scale hunter-gatherers, where time is *not* invested in planning ahead in subsistence activity. The opposite of **delayed-return**.

incest In social anthropology, sex with a member of a prohibited category of relative (not necessarily with close kin).

indexical In contrast to symbolic (arbitrary), acquiring meaning through natural, associational or metonymic relations. For example, a crown represents sovereignty not in a totally arbitrary way, but as a physical manifestation of the status and power it implies.

indigenous Relating to original occupation or simply to local cultural tradition. The validity of the term cross-culturally, in the former sense, is in dispute, and some anthropologists prefer either not to employ the term or to use instead **autochthonous**.

interpretivism Anti-structuralist, anti-scientistic perspective that uses the analogy that cultures are like languages in that they can be 'translated', one to another.

Inuit A preferred term for 'Eskimo' (the grouping of peoples of the North American Arctic, but not the kinship terminology structure).

Iron Age In most of Africa, the age associated with the coming of agriculture and with the Bantu-speaking populations and their migrations. Elsewhere, the age of iron-using populations, following the Bronze Age, from about 1300 BCE.

'Iroquois' A kinship terminology structure which distinguishes parallel cousins from cross-cousins. Usually siblings and parallel cousins are classed together.

Iwo Eleru Rock shelter in southwestern Nigeria, the site of the burial of a very late (11,700 BP) part 'archaic', part 'modern' skull.

jasperite The mineral jasper: an opaque, often reddish, variety of quartz.

'Java Man' Informal name of the first specimen of *H. erectus*, discovered by Eugene Dubois on Java in 1893. Also known as *Pithecanthropus*.

joking relationship A kin relationship with permitted licence and informality. The opposite is an **avoidance relationship**.

Kabwe A town in central Zambia formerly known as Broken Hill. The location of the discovery of 'Rhodesian Man'.

Kebara Site of a Neanderthal burial in Israel, dating to about 60,000 BP.

Khoekhoe Cattle- and sheep-herding populations of southern Africa. Their archaeological culture is sometimes said to be 'Neolithic', but this classification is in dispute. They reached the Cape around 2,000 years ago, before the arrival of Bantu-speaking peoples.

kinship The study of relatedness, including descent, alliance and terminology structures.

Kulturkreis German for 'culture circle'. The school of thought which emphasizes the existence of such 'culture circles' was called the *Kulturkreislehre*. See also **culture circle**.

Lake Mungo A site, in New South Wales, of early habitation in Australia. The site includes evidence of both burial and cremation. The date is in dispute, but it is usually assumed to be before around 40,000 BP.

Lake Toba See **Toba**.

Lamarckian Referring to the ideas of Jean-Baptiste Lamarck (1744–1829). Specifically, the notion that acquired characteristics may be inherited. Cf. **Darwinian**.

language The specifically human ability for thought and communication through words and grammar. All humans have this ability, but other higher primates do not. (All human societies have the potential for languages of equal complexity, and the most complex are those spoken by Inuit peoples.)

langue Ferdinand de Saussure's term for language in the sense of linguistic structure or grammar. By analogy, this can be the 'grammar' of culture as well as of language proper. Cf. ***parole***.

Lascaux Rock art site in the Dordogne, France, famous for its Upper Palaeolithic art dated to about 17,000 BP.

Later Stone Age (LSA) The term employed in southern Africa for the most recent stone tool traditions and associated social organization. It comprises modern hunter-gatherers and herders of southern Africa whose lifestyles predate the arrival of Iron Age Bantu-speaking populations.

level of intentionality In psychology, one of the five or six levels of theory of mind. Second-level intentionality, for example, is believing (first-level) that someone else believes (second-level) something. See also **theory of mind**.

Lévi-Straussian Referring to the ideas of Claude Lévi-Strauss (1908–2009). See also **structuralism**.

liminality An in-between status in a ritual, when an individual is in the process of making a transition from one social status or phase in life to another.

lineage A line of descent (patrilineal or matrilineal). Lineages are often grouped into clans. See also **clan**.

linguistics The scientific study of language in the abstract, or of languages.

'lion man' A statuette with the head of a lion and the body of a man.

lithic In relation to stone tools. Often used as a suffix (as in **Neolithic**).

Lower Palaeolithic Early period of the Palaeolithic, roughly from 2,600,000 to 100,000 BP. The period of the *Homo erectus* Out of Africa migrations.

Lupemban Archaeological industries of central and western Africa, 32,000 to 17,000 BP. They were characterized by long, thin bifacial and two-pointed blades.

Makapansgat An archaeological site along a valley in the Limpopo province of South Africa. A number of australopithecines have been found there.

material culture The artefacts created by people according to presumed cultural traditions, for example stone tools uncovered by archaeologists, or the material aspects of cultural life recorded by ethnographers.

matrilineal descent Descent through females (mother to children). Also known as uterine descent.

matriliny Descent through females. See also **matrilineal descent**.

Mesolithic The European and Asian stone tool tradition between the Palaeolithic and the Neolithic. The term means 'middle stone age', but is not to be confused with the southern African Middle Stone Age, which is roughly the equivalent of the European Upper Palaeolithic.

metaphor An analogy or relation of similarity across different levels of meaning (e.g., a red traffic light stands for 'stop').

metonym A part that stands for the whole, or an object that represents something closely associated with it (for example, a crown representing sovereignty).

microlith A tiny stone tool such as a small projectile point.

Middle Kingdom In China, the central states both geographically and according to the political organization of earlier times. (The precise meaning depends on context, but in ancient China it is geographical rather than, as in ancient Egypt, a historical period.)

Middle Palaeolithic Middle period of the Palaeolithic, roughly from 300,000 to 30,000 BP. The period associated with Neanderthals in Europe and with the emergence of modern *Homo sapiens* in Africa.

Middle Stone Age (MSA) The southern African stone tool tradition, around 300,000 to 50,000 BP. Associated with early modern and modern humans, and the symbolic revolution.

modern A term whose meaning depends heavily on context. It can refer, for example, to 'modern humans' (emerging 200,000 BP) or to 'modern society' (emerging, depending on context, in the Neolithic, in the Enlightenment or in the twentieth century).

modernity The nominal form of the adjective **modern** (see above). 'Behavioural modernity' usually refers to the emergence of symbolic thought.

Modes 1, 2, 3, 4, 5 A classification system for stone tools, designed in the 1960s by Grahame Clark in order to unify African and European classifications. See also **five modes**.

moiety Literally, 'half' (French *moitié*): entailing a division of society into two halves, and a rule that one marries into the half to which he or she does not belong. The division is through either patrilineal or matrilineal descent. Common in Australia and South America.

molecular biology The study of biology at the molecular level.

molecular clock A time measure for genetic divergence: it assumes a constant mutation rate between genomes.

monogenesis One origin of humankind. Cf. **polygenesis**.

monotheism Belief in one deity, rather than more than one. Cf. **polytheism**.

Mousterian Middle Palaeolithic, including Neanderthal, stone tool tradition dating from 100,000 to 35,000 BP. Named after the rock shelter Le Moustier in the Dordogne and characterized by reshaped flakes.

mtDNA Mitochondrial DNA: a form of DNA that performs specific functions within the cell. Its significance in genetic studies is that, in humans and many other species, it is inherited only through females and thus indicates matrilineal descent.

Multiregional Continuity Model (MCM) Another name for the **multiregional hypothesis** (see below). More specifically, the model that suggests that, for example, Asians have evolved from Asian *Homo erectus* and Europeans from European *H. erectus* or from Neanderthals.

multiregional hypothesis A theory that modern humankind is the product of evolution from several different earlier forms. Cf. **Out of Africa**, **Recent African Origin (RAO model)**.

mutation In genetics, the change in a DNA sequence that will affect the fitness of an individual and their progeny.

mystical thought Lucien Lévy-Bruhl's term for thought processes present in every human mind but commonly associated with 'primitive' thinking: communication with nature or with the spirit world.

mythology A body of oral literature (myths) that deals with origins, symbolic relations and the explanation of natural or supernatural phenomena. Characteristically, mythology blurs the relation between people and animals, invokes deities and/or employs metaphor, often deep with meaning.

Nachikufan Zambian archaeological industries dating from about 20,000 to 10,000 BP and characterized by the development of small blades, scrapers and bored stones. Named after a cave in northern Zambia.

natural selection The mechanism of Darwinian evolution, through which heritable traits are passed from generation to generation. This can involve either sexual selection (i.e., competition for mates) or ecological selection. Either way, those who live to breed will propagate future generations.

Neanderthal, Neandertal The English name for *Homo neanderthalensis* or *H. sapiens neanderthalensis*.

'Neanderthal flute' A purported, prehistoric musical instrument, the prototype of which is the femur of a cave bear in which four holes (as in a modern recorder) have been made.

neocortex The main part of the brain, excluding the brain stem and limbic system.

Neolithic Stone tool industry characterized by polished tools and by ceramics. The term is also employed very commonly for the types of social organization and subsistence lifestyles which characterize this industry. These include permanent settlement, village life and animal husbandry and agriculture. The term means 'new stone age'. See also **Mesolithic**.

Neolithization The transition from food-gathering to food production, along with accompanying changes in economic and social organization.

neuroscience Traditionally, the scientific study of the nervous system, and today associated also with implications for understanding cognition and the evolution of the human mind.

norms Socially accepted behaviour.

Northwest Coast A culture area of North America characterized by complex, hierarchical hunter-gatherer-fisher societies and specific patterns of environmental exploitation and exchange.

ochre Red, orange or yellow mineral pigment believed to be used for decoration or painting.

Oedipus myth A complex Greek myth that involves unknowing incest (on the part of Oedipus, the lead character) and the breach of several other taboos.

Oldowan The oldest known stone tool tradition, dated to 2,500,000 BP or older and associated with *Homo habilis* or possibly *Australopithecus garhi*.

orang-utan Southeast Asian species *Pongo pygmaeus*

'original affluent society' Marshall Sahlins' term for hunter-gatherer social life, in which 'affluence' is measured by free time rather than by accumulated wealth. Hunter-gatherers spend *less* time in subsistence-related activities than non-hunter-gatherers.

Orrorin An early eastern African hominin, the genus of *Orrorin tugenensis*, dating from approximately 6,000,000 years ago.

Glossary

Out of Africa   The theory, developed especially since the 1980s, that all modern humankind is descended from a small and relatively recent (less than 200,000 years ago) group of Africans. (The allusion is to the title of an unrelated 1937 book, made into a film in 1985.) Also called the **Recent African Origin** model. Cf. **Multiregional Continuity Model, multiregional hypothesis.**

ovum   The egg, or female reproductive cell.

own-kill rule   Chris Knight's term for a rule that forbids a person from eating meat that he (normally a male) kills himself. This taboo is often likened to incest, and the meat is given to or exchanged with others.

palaeo-anthropologist   A biological anthropologist who specializes in fossil remains.

Palaeolithic   The term means 'old stone age'. Divided into Early or Lower (including Oldowan and Acheulean, from 3,600,000 or 3,500,000 to 100,000 BP), Middle (including Mousterian, from 300,000 to 30,000 BP) and Late or Upper (including several traditions from about 45,000 to 10,000 BP).

palaeontologist   A specialist in prehistoric life forms, including the study of human origins through fossil remains.

parallel cousin   Father's brother's child or mother's sister's child. Cf. **cross-cousin.**

parallel relative   A collateral relative related through a same-sex sibling link.

Paranthropus   The genus name for a robust form of australopithecine. See **australopithecines.**

parole   Ferdinand de Saussure's term for speech in the sense of actual utterances. By analogy, it also refers to social action as opposed to social structure (*langue*). Cf. *langue.*

patrilineal descent   Descent through males (father to children). Also known as agnatic descent.

patriliny   Descent through males. See also **patrilineal descent.**

'Peking Man'   *Homo erectus* fossils discovered at Zhoukoudian, near Beijing, in 1923 and subsequently. Originally labelled *Sinanthropus pekinensis.*

performance   Noam Chomsky's earlier term for the practical aspect of language, i.e., speaking. Cf. **competence.**

person-number-gender marker   A noun or pronoun that identifies person (first, second or third), gender (e.g., masculine, feminine, neuter or common) and number (e.g., singular, dual or plural).

phememe   In Mary LeCron Foster's usage, a unit of meaning in primitive forms of language. It implies metaphorical associations that came into consciousness in such times.

philology Historical linguistics, especially as characterized the method and theory of linguistic studies in the nineteenth century.

phoneme The smallest meaningful unit of sound in a given language.

phonetics The study of the objective auditory or acoustic nature of sounds, independent of their place in a sound system (phonemics or phonology).

phonology The study of sounds as part of the sound system of a particular language. For example, in English the sounds **p**, **t** and **k** form one sequence (unvoiced stops, in order from front to back of the mouth) and **b**, **d** and **g** another (the equivalent voiced stops). Other languages may have fewer or more of these, or lack the distinction between unvoiced and voiced.

phratry A very large kin group, composed of several clans and formed through either patrilineal or matrilineal descent.

phylogegraphy A genetic approach to the geography of human migration, literally 'geography of the gene-tree'.

physical anthropology Earlier, and narrower, term for what is now usually called biological anthropology.

'Piltdown Man' A supposed fossil 'discovered' in Kent, southeastern England, in 1912 and exposed as a fake in 1953. At the time named *Eoanthropus dawsoni* (a name no longer in use).

Pirahã An Amerindian language of South America, of interest in linguistics because it is supposed to be the only language which lacks the property of recursion.

Pithecanthropus The genus name once used for *Homo erectus*, especially for the type find 'Java Man'. It means 'ape-man'.

Pithecanthropus alalus Ernst Haekel's name for a hypothetical 'missing link'. It is not associated with any fossil.

Pithecanthropus erectus An early name for *Homo erectus*, especially 'Java man'.

P-language The idealized notion of language in existence independently of any people. Cf. **E-language** and **I-language**.

Pleistocene Geological epoch from about 2,600,000 to 10,000 BP (followed by the Holocene). It was characterized by stages of repeated glaciation.

Pliocene Geological epoch before the Pleistocene. From about 5,400,000 to 2,600,000 BP.

polygamous marriage Marriage to more than one person at a time: either polygyny (more than one wife), polyandry (more than one husband) or 'group marriage'.

polygenesis More than one origin for humankind. Cf. **monogenesis**.

polytheism   Belief in more than one deity. Cf. **monotheism**.

population bottleneck   A population decrease that causes a reduction in the genetic variation of a population. Past population bottlenecks (such as one following the Toba volcanic eruption) may be deduced through genetic studies.

postmodern   Originally meaning the reaction against modernism (e.g., in architecture), the term today is imprecise in meaning. It tends to refer to anti-objectivist or anti-scientific viewpoints.

postmodernism   Any theoretical perspective, for example in social anthropology, which involves the rejection of the validity of objective categories or scientific methods.

post-processual archaeology   A trend in archaeological theory which emphasizes the subjectivity of archaeological interpretation. It originated in the late 1970s as a reaction against processual archaeology.

post-vocalic /r/   In English, phonetic [r] pronounced at the end of a word (as in Ireland, Canada, most of the United States, etc.). In much of the English-speaking world (parts of England, New England, Australia, etc.), this historical phonemic /r/ is not pronounced at all. Cf. **pre-consonantal /r/**.

potassium-argon dating   Dating method employing the measure of the rate of decay of an isotope of potassium into argon. It is used when radiocarbon dating is not possible.

pre-consonantal /r/   In English, phonetic [r] before a consonant. Depending on dialect, English phonemic /r/ before a consonant may be rendered as either a phonetic [r] (e.g., in Canada) or as the lengthening of the previous consonant (e.g., as in Australia). Cf. **post-vocalic /r/**.

prehistory   The period before written records.

primate   A member of the biological order *primates*, including lemurs, monkeys and apes.

primatologist   One who studies primates.

primitive revelation   The notion that God revealed his presence to early humans or primitive peoples before the Judeo-Christian era.

processual archaeology   The trend in archaeological theory that advocates a scientific methodology and an emphasis on evolution and cultural ecology. It became prominent in the 1960s, especially in North America. Cf. **post-processual archaeology**.

proto-language   In my theory of language (derived from Derek Bickerton's), words and phrases only, without simple sentences or rules for word order. Cf. **rudimentary language**.

psychic unity   The notion that all humans, irrespective of cultural tradition, think in the same way.

quadruped   A four-footed animal.

radiocarbon dating   Dating method employing the measure of the rate of decay of the radioactive isotope carbon-14. Its limit is about 60,000 years. For earlier dates, other methods (such as potassium-argon dating) are required.

Recent African Origin (RAO) model   Another name for the **Out of Africa** theory: that modern *Homo sapiens* have evolved exclusively or mainly from a small African population. Cf. **Multiregional Continuity Model**.

recursion   In linguistics, the property of embedding one unit into another of the same kind, such as sentences within sentences.

relatedness   A recent anthropological notion replacing the older and supposedly more ethnocentric idea kinship.

relativism   A view of the world that opposes the assumption of cultural universals or universal values. In social anthropology, it usually refers to a form of cultural relativism rather than a theory of values.

relativist   One who follows a relativist perspective.

religion   A system of beliefs in spiritual entities and the set of rites that support such beliefs.

'Rhodesian Man'   The *Homo rhodesiensis* or *Homo heidelbergensis* fossil discovered at the Broken Hill mine in then Northern Rhodesia (modern Zambia) in 1921.

ritual   The actions or rites that support a system of religious belief. Ritual is symbolic in meaning and often collective in performance.

rock art   Ancient or recent art depicted on rock surfaces. Broadly, there are two forms: engraving and painting.

rudimentary language   In my theory of language (derived from Derek Bickerton's), language possessing only simple syntax. Cf. **proto-language**.

Sahelanthropus   The genus of *Sahelanthropus tchadensis* (7,000,000 years ago), significant because it predates the divergence between chimpanzees and humans and could represent a common ancestor.

Sahul   The continental shelf of Australia and New Guinea and the Pleistocene land mass which once occupied much of it.

Sally-Ann test   A psychological test of cognitive abilities, involving the recognition of another (imaginary) person's perceptions.

sambandham   Among the Nayars of Kerela in South India, a high-status man taken by a woman as her lover.

San   Southern African hunter-gatherers, including Ju/'hoansi (!Kung), /Gui, //Gana, Naro, /Xam and other groups. Also known collectively as Bushmen.

Saussurian   Referring to the ideas of Ferdinand de Saussure (1857–1913). Specifically the ideas on the synchronic study of language from the posthumous *Course in general linguistics* (French edition, 1916).

'Scheherezade effect'   Geoffrey Miller's term for his theory of the origin of language: that it developed in order to attract potential mates.

section   In Australian Aboriginal kinship, one of four or eight units into which things, including people, are classified. Every person belongs to one of these, and marries a member of one specific one of the other sections. In a four-section system, for example, a man belongs to the same section as his father's father and marries into the same section as his father's father did. This happens to be also the section of his cross-cousin.

sexual selection   In Darwinian theory, the primary means of natural selection: through competition for mates.

shamanism   Religion based on the activities of shamans, ritual specialists with the ability to communicate with the spirit world. Trance performance, healing practice, metamorphosis into animal form and out-of-body travel are common.

signifying   Relating to the relationship between a word (or morpheme) and meaning, or by extension, between any object and its meaning.

signifying revolution   My term for the revolutionary linguist change to the use of words to signify meaning.

simile   Like **metaphor**, an analogy or relation of similarity across different levels of meaning, but expressed in the form 'as a . . .', or 'like a . . .'.

social and cultural anthropology   A term which includes both the 'social' and the 'cultural' traditions of anthropology. The term is growing in popularity in the United Kingdom.

social anthropology   The field which is concerned with the study of society in the abstract, and in the comparative understanding of society and societies. It is the preferred term in the United Kingdom and some other countries, whereas 'cultural anthropology' is more common in the United States. In the United States, the term 'social anthropology' sometimes connotes a narrower, British theoretical perspective within cultural anthropology.

social contract   The seventeenth- and eighteenth-century idea that the essence of society is a 'contract' among its members to live peaceably together.

social theory   Theoretical branch of the social sciences generally, especially sociology. It is sometimes distinguished from empirical studies.

sociality   The capacity for being social or sociable. Employed in seventeenth- and eighteenth-century philosophy and reintroduced into biological and anthropological sciences in the twentieth century.

society   The largest group of people or animals that share common cultural tradition, or share a recognition that they are indeed the same group.

sociobiology   The study of social relations in a biological framework. More precisely, the discipline or theoretical position that treats human culture and society as adjuncts of humankind's animal nature.

socio-centric category   A category of kin defined in the same way for all members of society (e.g., a **moiety** or a **section**). Cf. **egocentric category**.

sociology   The study of society. The term usually refers to the discipline that includes both social theory and the empirical study of social facts, but it can also refer to (part of) social anthropology, especially when the latter is understood as a form of 'comparative sociology'.

speech   Actual vocalized communication. See also *parole*.

spermatozoon   The male reproductive cell.

Still Bay   Also known as Stillbay or Stillbaai, an advanced Palaeolithic or Middle Stone Age cultural tradition, very roughly 77,000 to 72,000 BP. It was identified in the 1920s, and questioned in the 1970s, but has since taken on renewed interest in view of cave sites such as Sibudu and Blombos.

structural-functionalism   The theoretical perspective associated with A. R. Radcliffe-Brown and his followers. It emphasizes the synchronic study of society, and the systematic nature of society and social institutions.

structuralism   The perspective that emphasizes relations over substance. To a structuralist, things derive meaning only through such relations.

Subarctic   A region of the northern hemisphere, especially the culture area of North America inhabited by societies made up of large, cognatically structured hunter-gatherer bands.

subsection   In Australian Aboriginal kinship, a section divided into two, with alternate forms of marriage permissible within it. Cf. **section**.

sui generis   Literally 'of its own kind', referring to that which can only be explained in its own terms. For example, culture can be explained only with reference to culture itself.

symbol   Loosely, a thing represented by something else.

symbolic, symbolism   Relating to the use of symbols.

symbolic revolution   My preferred term for the 'human revolution' of early *Homo sapiens sapiens*, related to full language and to elementary structures of kinship.

synchronic   Literally, 'in the same time'. The opposite is **diachronic**.

syntactic   Relating to sentences, or, more broadly, to grammar.

tetradic   A four-part system similar to an Australian section system. Hypothesized by N. J. Allen as the primal human kinship structure.

theory of mind   The ability to understand another person's point of view, in other words to anticipate the thinking of another person or being. This facility is limited in small children, primates and, presumably too, in early hominins.

therianthrope   A creature that is part human and part animal. Common in rock art, where the figure is presumed to represent a shaman.

Toba   A super-volcano that exploded approximately 74,000 years ago, causing a 'volcanic winter' of perhaps ten years and, arguably, a significant reduction in the world's population and a population bottleneck. The remnants of the Toba volcano today comprise Lake Toba on the island of Sumatra.

totem   In the Ojibwa language, the spirit of a patrilineal clan. By extension, a similar spirit among any people.

totemism   Any belief system which entails the symbolic representation of the social (e.g., clan membership) by the natural (e.g., animal species and their characteristics). Some anthropologists question the validity of referring to such a variety of belief systems by a single term.

Tower of Babel   Mythical tower which, according to the Bible, caused offence to God, who destroyed it, confounded the language of the earth and forced its speakers to scatter.

transhumant   Referring to seasonal movement, for example winter coastal aggregation and summer upland dispersal.

Twin Rivers   A site in Zambia with the earliest evidence of pigment use. Dated to 300,000 years and attributed to *Homo heidelbergensis*.

Type I   My term for a kinship system, such as San or Bushman ones, which emphasize flexibility in group structure and cosmological association.

Type II   My term for a kinship system, such as Australian Aboriginal and South American ones, which emphasize structured internal relations and cosmological associations.

unilineal descent   Descent through one line. It includes patrilineal and matrilineal descent systems.

universal kinship   Systems in which everyone in a society is classified by a relationship term and treated appropriately. In such systems there is no concept of someone being 'non-kin'.

'untamed thought'   The more accurate translation of Claude Lévi-Strauss' book title *La pensée sauvage* (English title: *The savage mind*).

Upper Palaeolithic   Late period of the Palaeolithic, roughly from 45,000 to (in some regions) 10,000 BP. Comprises a number of diverse stone tool traditions.

uxorilocality   Postmarital residence in the wife's home. Also called matrilocality. (Related to female philopatry in primatology, the tendency of groups to form around related females.)

'Venus' figurines   Stone, ivory or clay female figures commonly associated with the European Upper Palaeolithic.

virilocality   Postmarital residence in the husband's home. Also called patrilocality. (Related to male philopatry in primatology, the tendency of groups to form around related males.)

worldview   A broad perspective on the world by people within their culture. Common in the American tradition. From the German *Weltanschauung*.

yin* and *yang   In Chinese cosmology, the interdependent but opposite elements of the natural world.

Zinjanthropus   The robust australopithecine now classified as *Paranthropus boisei*.

References

Allen, Nicholas J. 2008. 'Tetradic theory and the origin of human kinship systems', in Allen *et al.*, pp. 96–112

Allen, Nicholas J., Hilary Callan, Robin Dunbar and Wendy James (eds.). 2008. *Early human kinship: from sex to social reproduction*. Oxford: Blackwell Publishing

Ambrose, Stanley H. 1998. 'Late Pleistocene human population bottlenecks, volcanic winter, and differentiation of modern humans', *Journal of Human Evolution* 34 (6): 623–51

Arbib, Michael A. 2005. 'From monkey-like action recognition to human language: an evolutionary framework for neurolinguistics', *Behavioral and Brain Sciences* 28: 105–67

Arcand, Bernard. 1977. 'The logic of kinship, an example from the Cuiva', *Actes du XLIIe Congrès Internationals des Américanistes*, vol. II, pp. 19–34

Astuti, Rita, Jonathan Parry and Charles Stafford (eds.). 2007. *Questions of anthropology* (London School of Economics Monographs on Social Anthropology 76). Oxford: Berg

Avebury, Lord [Sir John Lubbock]. 1911. *The pleasures of life*. London: Macmillan and Co.

Bancel, Pierre J., Alain Matthey de l'Etang and John D. Bengtson. 2006. 'Back to Proto-Sapiens (part 2): the global kinship terms PAPA, MAMA and KAKA', paper presented at the American Anthropological Association 105th Annual Meeting, San Jose, CA, November 2006

Barham, Lawrence S. 2000. *The Middle Stone Age of Zambia, south central Africa*. Bristol: Western Academic and Specialist Press

  2002. 'Systematic pigment use in the Middle Pleistocene of south-central Africa', *Current Anthropology* 43: 181–90

  2004. 'Art in human evolution', in Gunter Berghaus (ed.), *New perspectives on prehistoric art*. New York: Praeger, pp. 105–30

  2007. 'Modern is as modern does? Technological trends and thresholds in the south-central African record', in Mellars *et al.*, pp. 165–76

Barham, Lawrence and Peter Mitchell. 2008. *The first Africans: African archaeology from the earliest toolmakers to most recent foragers*. Cambridge University Press

Barnard, Alan. 1978. 'Universal systems of kin categorization', *African Studies* 37: 69–81
  1988. 'Structure and fluidity in Khoisan religious ideas', *Journal of Religion in Africa* 18: 216–36
  1992. *Hunters and herders of southern Africa: a comparative ethnography of the Khoisan peoples*. Cambridge University Press
  1999. 'Modern hunter-gatherers and early symbolic culture', in Dunbar *et al.*, pp. 50–68
  2000. *History and theory in anthropology*. Cambridge University Press
  2002. 'The foraging mode of thought', *Senri Ethnological Studies* 60: 5–24
  2004. 'Hunting-and-gathering society: an eighteenth-century Scottish invention', in Alan Barnard (ed.), *Hunter-gatherers in history, archaeology and anthropology*. Oxford: Berg, pp. 31–43
  2007a. *Anthropology and the Bushman*. Oxford: Berg
  2007b. 'From Mesolithic to Neolithic modes of thought', in Whittle and Cummings, pp. 5–19
  2008. 'The co-evolution of language and kinship', in Allen *et al.*, pp. 232–43
  2009. 'Social origins: sharing, exchange, kinship', in Botha and Knight, pp. 219–35
  2010a. 'Mythology and the evolution of language', in Andrew D. M. Smith, Marieke Schouwstra, Bart de Boer and Kenny Smith (eds.), *The Evolution of Language: Proceedings of the 8th International Conference (EVOLANG8)*. Hackensack, NJ: World Scientific, pp. 11–18
  2010b. 'When individuals do not stop at the skin', in Robin Dunbar, Clive Gamble and John Gowlett (eds.), *Social brain, distributed mind* (Proceedings of the British Academy 158). Oxford University Press for the British Academy, pp. 249–67
  2011. *Social anthropology and human origins*. Cambridge University Press
Barnes, J. A. 1973. 'Genetrix: genitor: nature: culture?', in Jack Goody (ed.), *The character of kinship*. Cambridge University Press, pp. 61–73
Bastian, Adolf. 2005 [1893–4]. 'Elementary ideas, folk ideas and geographical provinces', in Koepping, pp. 170–8
Bateson, Gregory. 1936. *Naven: survey of the problems suggested by a composite picture of the culture of a New Guinea tribe drawn from three points of view*. Cambridge University Press
  1973. *Steps to an ecology of mind: collected essays in anthropology, psychiatry, evolution and epistemology*. London: Paladin
Beaune, Sophie de, Frederick L. Coolidge and Thomas Wynn (eds.). 2009. *Cognitive archaeology and human evolution*. Cambridge University Press
Bednarik, Robert G. 1996. 'The cupules on Chief's Rock, Auditorium Cave, Bhimbetka', *The Artefact* 19: 63–72
  1998. 'The "australopithecine" cobble from Makapansgat, South Africa', *South African Archaeological Bulletin* 53: 4–8
  2003. 'The earliest evidence of palaeoart', *Rock Art Research* 20 (2): 89–135
Behar, Doron M., Richard Villems, Himla Soodyall, Jason Blue-Smith, Luisa Pereira, Ene Metspalu, Rosaria Scozzari, Heeran Makkan, Shay Tzur,

David Comas, Jaume Bertranpetit, Lluis Quintana-Murci, Chris Tyler-Smith, R. Spencer Wells, Saharon Rosset and the Genographic Consortium. 2008. 'The dawn of human matrilineal diversity', *American Journal of Human Genetics* 82: 1–11

Berger, Lee R., Darryl J. de Ruiter, Steven E. Churchill, Peter Schmidt, Kristian J. Carlson, Paul H. G. M. Dirks and Job M. Kibil. 2010. 'Australopithecus sediba: a new species of Homo-like australopith from South Africa', *Science* 328: 195–204

Bermúdez de Castro, J. M., M. Martinón-Torrez, E. Carbonell, S. Sarmiento, A. Rosas, J. van der Made and M. Lozano. 2004. 'The Atapuerca sites and their contribution to the knowledge of human evolution in Europe', *Evolutionary Anthropology* 13: 25–41

Bicchieri, M. G. (ed.). 1972. *Hunter-gatherers today: a socioeconomic study of eleven such cultures in the twentieth century*. New York: Holt, Rinehart and Winston

Bickerton, Derek. 2003. 'Symbol and structure: a comprehensive framework for language evolution', in Christiansen and Kirby, pp. 77–93

Biesele, Megan. 1976. 'Aspects of !Kung folklore', in Lee and DeVore, pp. 302–24

Binford, Lewis R. 2002 [1983]. *In pursuit of the past: decoding the archaeological record*. Berkeley: University of California Press

Bird-David, Nurit. 1990. 'The giving environment: another perspective on the economic system of hunter-gatherers', *Current Anthropology* 31: 183–96

  1999. '"Animism" revisited: personhood, environment, and relational epistemology', *Current Anthropology* 40 (Supplement): S67–S91

Blacking, John. 1976. *How musical is man?* London: Faber and Faber

Bleek, Dorothea F. 1928/9. 'Bushman grammar: a grammatical sketch of the language of the /xam-ka-!k'e', *Zeitschrift für Eingeborenen-Sprachen* 19: 81–98

  1929/30. 'Bushman grammar: a grammatical sketch of the language of the /xam-ka-!k'e (continuation)', *Zeitschrift für Eingeborenen-Sprachen* 20: 161–74

Bleek, W. H. I. and L. C. Lloyd. 1911. *Specimens of Bushman folklore*. London: George Allen and Company

Bloch, Maurice. 1971. *Placing the dead: tombs, ancestral villages, and kinship organisation in Madagascar*. London: Seminar Press

Bloch, R. Howard. 1991. *Medieval misogyny and the invention of Western romantic love*. University of Chicago Press

Blurton Jones, Nicolas and Melvin Konner. 1976. '!Kung knowledge of animal behaviour or: the proper study of mankind is animals', in Lee and DeVore, pp. 325–48

Botha, Rudolf. 2009. 'Theoretical underpinnings of inferences about language evolution: the syntax used at Blombos Cave', in Botha and Knight, pp. 93–111

Botha, Rudolf and Chris Knight (eds.). 2009. *The cradle of language*. Oxford University Press

Bowern, Claire and Harold Koch (eds.). 2004. *Australian languages: classification and the comparative method*. Amsterdam: John Benjamins

References

Bowler, J. M. Rhys Jones, Harry Allen and A. G. Thorne. 1970. 'Pleistocene human remains from Australia: a living site and human cremation from Lake Mungo, western New South Wales', *World Archaeology* 2: 39–60

Brody, Hugh. 2000. *The other side of Eden: hunter-gatherers, farmers and the shaping of the world*. Vancouver: Douglas and McIntyre

Brumm, Adam and Mark W. Moore. 2005. 'Symbolic revolutions and the Australian archaeological record', *Cambridge Archaeological Journal* 15 (2): 157–75

Cann, Rebecca L., Mark Stoneking and Allan C. Wilson. 1987. 'Mitochondrial DNA and human evolution', *Nature* 329 (6099): 31–6

Carsten, Janet. 2000. 'Introduction: cultures of relatedness', in Janet Carsten (ed.), *Cultures of relatedness: new approaches to the study of kinship*. Cambridge University Press, pp. 1–10

Childe, V. Gordon. 1936. *Man makes himself*. London: Watts and Co.

Chomsky, Noam. 1965. *Aspects of a theory of syntax*. Cambridge, MA: MIT Press
   1986. *Knowledge of language: its nature, origin, and use*. New York: Praeger
   2006. *Language and mind* (3rd edn). Cambridge University Press

Christiansen, Morten H. and Simon Kirby (eds.). 2003. *Language evolution*. Oxford University Press

Clark, J. G. D. 1969. *World prehistory: a new outline* (2nd edn). Cambridge University Press

Cochran, Gregory and Henry Harpending. 2009. *The 10,000 year explosion: how civilization accelerated human evolution*. New York: Basic Books

Conkey, Margaret W. 1999. 'A history of the interpretation of European "palaeolithic art": magic, mythogram, and metaphors for modernity', in Lock and Peters, pp. 288–349

Coolidge, Frederick L. and Thomas Wynn. 2009. *The rise of Homo sapiens: the evolution of modern thinking*. Oxford: Wiley-Blackwell
   2011. 'Comment', in Henshilwood and Dubreuil, pp. 380–2

Coon, Carlton S. 1962. *The origin of races*. New York: Alfred A. Knopf

Corballis, Michael C. 2002. *From hand to mouth: the origins of language*. Princeton University Press
   2003. 'From hand to mouth: the gestural origins of language', in Christiansen and Kirby, pp. 201–18
   2011. *The recursive mind: the origins of human language, thought, and civilization*. Princeton University Press

Cowan, James G. 1992. *The elements of the Aboriginal tradition*. Shaftesbury: Element

Curnoe, D. 2010. 'A review of early Homo in southern Africa focusing on cranial, mandibular and dental remains, with the description of a new species (Homo gautengensis sp. nov.)', *Homo: Journal of Comparative Human Biology* 61 (3): 151–77

Damas, David (ed.). 1969. *Contributions to anthropology: band societies* (National Museums of Canada Bulletin 228). Ottawa: National Museums of Canada
   1972. 'The Copper Eskimo', in Bicchieri, pp. 3–50

Davidson, Iain. 2003. 'The archaeological evidence of language origins: states of art', in Christiansen and Kirby, pp. 140–57

Deacon, Jeanette. 1990. 'Weaving the fabric of Stone Age research in southern Africa', in Peter Robertshaw (ed.), *A history of African archaeology*. London: James Currey, pp. 39–58

Deacon, Terrence W. 1997. *The symbolic species: the coevolution of language and the brain*. New York: W. W. Norton & Co.

Derevianko, A., M. Shunkov and P. Volkov. 2008. 'A Paleolithic bracelet from Denisova Cave', *Archaeology, Ethnology and Anthropology of Eurasia* 34 (2): 13–25

d'Errico, Francesco and Lucinda Backwell (eds.). 2005. *From tools to symbols: from early hominids to modern humans*. Johannesburg: Witwatersrand University Press

d'Errico, Francesco, Christopher Henshilwood, Graeme Lawson, Marian Vanhaeren, Anne-Marie Tillier, Marie Soressi, Frédérique Bresson, Bruno Maureille, April Nowell, Joseba Lakarra, Lucinda Backwell and Michèle Julien. 2003. 'Archaeological evidence for the emergence of language, symbolism, and music – an alternative multidisciplinary perspective', *Journal of World Prehistory* 17: 1–70

d'Errico, Francesco, Christopher Henshilwood, Marian Vanhaeren and Karen Van Niekerk. 2005. 'Nassarius kraussianus shell beads from Blombos Cave: evidence for symbolic behaviour in the Middle Stone Age', *Journal of Human Evolution* 48: 3–24

Descola, Philippe. 1994. *In the society of nature: a native ecology in Amazonia* (translated by Nora Scott). Cambridge University Press
  2005. *Par-delá nature et culture*. Paris: Gallimard

Dixon, R. M. W. 2002. *Australian languages: their nature and development*. Cambridge University Press

Doniger, Wendy. 2009. 'Claude Lévi-Strauss's theoretical and actual approaches to myth', in Boris Wiseman (ed.), *The Cambridge companion to Lévi-Strauss*. Cambridge University Press, pp. 196–215

Dorais, Louis-Jacques. 1990. 'The Canadian Inuit and their language', in Dirmid R. F. Collis (ed.), *Arctic languages: an awakening*. Paris: UNESCO, pp. 185–289

Douglas, Mary. 1969. *Natural symbols: exploration in cosmology*. London: Routledge and Kegan Paul
  1982. 'Introduction to grid/group analysis', in Mary Douglas (ed.), *Essays in the sociology of perception*. London: Routledge and Kegan Paul, pp. 1–8

Dunbar, Robin I. M. 1996. *Grooming, gossip and the evolution of language*. London: Faber and Faber
  2003. 'The social brain: mind, language and society in evolutionary perspective', *Annual Review of Anthropology* 32: 163–81
  2004. *The human story: a new history of mankind's evolution*. London: Faber and Faber
  2007. 'Why are humans not just great apes?', in Pasternak, pp. 37–48

Dunbar, Robin, Chris Knight and Camilla Power (eds.). 1999. *The evolution of culture: an interdisciplinary view*. Edinburgh University Press

Durkheim, Émile. 1915 [1912]. *The elementary forms of the religious life*. London: George Allen and Unwin

   1963 [1898]. *Incest: the nature and origin of the taboo* (translated by Edward Sagarin). New York: Stuart

Durkheim, Émile and Marcel Mauss. 1963 [1903]. *Primitive classification* (translated and edited by Rodney Needham). London: Cohen and West

Dziebel, German Valentinovich. 2007. *The genius of kinship: the phenomenon of human kinship and the global diversity of kinship terminologies*. Youngstown, NY: Cambria Press

Edwardes, Martin. 2010. *The origins of grammar: an anthropological perspective*. London: Continuum

Eibl-Eibesfeldt, Irenäus. 1979. *The biology of peace and war: men, animals, and aggression*. London: Thames and Hudson

Enard, Wolfgang, Molly Przeworski, Simon E. Fisher, Cecilia S. L. Lai, Victor Wiebe, Takashi Kitano, Anthony P. Monaco and Svante Pääbo. 2002. 'Molecular evolution of FOXP2, a gene involved in speech and language', *Nature* 418 (6900): 869–72

Evans-Pritchard, E. E. 1956. *Nuer religion*. Oxford: Clarendon Press

   1973. 'Genesis of a social anthropologist: an autobiographical note', *New Diffusionist* 3 (10): 17–23

Everett, Daniel L. 2005. 'Cultural constraints on grammar and cognition in Pirahã: another look at the design features of human language', *Current Anthropology* 46: 621–46

Foley, Robert. 2004. 'The evolutionary ecology of linguistic diversity in human populations', in Martin Jones (ed.), *Traces of ancestry: studies in honour of Colin Renfrew*. Cambridge: McDonald Institute for Archaeological Research, pp. 61–71

Foster, Mary LeCron. 1999. 'The reconstruction of the evolution of human spoken language', in Lock and Peters, pp. 747–75

Fox, Robin. 1967. *Kinship and marriage: an anthropological perspective*. Harmondsworth: Penguin Books

Frazer, James George. 1910. *Totemism and exogamy: a treatise on certain early forms of superstition and society* (4 vols.). London: Macmillan and Co.

   1919. *Folk-lore in the Old Testament: studies in comparative religion, legend and law* (3 vols.). London: Macmillan and Co.

   1922. *The Golden Bough: a study in magic and religion* (abridged edition). London: Macmillan and Co.

Freud, Sigmund. 1960 [1913]. *Totem and taboo: some points of agreement between the mental lives of savages and neurotics*. London: Routledge and Kegan Paul

Fukuyama, Francis. 2011. *The origins of political order, from prehuman times to the French Revolution*. London: Profile Books

Fuller, C. J. 1976. *The Nayars today*. Cambridge University Press

Gamble, Clive. 2007. *Origins and revolutions: human identity in earliest prehistory.* Cambridge University Press

Geertz, Clifford. 1966. 'Religion as a cultural system', in Michael Banton (ed.), *Anthropological approaches to the study of religion* (ASA Monographs 3). London: Tavistock Publications, pp. 1–46

1973. *The interpretation of cultures: selected essays.* New York: Basic Books

1983. *Local knowledge: further essays in interpretive anthropology.* New York: Basic Books

Gibbons, Ann. 2011. 'Aboriginal genome shows two-wave settlement of Asia', *Science* 333: 1689–91

Giddens, Anthony. 1993. *The transformation of intimacy: sexuality, love and eroticism in modern society.* Cambridge: Polity Press

Goody, Jack. 1977. *The domestication of the savage mind.* Cambridge University Press

Goren-Inbar, Naama, Nira Alperson, Mordechai E. Kislev, Orit Simchoni, Yoel Melamed, Adi Ben-Nun and Ella Werker. 2004. 'Evidence of hominin control of fire at Gesher Benot Ya'aqov, Israel', *Science* 304: 725–7

Graebner, Fritz. 1911. *Die Methode der Ethnologie.* Heidelberg: Carl Winters Universitäts Buchhandlung

Guenther, Mathias. 1979. 'Bushman religion and the (non)sense of anthropological theory of religion', *Sociologus* 29: 102–32

1999. *Tricksters and trancers: Bushman religion and society.* Bloomington: Indiana University Press

Güldemann, Tom. 1998. 'The Kalahari Basin as an object of areal typology – a first approach', in Mathias Schladt (ed.), *Language, identity, and conceptualization among the Khoisan.* Cologne: Rüdiger Köppe, pp. 137–96

Harris, D. R. 1989. 'An evolutionary continuum of people-plant interaction', in D. R. Harris and C. G. Hillman (eds.), *Foraging and farming: the evolution of plant exploitation.* London: Unwin Hyman, pp. 11–24

Harvati, Katerina, Chris Stringer, Rainer Grün, Maxime Aubert, Philip Allsworth-Jones and Caleb Adebayo Folorunso. 2011. 'The Later Stone Age calvaria from Iwo Eleru, Nigeria: morphology and chronology', *PLoS ONE* 6 (9): e24024. doi:10.1371/journal.pone.0024024

Hauser, Marc, Noam Chomsky and W. Tecumseh Fitch. 2002. 'The faculty of language: what is it, who has it, and how did it evolve?', *Science* 298: 1569–79

Helm, June. 1972. 'The Dogrib Indians', in Bicchieri, pp. 51–89

Henn, Brenna M., Christopher R. Gignoux, Matthew Jobin, Julie M. Granka, J. M. Macpherson, Jeffrey M. Kidd, Laura Rodríguez-Botigué, Sohini Ramachandran, Lawrence Hon, Abra Brisbin, Alice A. Lin, Peter A. Underhill, David Comas, Kenneth K. Kidd, Paul J. Norman, Peter Parham, Carlos D. Bustamante, Joanna L. Mountain and Marcus W. Feldman. 2011. 'Hunter-gatherer genomic diversity suggests a southern African origin for modern humans', *Proceedings of the National Academy of Sciences (PNAS)* 108 (13): 5154–62

Henshilwood, Christopher. 2009. 'The origins of symbolism, spirituality, and shamans: exploring Middle Stone Age material culture in South Africa', in Renfrew and Morley, pp. 29–49

Henshilwood, Christopher S., Francesco d'Errico, Curtis W. Marean, Richard G. Milo and Royden Yates. 2001. 'An early bone tool industry from the Middle Stone Age at Blombos Cave, South Africa: implications for the origins of modern human behaviour, symbolism and language', *Journal of Human Evolution* 41: 631–78

Henshilwood, Christopher S., Francesco d'Errico and Ian Watts. 2009. 'Engraved ochres from the Middle Stone Age levels at Blombos Cave, South Africa', *Journal of Human Evolution* 57: 27–47

Henshilwood, Christopher Stuart and Benoît Dubreuil. 2011. 'The Still Bay and Howiesons Poort, 77–59 ka: symbolic material culture and the evolution of the mind during the African Middle Stone Age', *Current Anthropology* 52: 361–400

Henshilwood, Christopher S. and Curtis W. Marean. 2003. 'The origin of modern human behaviour: critique of the models and their test implications', *Current Anthropology* 44: 627–51

  2006. 'Remodelling the origins of modern human behaviour', in Soodyall, pp. 31–48

Hewlett, Barry S. 1991. *Intimate fathers: the nature and context of Aka Pygmy paternal infant care*. Ann Arbor: University of Michigan Press

Hiatt, L. R. 1996. *Arguments about Aborigines: Australia and the evolution of social anthropology*. Cambridge University Press

Hobbes, Thomas. 1991 [1651]. *Leviathan*. Cambridge University Press

Hockett, Charles F. and Robert Ascher. 1964. 'The human revolution', *Current Anthropology* 5: 135–68

Hodder, Ian and Scott Hutson. 2003. *Reading the past: current approaches to interpretation in archaeology*. Cambridge University Press

Ingold, 1999. 'On the social relations of the hunter-gatherer band', in Richard Lee and Richard Daly (eds.), *The Cambridge encyclopedia of hunters and gatherers*. Cambridge University Press, pp. 399–410

  2000. *The perception of the environment: essays in livelihood, dwelling and skill*. London: Routledge

Isac, Daniela and Charles Reiss. 2008. *I-language: an introduction to linguistics as cognitive science*. Oxford University Press

James, Steven R. 1989. 'Hominid use of fire in the Lower and Middle Pleistocene', *Current Anthropology* 30: 1–26

Johnson, Matthew. 2010. *Archaeological theory: an introduction* (2nd edn). Oxford: Wiley-Blackwell

Jordan, Fiona M., Russell D. Gray, Simon J. Greenhill and Ruth Mace. 2009. 'Matrilocal residence is ancestral in Austronesian societies', *Proceedings of the Royal Society B* 276: 1957–64

Kaplan, Joanna Overing. 1975. *The Piaroa: a people of the Orinoco Basin*. Oxford: Clarendon Press

Kaufman, Daniel. 2002. 'Mind the gap: questions of continuity in the evolution of anatomically modern humans as seen from the Levant', *Archaeology, Ethnology and Anthropology of Eurasia* 4 (12): 53–61

Keinan, Alon, James C. Mullikin, Nick Patterson and David Reich. 2008. 'Accelerated genetic drift on chromosome X during the human dispersal out of Africa', *Nature Genetics* 41 (1): 66–70

Kelly, Robert L. 1995. *The foraging spectrum: diversity in hunter-gatherer lifeways*. Washington, DC: Smithsonian Institution Press

Kirby, Simon. 2011. 'The language organism in evolution, culture and what it means to be human', Inaugural Lecture as Professor of Language Evolution, University of Edinburgh, 22 Mar. 2011

Klein, Richard G. 2008. 'Out of Africa and the evolution of human behavior', *Evolutionary Anthropology* 17: 267–81

Klein, Richard G. (with Blake Edgar). 2002. *The dawn of human culture*. New York: John Wiley and Sons

Knight, Chris. 1991. *Blood relations: menstruation and the origins of culture*. New Haven: Yale University Press
  1997. 'The wives of the sun and the moon', *Journal of the Royal Anthropological Institute* 3: 133–53

Knight, Chris, Camilla Power and Ian Watts. 1995. 'The human symbolic revolution: a Darwinian account', *Cambridge Archaeological Journal* 5 (1): 75–114

Koepping, Klaus-Peter. 2005 [1983]. *Adolf Bastian and the psychic unity of mankind: the foundations of anthropology in nineteenth century Germany*. Münster: LIT Verlag

Krause, Johannes, Qiaomei Fu, Jeffrey M. Good, Bence Viola, Michael V. Shunkov, Anatoli P. Derevianko and Svante Pääbo. 2010. 'The complete mitochondrial DNA genome of an unknown hominin from southern Siberia', *Nature* 464 (7290): 894–7

Krause, Johannes, Carles Lalueza-Fox, Ludovic Orlando, Wolfgang Enard, Richard E. Green, Hernán A. Burbano, Jean-Jacques Hublin, Catherine Hänni, Javier Fortea, Marco de la Rasilla, Jaume Bertranpetit, Antonio Rosas and Svante Pääbo. 2007. 'The derived FOXP2 variant of modern humans was shared with Neandertals', *Current Biology* 17 (21): 1908–12

Kroeber, A. L. 1931. 'The culture-area and age-area concepts of Clark Wissler', in Stuart A. Rice (ed.), *Methods in social science: a case book*. University of Chicago Press, pp. 248–65

Kuper, Adam. 1996. *Anthropology and anthropologists: the modern British school* (3rd edn). London: Routledge
  1999. *Culture: the anthropologists' account*. Cambridge, MA: Harvard University Press
  2005. *The reinvention of primitive society: transformations of a myth*. Oxford: Routledge

Kuper, Adam and Jonathan Marks. 2011. 'Anthropologists unite!', *Nature* 470 (7333): 166–8

Kusimba, Sibul Barut. 2003. *African foragers: environment, technology, interactions*. Walnut Creek: AltaMira Press

Lakoff, George and Mark Johnson. 1980. *Metaphors we live by*. University of Chicago Press

Lang, Andrew. 1898. *The making of religion*. London: Longmans, Green and Co.
  1905. *The secret of the totem*. London: Longmans, Green and Co.

Latham, R. G. 1851. *Man and his migrations*. London: Jan van Voorst

Latour, Bruno. 1993. *We have never been modern* (translated by Catherine Porter). Cambridge, MA: Harvard University Press

Layton, Robert. 2008. 'What can ethnography tell us about human social evolution?', in Allen *et al.*, pp. 113–27

Leach, E. R. 1967. 'Virgin birth', *Proceedings of the Royal Anthropological Institute for 1966*, pp. 39–50

Lee, Richard B. 1969. '!Kung Bushman subsistence: an input-output analysis', in Andrew P. Vayda (ed.), *Environment and cultural behavior: ecological studies in cultural anthropology*. New York: Natural History Press, pp. 47–79
  1976. 'Introduction', in Lee and DeVore, pp. 1–24
  1979. *The !Kung San: men, women, and work in a foraging society*. Cambridge University Press

Lee, Richard B. and Richard Daly (eds.). 1999. *The Cambridge encyclopedia of hunters and gatherers*. Cambridge University Press

Lee, Richard B. and Irven DeVore. 1968a. 'Preface', in Lee and DeVore (1968b), pp. vii–ix
  (eds.). 1968b. *Man the Hunter*. Chicago: Aldine Publishing Co.
  (eds.). 1976. *Kalahari hunter-gatherers: studies of the !Kung San and their neighbours*. Cambridge, MA: Harvard University Press

Lévi-Strauss, Claude. 1945. 'French sociology', in Georges Gurvitch and Wilbert E. Moore (eds.), *Twentieth century sociology*. New York: The Philosophical Library, pp. 503–37
  1963. *Structural anthropology* (translated by Clare Jacobson and Brook Grundfest Schoepf). New York: Basic Books
  1966 [1962]. *The savage mind*. University of Chicago Press
  1968. 'The concept of primitiveness', in Lee and DeVore (1968b), pp. 349–52
  1969a [1964]. *The raw and the cooked: introduction to a science of mythology, volume I* (translated by John and Doreen Weightman). New York: Harper and Row
  1969b [1962]. *Totemism*. Harmondsworth: Penguin Books
  1969c [1949]. *The elementary structures of kinship* (rev. edn, translated by James Harle Bell, John Richard von Sturmer and Rodney Needham). Boston: Beacon Press
  1978. *Structural anthropology 2* (translated by Monique Layton). Harmondsworth: Penguin Books

Lévy-Bruhl, Lucien. 1975 [1949]. *The notebooks on primitive mentality* (translated by Peter Rivière). Oxford: Basil Blackwell

Lewis-Williams, J. David. 1981. *Believing and seeing: symbolic meanings in southern San rock paintings*. London: Academic Press

2002. *The mind in the cave: consciousness and the origins of art*. New York: Thames and Hudson

2010. *Conceiving God: the cognitive origin and evolution of religion*. London: Thames and Hudson

Lewis-Williams, David and Sam Challis. 2011. *Deciphering ancient minds: the mystery of San Bushman rock art*. London: Thames and Hudson

Lewis-Williams, David and David Pearce. 2005. *Inside the Neolithic mind: consciousness, cosmos and the realm of the gods*. London: Thames and Hudson

Li, Heng and Richard Durbin. 2011. 'Inference of human population history from individual whole-genome sequences', *Nature* 475 (7357): 493–6

Lock, Andrew and Charles R. Peters (eds.). 1999. *Handbook of symbolic evolution*. Oxford: Blackwell Publishers

Locke, John. 1988 [1690]. *Two treatises of government*. Cambridge University Press

Lombard, Marlize and Laurel Phillipson. 2010. 'Indications of bow and stone-tipped arrow use 64,000 years ago in KwaZulu-Natal, South Africa', *Antiquity* 84: 635–48

London, Jack. *Before Adam*. London: T. Werner Laurie.

Lubbock, Sir John. 1865. *Pre-historic times, as illustrated by ancient remains, and the manners and customs of modern savages*. London: Williams and Norgate

Lyotard, Jean-François. 1984 [1979]. *The postmodern condition: a report on knowledge* (translated by Geoff Bennington and Brian Massumi). Manchester University Press

Macaulay, Vincent, Catherine Hill, Alessandro Achilli, Chiara Rengo, Douglas Clarke, William Meehan, James Blackburn, Ornella Semino, Rosaria Scozzari, Fulvio Cruciani, Adi Taha, Norazila Kassim Shaari, Joseph Maripa Raja, Patimah Ismail, Zafarina Zainuddin, William Goodwin, David Bulbeck, Hans-Jürgen Bandelt, Stephen Oppenheimer, Antonio Torroni and Martin Richards. 2005. 'Single, rapid coastal settlement of Asia revealed by analysis of complete mitochondrial genomes', *Science* 308: 1034–6

Maddock, Kenneth. 1972. *The Australian Aborigines: a portrait of their society*. London: Allen Lane

Malinowski, B. 1916. 'Baloma: the spirits of the dead in the Trobriand Islands', *Journal of the Royal Anthropological Institute* 46: 353–430

1930. 'Kinship', *Man* 30: 19–29

McBrearty, Sally and Alison Brooks. 2000. 'The revolution that wasn't: a new interpretation of the origin of modern human behavior', *Journal of Human Evolution* 39: 453–563

McPherron, Shannon P., Zeresenay Alemseged, Curtis W. Marean, Jonathan G. Wynn, Denne Reed, Denis Geraads, Rene Bobe and Hamdallah A. Bearat. 2010. 'Evidence for stone-tool-assisted consumption of animal tissues before 3.39 million years ago at Dikika, Ethiopia', *Nature* 466 (7308): 857–60

Marcus, Joyce and Kent Flannery. 2004. 'The coevolution of ritual and society: new ^{14}C dates from ancient Mexico', *Proceedings of the National Academy of Sciences (PNAS)* 101 (52): 18257–61

Marshall, Lorna. 1999. *Nyae Nyae !Kung beliefs and rites*. Cambridge, MA: Peabody Museum of Archaeology and Ethnology

Masson, John. 2006. 'Apollo 11 Cave in southwest Namibia: some observations on the site and its rock art', *South African Archaeological Bulletin* 61: 76–89

Maybury-Lewis, Davd. 1967. *Akwê-Shavante society: social organization of a Brazilian tribe*. Oxford: Clarendon Press

Mellars, Paul. 2002. 'Archaeology and the origins of modern humans: European and African perspectives', in Tim J. Crow (ed.), *The speciation of modern Homo sapiens* (Proceedings of the British Academy 106). Oxford University Press for the British Academy, pp. 31–47

  2006. 'Why did modern human populations disperse from Africa ca. 60,000 years ago? A new model', *Proceedings of the National Academy of Sciences (PNAS)* 103 (25): 9381–6

Mellars, Paul, Katie Boyle, Ofer Bar-Yosef and Chris Stringer (eds.). 2007. *Rethinking the human revolution: new behavioural and biological perspectives on the origin and dispersal of modern humans*. Cambridge: McDonald Institute for Archaeological Research

Mellars, Paul and Chris Stringer (eds.). 1989. *The human revolution: behavioural and biological perspectives in the origins of modern humans*. Edinburgh University Press

Miller, Geoffrey. 2000. *The mating mind: how sexual choice shaped the evolution of human nature*. New York: Anchor Books

Miller, G. H., P. B. Beaumont, H. J. Deacon, A. S. Brooks, P. E. Hare and A. J. T. Jull. 1999. 'Earliest modern humans in South Africa dated by isoleucine epimerization in ostrich eggshell', *Quaternary Science Reviews* 18: 1537–48

Mitchell, Peter. 2002. *The archaeology of southern Africa*. Cambridge University Press

  2010. 'Making history at Sehonghong: Soai and the last Bushman occupants of his shelter', *Southern African Humanities* 22: 149–70

Mithen, Steven. 2005. *The singing Neanderthals: the origins of music, language, mind and body*. London: Weidenfeld and Nicolson

Morgan, Lewis Henry. 1877. *Ancient society, or researches in the lines of human progress from savagery through barbarism to civilization*. New York: Henry Holt

Morris, Job. 2011. 'Indigenous leadership: value driven development: a San perspective'. Paper presented at the one-day seminar 'Responsible Leadership: Lessons Learned', University of Pretoria, 15 Sept. 2011

Murdock, George Peter. 1949. *Social structure*. New York: Macmillan

Newmeyer, Frederick J. 1983. *Grammatical theory: its limits and its possibilities*. University of Chicago Press

Noble, William and Iain Davidson. 1996. *Human evolution, language and mind: a psychological and archaeological enquiry*. Cambridge University Press

O'Connell, J. F. and J. Allen. 2004. 'Dating the colonization of Sahul (Pleistocene Australia – New Guinea): a review of recent research', *Journal of Archaeological Research* 31: 835–53

Oppenheimer, Stephen. 2004. *The real Eve: modern man's journey out of Africa*. New York: Carroll and Graf
  2007. 'What makes us human? Our ancestors and the weather', in Pasternak, pp. 93–113
  2009. 'The great arc of dispersal of modern humans: Africa to Australia', *Quaternary International* 202: 2–13
Pasternak, Charles (ed.). 2007. *What makes us human?* Oxford: Oneworld
Peterson, Nicolas. 1999. 'Introduction: Australia', in Richard B. Lee and Richard Daly (eds.), *The Cambridge encyclopedia of hunters and gatherers*. Cambridge University Press, pp. 317–23
Pettitt, Paul. 2011. *The Palaeolithic origins of human burial*. London: Routledge.
Phillipson, David W. 2005. *African archaeology* (3rd edn). Cambridge University Press
Pickering, Robyn, Paul H. G. M. Dirks, Zubair Jinnah, Darryl J. de Ruiter, Steven E. Churchill, Andy I. R. Herries, Jon D. Woodhead, John C. Hellstrom and Lee R. Berger. 2011. 'Australopithecus sediba at 1.977 Ma and implications for the origin of the genus Homo', *Science* 333: 1421–3
Pinhasi, Ron and Jay T. Stock (eds.). 2011. *Human bioarchaeology of the transition to agriculture*. Chichester: Wiley-Blackwell
Price, T. Douglas (ed.). 2000. *Europe's first farmers*. Cambridge University Press
Ptak, Susan E., Wolfgang Enard, Victor Wiebe, Ines Hellmann, Johannes Krause, Michael Lachmann and Svante Pääbo. 2009. 'Linkage disequilibrium extends across putative selected sites in FOXP2', *Molecular Biology and Evolution* 26: 2181–4
Pufendorf, Samuel von. 1927 [1682]. *De officio hominis et civis juxta legem naturalem libri duo*. Volume I: the photographic reproduction. Concord, NH: Rumford Press
Quiatt, Duane and Vernon Reynolds. 1993. *Primate behaviour: information, social knowledge, and the evolution of culture*. Cambridge University Press
Radcliffe-Brown, A. R. 1951. 'The comparative method in social anthropology', *Journal of the Royal Anthropological Institute* 81: 15–22
  1952. *Structure and function in primitive society: essays and addresses*. London: Cohen and West
  1964 [1922]. *The Andaman Islanders*. New York: Free Press of Glencoe
Rappaport, Roy A. 1971. 'The sacred in human evolution', *Annual Review of Ecology and Systematics* 2: 23–44
  1999. *Ritual and religion in the making of humanity*. Cambridge University Press
Ratzel, Friedrich. 1896–8 [1885–8]. *The history of mankind* (translated by A. J. Butler) (3 vols.). London: Macmillan
Reich, David, Richard E. Green, Martin Kircher, Johannes Krause, Nick Patterson, Eric Y. Durand, Bence Viola, Adrian W. Briggs, Udo Stenzel, Philip L. F. Johnson, Tomislav Maricic, Jeffrey M. Good, Tomas Marques-Bonet, Can Alkan, Qiaomei Fu, Swapan Mallick, Heng Li, Matthias Meyer, Evan E. Eichler, Mark Stoneking, Michael Richards, Sahra Talamo, Michael V. Shunkov, Anatoli P. Derevianko, Jean-Jacques Hublin, Janet Kelso,

Montgomery Slatkin and Svante Pääbo. 2010. 'Genetic history of an archaic hominin group from Denisova Cave in Siberia', *Nature* 468 (7327): 1053–60

Renfrew, Colin and Paul Bahn (eds.). 2008. *Archaeology: theories, methods and practice* (5th edn). London: Thames and Hudson

Renfrew, Colin and Iain Morley (eds.). 2009. *Becoming human: innovation and prehistoric material and spiritual culture.* Cambridge University Press

Renfrew, Jane M. 2009. 'Neanderthal symbolic behaviour?', in Renfrew and Morley, pp. 50–60

Ride, W. D. L., H. G. Cogger, C. Dupuis, O. Kraus, A. Minelli, F. C. Thompson and P. K. Tubbs. 2000. *International code of zoological nomenclature* (4th edn). London: Natural History Museum

Rivière, Peter. 1969. *Marriage among the Trio: a principle of social organization.* Oxford: Clarendon Press
　1984. *Individual and society in Guiana: a comparative study of Amerindian social organization.* Cambridge University Press

Rogers, Edward S. 1972. 'The Mistassini Cree', in Bicchieri, pp. 90–137

Rohde, Douglas L. T., Steve Olsen and Joseph T. Chang. 2004. 'Modelling the recent common ancestry of all living humans', *Nature* 431 (7008): 562–6

Rousseau, Jean-Jacques. 1997a. *The Discourses and other early political writings.* Cambridge University Press
　1997b. *The social contract and other later political writings.* Cambridge University Press

Rowley-Conwy, Peter. 2007. *From Genesis to prehistory: the archaeological Three Age System and its contested reception in Denmark, Britain, and Ireland.* Oxford University Press

Sadr, Karim. 2003. 'The Neolithic of southern Africa', *Journal of African History* 44: 195–209

Sahlins, Marshall. 1974. *Stone age economics.* London: Tavistock Publications

Salzman, Philip Carl. 2008. *Culture and conflict in the Middle East.* Amherst, NY: Humanity Books

Sarmiento, Esteban. 2007. 'Twenty-two species of extinct human ancestors', in G. J. Sawyer and Viktor Deak (creators), *The last human: a guide to twenty-two species of extinct humans.* New Haven: Yale University Press, pp. 24–229

Saussure, Ferdinand de. 1974 [1916]. *Course in general linguistics* (edited by Charles Bally and Albert Sechehaye, translated by Wade Baskin). Glasgow: Fontana/Collins

Schmidt, Wilhelm. 1931. *The origin and growth of religion: facts and theories* (translated by H. J. Rose). London: Methuen.
　1939. *Primitive revelation* (translated by Joseph J. Baierl). St Louis. B. Herder Book Co.

Schneider, David M. 1980 [1968]. *American kinship: a cultural account* (2nd edn). University of Chicago Press
　1984. *A critique of the study of kinship.* Ann Arbor: University of Michigan Press

Scholz, Christopher A., Thomas C. Johnson, Andrew S. Cohen, John W. King, John A. Peck, Jonathan T. Overpeck, Michael R. Talbot, Erik T. Brown,

Leonard Kalindekafe, Philip Y. O. Amoako, Robert P. Lyons, Timothy M. Shanahan, Isla S. Castañeda, Clifford W. Heil, Steven L. Forman, Lanny R. McHargue, Kristina R. Beuning, Jeanette Gomez and James Pierson. 2007. 'East African megadroughts between 135 and 75 thousand years ago and bearing on early-modern human origins', *Proceedings of the National Academy of Sciences (PNAS)* 104 (42): 16416–21

Shea, John J. 2011. 'Homo sapiens is as Homo sapiens was: behavioral variability versus "behavioral modernity" in Palaeolithic archaeology', *Current Anthropology* 52: 1–35

Silberbauer, George B. 1981. *Hunter and habitat in the central Kalahari Desert*. Cambridge University Press

Smith, William Robertson. 2002 [1894]. *Religion of the Semites*. New Brunswick, NJ: Transaction Publishers

Soodyall, Himla (ed.). 2006. *The prehistory of Africa: tracing the lineage of modern man*. Johannesburg: Jonathan Ball

Spencer, Baldwin and F. J. Gillen. 1899. *The native tribes of central Australia*. London: Macmillan and Co.

Sperber, Dan. 1975. *Rethinking symbolism*. Cambridge University Press
  1985. *On anthropological knowledge: three essays*. Cambridge University Press

Spiro, Melford. 1968. 'Virgin birth, parthenogenesis and physiological paternity: an essay in cultural interpretation', *Man* 3: 242–61

Stix, Gary. 2008. 'The migration history of humans: DNA study traces human origins across the continents', *Scientific American* 299 (1): 56–63

Stoneking, Mark. 2006. 'Genetic evidence for our recent African ancestry', in Soodyall, pp. 21–30

Stringer, Chris. 2011. *The origin of our species*. London: Allen Lane

Stutley, Margaret. 2003. *Shamanism: an introduction*. London: Routledge

Tanaka, Jiro and Kazuyoshi Sugawara (eds.). 2010. *An encyclopedia of /Gui and //Gana culture and society*. Kyoto: Laboratory of Cultural Anthropology, Graduate School of Human and Environmental Studies, Kyoto University

Testart, Alain. 1982a. *Les Chasseur-cueilleurs, ou l'origine des inégalités*. Paris: Société d'Ethnographie
  1982b.'The significance of food storage among hunter-gatherers: residence patterns, population densities, and social inequalities', *Current Anthropology* 23: 523–37

Tomasello, Michael. 2008. *Origins of human communication*. Cambridge, MA: MIT Press

Tonkinson, Robert. 1978. *The Mardudjara Aborigines: living the Dreamtime in Australia's desert*. New York: Holt, Rinehart and Winston

Towner, Sarah. 2010. 'Concept of mind in non-human primates', *Bioscience Horizons* 3 (1): 1–9

Traill, A. 1994. *A !Xóõ dictionary*. Cologne: Rüdiger Köppe Verlag

Turnbull, Colin. 1968. *Wayward servants: the two worlds of the African Pygmies*. London Eyre and Spottiswoode
  1985. *The human cycle*. London: Triad/Paladin Books

Turner, David H. 1985. *Life before Genesis: a conclusion. An understanding of the significance of Australian Aboriginal culture*. New York: Peter Lang

Turner, Victor. 1967. *The forest of symbols: aspects of Ndembu ritual*. Ithaca, NY: Cornell University Press

Tylor, Edward Burnett. 1871. *Primitive culture: researches into the development of mythology, philosophy, religion, language, art, and custom* (2 vols.). London: John Murray

Underhill, David. 2011. 'A history of Stone Age archaeological study in South Africa', *South African Archaeological Bulletin* 66: 3–14

Valiente Noailles, Carlos. 1988. *El circulo y el fuego: sociedad y derecho de los kúa*. Buenos Aires: Ediar

Vaz, Ruth Manimekalai. 2010. 'The Hill Madia of central India: early human kinship?', *Journal of the Anthropological Society of Oxford* (n.s.) 2 (1–2): 9–30
  2011. 'The 'Big Bang' of Dravidian kinship', *Journal of the Anthropological Society of Oxford* (n.s.) 3 (1): 38–66

Vico, Giambattista. 1982. *Vico: selected writings* (edited and translated by Leon Pompa). Cambridge University Press

Vinnicombe, Patricia. 1972. 'Myth, motive and selection in southern African rock art', *Africa* 42: 192–204

von Brandenstein, C. G. 1970. 'The meaning of section and section names', *Oceania* 41: 39–49
  1982. *Names and substance of the Australian section system*. University of Chicago Press

Wadley, Lyn. 2001. 'What is cultural modernity? A general view and a South African perspective from Rose Cottage Cave', *Cambridge Archaeological Journal* 11: 201–21
  2006. 'Revisiting cultural modernity and the role of ochre in the Middle Stone Age', in Soodyall, pp. 49–63

Wagner, Roy. 1986. *Symbols that stand for themselves*. University of Chicago Press

Warren, William W. 1885. 'History of the Ojibway people, based upon tradition and oral statements', *Collections of the Minnesota Historical Society* 5: 21–394

Watts, Ian. 1999. 'The origin of symbolic culture', in Dunbar *et al.*, pp. 113–46

Weidenreich, Franz. 1947. 'Facts and speculations concerning the origin of Homo sapiens', *American Anthropologist* 49: 187–203

Wells, J. C. 1982. *Accents of English I: an introduction*. Cambridge University Press

Wells, Spencer. 2007. *Deep ancestry: inside the genographic project*. Washington, DC: National Geographic
  2011. *Pandora's seed: why the hunter-gatherer holds the key to our survival*. London: Penguin Books

Wendt, W. E. 1976. '"Art mobilier" from the Apollo 11 Cave, South West Africa's oldest dated works of art', *South African Archaeological Bulletin* 31: 5–11

Whittle, Alasdair. 2003. *The archaeology of people: dimensions of Neolithic life*. London: Routledge

Whittle, Alasdair and Vicki Cummings (eds.). 2007. *Going over: the Mesolithic–Neolithic transition in north-west Europe* (Proceedings of the British Academy 144). Oxford University Press for the British Academy

Wikipedia contributors. 2011. 'Lunar deity'. *Wikipedia: the free encyclopedia*. San Francisco: Wikimedia Foundation, Inc. http://en.wikipedia.org/wiki/Lunar_deity (accessed 2 Oct. 2011)

Willoughby, Pamela R. 2007. *The evolution of modern humans in Africa: a comprehensive guide*. Lanham, MD: AltaMira Press

Wissler, Clark. 1923. *Man and culture*. New York: Thomas Y. Crowell
 1927. 'The culture-area concept in American anthropology', *American Journal of Sociology* 32: 881–91

Woodburn, James. 1982. 'Egalitarian societies', *Man* (n.s.) 17: 431–51

Wrangham, Richard. 2009. *Catching fire: how cooking made us human*. London: Profile Books

Wynn, Thomas and Frederick L. Coolidge. 2009. 'Implications of a strict standard for recognizing modern cognition in prehistory', in Beaune *et al.* 2009, pp. 117–27

Zhivotovsky, Lev A., Noah A. Rosenberg and Marcus W. Feldman. 2003. 'Features of evolution and expansion of modern humans, inferred from genomewide microsatellite markers', *American Journal of Human Genetics* 72 (5): 1171–86

Zilhão, João. 2007. 'The emergence of ornaments and art: an archaeological perspective on the origins of "behavioral modernity"', *Journal of Archaeological Research* 15: 1–54

Index

Aborigines, 11, 43
  Dreamtime, 73
  society, 57
accumulation, 134
age-area hypothesis, 36
agriculture, 121, 123, 128, 132
agro-pastoralists, 25, 32, 56, 130, 134
Ainu, 31
Allen, N. J., 53, 55, 58, 75
Altamira, 31
Andamanese, 43, 67, 109, 110
anthropology
  biological, 3
  cultural, 11, 38
  four-field, 3
  social, 3, 14, 15, 40, 71, 148
Apollo 11 Cave, 15, 31
Arab society, 46
Arabian Peninsula, 107
archaeology, 15, 114, 145
  prehistoric, 3
Ardipithecus, 19
Arrernte, 31, 50
art
  Palaeolithic, 59
  pictorial, 13
  San, 76
Ascher, R., 12, 40
Asia, 123
Australia, 95, 107, 110, 126, 141
  boomerang, 17
  central, 55
  cremation, 113
  evolution in, 13
  kinship in, 46
  migration, 119
  myth, 70
  Western, 64
australopithecines, 19, 20

Australopithecus africanus, 16
Avebury, Lord (Sir John Lubbock), 149

Babel, 97
Bantu languages, 25, 99
Barham, L., 24, 29, 79
Barnes, J. A., 52
Bastian, A., 132, 133–6
Bateson, G., 64, 87
Bednarik, R., 16
Behar, D., 22
Bering Land Bridge, 106
Bickerton, D., 99
Biesele, M., 96
Binford, L., 113
Bird-David, N., 46, 62
Blacking, J., 102
Bleek, W. H. I., 85
Blombos Cave, 13, 15, 23, 32–4, 79, 98, 136
Boas, F., 115
Border Cave, 28
Botswana, 77
brain, 100
Broken Hill (Kabwe), 27
Bronze Age, 91, 113, 123
Brooks, A., 111, 140
Brumm, A., 13
Burns, R., 92
Bushmen, *see* San

Cann, R., 115
Carsten, J., 49
Çatalhöyük, 132
Central African Republic, 51
Chad, 19
Challis, S., 76
Chauvet Cave, 32
Childe, V. G., 123
Chile, 106

Index

chimpanzee, 19
China, 20, 67, 106, 125
Chinese, 7
Chomsky, N., 86, 87, 103
Clark, G., 24
Cochran, G., 136–8
communication, 42, 86, 90, 99
  beginnings of, 3
  gestural, 8
  primate, 7
Condillac, E. B. de, 105
cooking, 101
Coolidge, F., 78
Coon, C., 21
Cowan, J. G., 96
Cree, 65
cultural complexity, 2
culture, 6
  definition of, 11
  material, 13, 17
  symbolic, 2, 14, 16
culture circles, 106
Cyrano effect, 93

Dart's child, 27
Darwin, C., 60
Davidson, I., 100
Deacon, T., 100
delayed-return, 131
Denisovans, 119
DeVore, I., 2
diffusionism, 97, 106, 115, 120
diffusionists, 60
Djebel Qafzeh, 28
Doniger, W., 88
Douglas, M., 29, 51
Drakensberg Mountains, 76, 77, 141
drought, 33
Dubreuil, B., 34, 78
Dunbar, R. I. M., 89
  on language, 8
  Sally-Ann test, 4
Durbin, R., 109
Durkheim, E., 5, 67, 70, 129, 144
Dziebel, G., 115

Edwardes, M., 90
Eemian interglacial period, 14
Egypt, 105
Eibl-Eibesfeldt, I., 89
elementary ideas, 133

England, 38
Enlightenment, 126
Ethiopia, 19
Evans-Pritchard, E. E., 81, 82, 120
evolutionary psychology, 145
evolutionism, 115

Fitch, T., 87
Flannery, K., 128
Foley, R., 29
folk ideas, 133
fossil record, 17–21
Foster, M. L., 90
Fox, R., 41
FOXP2, 83, 120
Frazer, J. G., 70, 97, 112
  on religion, 6
  on totemism, 50, 71
Freud, S., 72
functionalism, 106

Geertz, C., 80
Genesis, Book of, 97
genetic diversity, 115
genetics, 145
gesture, 1
Gillen, F., 50
global migration, 107
Goody, J. R., 127
Graebner, F., 109
grammar, 90
grid and group, 29
grooming, 7
group marriage, 41
Guenther, M. G., 126, 148

Hadar, 19
Haddon, A. C., 119
Haida, 68
Harpending, H. C., 136–8
Hauser, M., 87
Heidelberg, 28
Henshilwood, C., 33, 78
  symbolic culture, 106
Hewlett, B., 51
Hiatt, L. R., 50
Hill Madia, 54
Hindi, 98
Hobbes, T., 10, 11, 74
Hockett, C., 12, 40
Hodder, I., 114
Holocene, 14

Homo antecessor, 8
Homo erectus, 3, 20, 95, 104, 105, 146
  fire, 101
  longevity, 100
  migration, 130
Homo habilis, 19, 20
Homo heidelbergensis, 8, 15, 28, 40, 118, 138, 146
Homo helmei, 105
Homo rhodesiensis, 40
Howiesons Poort, 32, 34
human revolution, 13, 14
hunter-gatherers
  environment, 129
  ethnography, 14, 122
  language, 6
  living, 135
  modern, 40
  religion, 61
  sociality, 10
  work, 1

Iatmul, 63
Ice Age, 106
immediate-return, 131
incest taboo, 41
India, 15, 110, 111
Indian Ocean, 110
Indonesia, 13, 20
Ingold, T., 10, 65, 102
interpretivism, 80, 115
Inuit, 6
Iron Age, 25, 113
Israel, 83, 105

Jews, Ashkenazi, 137
Johanson, D., 19
Johnson, M., 9, 114

Kalahari, 93, 99, 130
K-Ar dating, 36
Kariera, 44
Katande, 23
Kaufman, D., 116
Kenya, 19
Khoekhoe, 23
Khoisan, 22, 109
kinship, 7, 53
  American, 47
Kirby, S., 93
Klasies River Mouth, 28
Klein, R., 136, 139
Knight, C., 72

Konner, M., 96
Kuper, A., 11, 143

Lake Mungo, 28
Lakoff, G., 9
Lang, A., 50, 60
language
  /Xam, 91
  and culture, 79
  and myth, 5
  complex, 6
  full, 83
  grammar, 71
  origin of, 8
  uses of, 94
Lascaux, 31, 77
Later Stone Age, 25, 124
Latham, R. G., 104
Latour, B., 11
Layton, R., 54, 58
Leach, E., 51
Leaky, L. S. B., 19
Lee, R. B., 2, 125
Lesotho, 141
levels of intentionality, 4
Lévi-Strauss, C., 53, 70, 72, 81, 97, 127
  genesis of symbolic thought, 5, 15, 150
  inequality, 131
  kinship, 41
  myth, 117
  'Mythologiques', 140
  science of the concrete, 147
  symbolism, 86
Lévy-Bruhl, L., 3
Lewis-Williams, J. D., 76, 132
Li, H., 109
linguistic complexity, 2
linguistics
  anthropological, 3
Lloyd, L. C., 85
Locke, J., 75
London, J., 1
Lubbock, J., 122
Lupemban industries, 30
Lyotard, J. F., 126

McBrearty, S., 111, 140
Madagascar, 112
Makapansgat, 16
Malinowski, B., 49, 50, 115
Marcus, J., 128
Mardudjara, 95
Marean, C., 34, 106

Index

Marks, J., 143
marriage, 41
Marxism, 114, 126
Mason, R., 27
Melanesia, 118
Mellars, P., 14, 22, 23, 110, 139
Mesolithic, 24, 25, 123
metaphor, 9
Middle Ages, 64
Middle East, 137
Middle Stone Age, 25, 34, 98, 123, 124
Miller, G., 93
Mitchell, P., 24, 141
Mitochondrial Eve, 109
modernity, 125
moon symbolism, 122
Moore, M., 13
Morgan, L. H., 114
Morley, I., 24
Morris, J., 96
Mousterian, 15
Multiregional Continuity Model, 21
music, 8, 9, 28
myth, 60, 68, 84, 87, 118, 122, 125
  /Xam, 84
  Oedipus, 88
  Roman, 71
  San, 76
  South American, 81

Nachikufan industries, 30
Namibia, 15, 77
narrative, 35
Nayar, 111
Ndembu, 87
Neanderthal burials, 136
Neanderthal flute, 15, 28
Neanderthals, 19, 34, 83, 89, 118, 149
  contact, 79
  discovery, 104
  extinction of, 14
  FOXP2, 120
Near East, 123
Needham, R., 12
Neolithic, 24, 91, 122
  definition of, 25
  end of, 138
  humanity, 3
  postmodernity, 14
  revolution, 123
  transition, 40
Neolithization, 126
neuroscience, 145

Newmeyer, F., 86
Nigeria, 119
Noble, W., 100
North Africa, 137
North America, 113, 117
Northwest Coast, 55, 67
Nuer, 81
Nyaka, 62

Oaxaca, 128
ochre, 33, 59
Oppenheimer, S., 105, 106
ornaments, 13, 119
Out of Africa, 105, 110, 111, 115, 121

Pacific, 119
Palaeolithic, 22, 23, 26
  evolution of, 13
  Upper, 59, 122
Palestine, 105
Papua New Guinea, 63
pastoralism, 121
pastoralists, 32, 46
Pearce, D., 132
Phillipson, D., 24
Pirahã, 7
Pleistocene, 14
post-Neolithic, 131
post-processualism, 114
pre-Neolithic, 140
primitive communism, 2
processualism, 114
Pufendorf, S., 10
Pygmies
  Aka, 51, 52
  Mbuti, 44, 46, 58

Qing, 141
Quiatt, D., 41

Radcliffe-Brown, A. R., 11, 66
radiocarbon dating, 36
Rappaport, R., 128
Ratzel, F., 109
Recent African Origin, 22
Red Sea, 107
relativism, 115
religion
  attributes of, 5
  belief, 60
  natural, 129
  ritual, 59
  totemism, 60

Renfrew, C., 24
Republic of Congo, 51
Reynolds, V., 41
'Rhodesian Man', 140
Robertson Smith, W., 73, 88
rock art, 75, 145
Rousseau, J. J., 75, 131

Sahelanthropus, 19
Sahelanthropus tchadensis, 2
Sahlins, M., 129
Sally-Ann test, 4
Salzman, C. P., 47
Sampson, G., 27
San, 44, 57, 134
  !Xóõ, 6
  /Gui and //Gana, 94, 98
  /Xam, 7, 76, 92
  Ju/'hoan, 6
  Ju/'hoansi, 51, 96
  Kua, 97
  languages, 98
  myth, 84
  Naro, 6, 56, 93, 94, 126
  religion, 126
Saussure, F. de, 103
Saussurianism, 9
Scheherezade effect, 93
Schmidt, W., 60, 114
Schneider, D. M., 47, 49
shamanism, 76, 102
sharing, 134
Shea, J., 125
Sibudu Cave, 17
Silberbauer, G. B., 63
Silk Road, 106
Slovenia, 15
sociality, 10, 41
society, 10
  and religion, 6
  theories of, 12
sociology, 15
South Africa, 13, 15, 16, 17
South America, 17, 116, 117
Southeast Asia, 113
Spain, 15
Spencer, B., 50
Sperber, D., 9, 127
Spiro, M., 51
Still Bay, 34
Stix, G., 107

Stoneking, M., 115
Stringer, C., 14, 22, 140
structuralism, 67, 80
Sugawara, K., 94
symbolic revolution, 12, 13, 14
symbolic thought, 2, 5, 13, 15, 32, 34, 39, 62, 71, 73, 78, 87
symbolism, 4, 8, 99, 100, 111, 125

Testart, A., 131
theory of mind, 4
Toba, 13, 97, 104
totemism, 50, 55, 57, 65–71, 125
trance, 76
Turnbull, C., 46
Turner, V., 87
Twin Rivers, 15, 29
Tylor, E. B., 61, 133

Underhill, D., 27
urban revolution, 124

Valiente-Noailles, C., 97
Vaz, R. M., 53
Venus figurines, 59
Vico, G., 113
Vinnicombe, P., 76
von Brandenstein, C. G., 44

Wadley, L., 33
Wagner, R., 9
Weidenreich, F., 21
West Africa, 123
Whittle, A., 131
Wikipedia, 72
Willoughby, P., 24
Wilson, A., 115
Wissler, C., 36, 117
Woodburn, J., 131
Wynn, T., 78

X-woman, 118

Yap, 49
Y-chromosomal Adam, 109

Zambia, 15, 27, 29, 79, 87
Zapotec state, 128
Zhivotovsky, L. A., 107
Zhou Dynasty, 125
Zilhão, J., 78